T0301577

Idle Threats

America and the Long 19th Century

GENERAL EDITORS
David Kazanjian, Elizabeth McHenry, and Priscilla Wald

Black Frankenstein: The Making of an American Metaphor
Elizabeth Young

Neither Fugitive nor Free: Atlantic Slavery, Freedom Suits,
and the Legal Culture of Travel
Edlie L. Wong

Shadowing the White Man's Burden: U.S. Imperialism
and the Problem of the Color Line
Gretchen Murphy

Bodies of Reform: The Rhetoric of Character in Gilded Age America
James B. Salazar

Empire's Proxy: American Literature and U.S. Imperialism
in the Philippines
Meg Wesling

Sites Unseen: Architecture, Race, and American Literature
William A. Gleason

Racial Innocence: Performing American Childhood
from Slavery to Civil Rights
Robin Bernstein

American Arabesque: Arabs and Islam in the
19th-Century Imaginary
Jacob Rama Berman

Racial Indigestion: Eating Bodies in the 19th Century
Kyla Wazana Tompkins

Idle Threats: Men and the Limits of Productivity
in 19th-Century America
Andrew Lyndon Knighton

Idle Threats

*Men and the Limits of Productivity
in 19th-Century America*

Andrew Lyndon Knighton

NEW YORK UNIVERSITY PRESS
New York and London

NEW YORK UNIVERSITY PRESS
New York and London
www.nyupress.org

Portions of Chapter 1 were originally published in *ESQ* 53 (2007): 184–215.
Copyright 2007 by the Board of Regents of Washington State University.

LIBRARY OF CONGRESS CATALOGING-IN-PUBLICATION DATA

Knighton, Andrew Lyndon.
Idle threats : men and the limits of productivity in 19th-Century America
/ Andrew Lyndon Knighton.
p. cm.
Includes bibliographical references and index.
ISBN 978-0-8147-4890-9 (cl : alk. paper)
ISBN 978-0-8147-8939-1 (pb : alk. paper)
ISBN 978-0-8147-4891-6 (ebook)
ISBN 978-0-8147-4944-9 (ebook)
1. Labor productivity—United States—History—19th century.
2. Leisure—United States—History—19th century. I. Title.
HC110.L3K65 2012
331.11'8097309034—dc23

2011051504

References to Internet Websites (URLs) were accurate at the time of
writing. Neither the author nor New York University Press is responsible
for URLs that may have expired or changed since the manuscript was
prepared.

New York University Press books are printed on acid-free paper, and
their binding materials are chosen for strength and durability. We
strive to use environmentally responsible suppliers and materials to the
greatest extent possible in publishing our books.

Manufactured in the United States of America
c 10 9 8 7 6 5 4 3 2 1
p 10 9 8 7 6 5 4 3 2 1

A book in the American Literatures Initiative (ALI), a collaborative
publishing project of NYU Press, Fordham University Press, Rutgers
University Press, Temple University Press, and the University of Virginia
Press. The Initiative is supported by The Andrew W. Mellon Foundation.
For more information, please visit www.americanliteratures.org.

THE
AMERICAN
LITERATURES
INITIATIVE

To the memory of Alex Chilton and MC David Mac

Contents

Acknowledgments

In response to inquiries about the progress of my work, I have sometimes glibly pointed out that a history of unproductivity adequate to its object would be perpetually not quite finished. Those who refused to accept such jesting deserve all the greater thanks for helping to bring this project to fruition. Foremost among them is Richard Leppert, who guided me through successive layers of professionalization with the same incisiveness that cut through successive waves of early drafts. I am indebted to Cesare Casarino for his theoretical provocations, to Paula Rabinowitz for her generosity, and to my overworked colleagues at California State University, Los Angeles, for their support and trust. The stewardship of those professional readers whose interest, encouragement, and keen comments have enriched this project at various stages—Jana Argersinger, Tom Augst, John Cleman, Maria Karafilis, Dan McCall, Tom Pepper, Jack Zipes, and a number of anonymous reviewers—should be palpable on each and every page.

I would be remiss if I did not extend my appreciation to others whose unsung exertions facilitated my research—especially the librarians. The familiar staffs at UCLA's Young Library, CSULA's Kennedy Library, and, most crucially, the University of Minnesota's Wilson Library deserve special mention; I also thank those who aided me at the Arthur and Elizabeth Schlesinger Library on the History of Women in America, the Huntington Library, the Minnesota Historical Society, the University of Minnesota Immigration History Research Center, the Columbia University Rare Books and Manuscripts Library, and the University of Virginia's Manuscripts Collection. Those familiar with her work will agree that Kim Anderson, now of the Multnomah County Public Library in Portland, is a credit to the profession and deserves a singular recognition. A number of institutions and individuals also supported my research in very tangible ways that enabled me to enjoy at least short intervals of comparatively noninstrumental thinking: the University of Minnesota's Doctoral

Dissertation Fellowship helped to build the foundations of the project, and crucial later support came from CSULA's Research and Creative Leave Award, a Barry Munitz Award, and an American Communities Program fellowship.

Brynnar Swenson is, without a doubt, one of the most adept theorists (and practitioners) of idleness I have known, and he has contributed to envisioning this project since its very inception. My collaborations with David Jenemann have made me wonder without fail at the restless energy of language. My parents cultivated in me the confidence to take on any project. And my deeply productive conversations over the years with Mazher Al-Zoby, Morgan Adamson, John Conley, Daniel del Castillo, Alicia Gibson, Astrid Kleiveland, Cecily Marcus, J. D. Mininger, Jennifer Ohlund, Yun Peng, Malcom Potek, Melissa Ray, Gauti Sigthorsson, Julietta Singh, Jakki Spicer, Karen Steigman, Paige Sweet, Kristin Swenson, and Collier White have generated considerable pleasure and necessary inspiration. Both intellectual and personal, these exchanges have demonstrated to me a fundamental continuity between the demands of work and the joys of play: both are best when enjoyed collectively.

Idle Threats

Introduction

Procrastination and Prolegomena

Now what is the cause of this absence of repose, this bottled-
lightning quality in us Americans? . . . We, here in America,
through following a succession of pattern-setters whom it is now
impossible to trace, and through influencing each other in a bad
direction, have at last settled down collectively into what, for better
or worse, is our own characteristic national type.
—William James, "The Gospel of Relaxation," 1899

Indolence is an impossibility of beginning. . . . It is, in its concrete
fullness, a holding back from the future. The tragedy of being it
reveals is then the more profound.
—Emmanuel Levinas, *Existence and Existents*, 1978

This introduction finds itself poised somewhere between Levinas and James; it harbors both a curiosity about the past and an apprehension about the future. It inaugurates my attention to what James calls an
"impossible" task—that of documenting the "pattern-setters" who, over
the course of a century rife with cultural negotiation, solidified the relationship between an American "national type" and the value of productivity. The task is daunting, both because of the considerable complexity
and discontinuity of the history involved, and because of the ambiguity
of the central concepts with which it will work—for the cultural meanings of productivity and unproductivity were, throughout the nineteenth
century, far from self-evident. Despite what we tend to think about the
primacy of hard work in the American experience, the nineteenth century
was marked by a profound ambivalence about productivity (and, for that
matter, about unproductivity, which was simultaneously regarded both as

a ruinous pathology of the poor and the seductive ideal of the prosperous). And in this regard, perhaps, the very ambivalence of this introduction—diffident before the chore that awaits, and furthermore saddled with all the procrastinatory preliminaries that have to be dispensed with before the *real work* can commence—provides an appropriate starting point.

That, however, is only one of the multitude of ambivalences that emerges whenever the topic of unproductivity is taken seriously. To speak of one's own unproductivity is of course already to have betrayed it in the very production of meaning; in the same way, nagging doubts should arise about whether a work dedicated to idleness may ever be truly adequate to its object. Such playful reversals mirror the serious complexities that have long accompanied the concept of unproductivity, and the tensions produced when its representation and its practice come into contradiction; these are the inherent complexities of discourses that only hazily can discuss laziness, and which, in their attempts to explain the meaning of work, sometimes produce nothing less than an *unworking* of the very concept. In the nineteenth century, ambiguities of this stripe manifest in a crisis of meaning that is both conceptual and economic. The familiar categories of industry and idleness are scrambled, if momentarily, and there, beyond the limits of what can be recognized as productivity, emerges an unusual, powerful, and often paradoxical force that I will here refer to as the productivity of the unproductive.

To understand the importance of unproductivity in the nineteenth century means injecting a shadow of doubt into a pervasive mythology that has long grounded the American "national type": the fundamental value of the work ethic, and of the individuated and heroic American self typically portrayed as shaped by that ethic. In accordance with that organizing myth, the nineteenth century tends to be plotted as an epochal triumph of industriousness—a national application of elbow grease that settles the frontier, erects the metropolis and builds the infrastructure, holds the nation together through war and panic, and forges an indefatigable identity sometimes taken to be synonymous with both American ideals and modernity itself.[1] The nineteenth century was "the Golden Age for the idea of work," as Adriano Tilgher put it. "It saw the acceptance of universal conscription in the army of labor, the spectacle of the whole race toiling."[2] Yet one must also acknowledge, beneath this homogenizing historical template, the ideological ferment that was necessary to construct, out of the infinite varieties and intensities of human activity, the primacy of the normative value of productivity and of modern "work" as its mode.

Among the fascinating characteristics of this cultural negotiation is the relative transparency of its premises. As we shall see in what follows, the distinction drawn between forms of putatively productive and unproductive activity—a distinction that masquerades as a moral matter bearing on the social or spiritual duty of the individual, or as a physiological concern reflecting the bodily limits imposed by fatigue, or even as an aesthetic question governing the desirability of formal and experiential repose—often exposes itself as a nakedly and unapologetically *economic* judgment. Nevertheless, the concept of unproductivity does perform an array of moral, political, and even spiritual functions, and circulates across a wide range of discursive practices that far exceed the capacity of any study seeking exhaustiveness in treating them. Conservatively, one might argue that the nineteenth-century field of cultural production (and especially the imaginative domains of literature, the visual arts, architecture, and even the living of everyday life, upon which much of this study will focus) is rich with experimentation with the possibilities of rethinking productivity. From Rip Van Winkle to Bartleby to George Hurstwood, for example, American literature is populated by a remarkable cast of characters who are defined by their idleness.[3] But a more radical claim, and one that I hope to sustain throughout the chapters that follow, is that virtually every nineteenth-century American discourse finds itself circling back repeatedly to nagging questions about unproductivity (or, perhaps to put it more provocatively: these seemingly productive discourses find themselves unworked by the force of the unproductive).

Despite the scope and the complexity of these discourses about productivity and its limits, discernable patterns do emerge; of particular interest here is the strenuous effort to stabilize the central binary pitting industry against idleness, by casting it as a permanent, essential, and immutable opposition. Repeatedly, we see these two poles represented as fixed alternatives, the relationship between them naturalized as a fact of spiritual, physiological, and moral life. The self-culture advocate James Freeman Clarke attempted in 1882 to articulate such a strict schema, in an account of idleness that reflects both the proscriptive spirit and the fragile premises of such discourse. Discussing amusement and other idle pursuits in his *Self-Culture: Physical, Intellectual, Moral, and Spiritual*, Clarke naturalizes the opposition between the clear alternatives of desirable productivity and its idle other. "All through creation runs this alternation from work to play, from play to work," he asserts, speculating further that "even animals which seem to be all work and no play, like bees and ants, probably have their recreations."[4] If we are tempted to laud Clarke for at least granting play a place in the human experience—which is more than some of his more puritanical ancestors would have done—it should also be noted that his endorsement is bound by certain caveats, including the admonition that amusements can be good only insofar as they do "not leav[e] one exhausted and with distaste for work, but more able to return to work," and are dedicated not to "degrading the tastes, but elevating them."[5] In this way, then, amusements must be made productive, whether of redoubled industrious energies or of improved subjects and citizens.

Predictably defining work and play as binarily opposed, and explicitly identifying productive work as the privileged term in that opposition, Clarke, however, finds that his inviolable "laws of the universe" nevertheless begin to unravel under closer consideration, requiring him to tie them up with ever-longer strings of rationalization. Like many of his contemporaries, he succumbs to the need to elaborate upon, qualify, and append exceptions to his basic premises about what constitutes productivity; in one telling instance, he spools out the following taxonomy, remarkable not only for its tone of moral certitude and its apparent exhaustiveness, but also for the way that the repressed ambiguities built into the concept of productivity persist in rising to the surface:

> We may place among productive laborers the poet, the painter, the judges and lawyers, the physician, the orators, the professors, the clergyman. These are all working-men, adding as much to the wealth of society as the farmer, the manufacturer, or the merchant.
>
> But if a man spends his labor in doing what adds no value to life, or diminishes its value, he is unproductive. The gambler, who merely tries to get another man's money; the man who adulterates food, or makes poor articles which seem like good ones; the quack doctor who persuades people to take medicines which do them no good; those who manufacture and sell poisonous liquors to destroy the peace of families and the health of the community; those who write books which corrupt the mind and heart—are plainly unproductive laborers. But I also call the man an unproductive laborer who, as a lawyer or politician, tries to make the worse appear the better reason; who seeks to gain wealth, reputation, fame, by any means, right or wrong. I call the man an unproductive laborer who seeks to grow rich suddenly by speculation; instead of by faithful, legitimate business. I call the preacher an unproductive laborer who, instead of helping men to lead good lives, teaches them only outside forms, sectarian self-satisfaction,

narrow dogmas, or sensational emotions. Such men, if they sincerely believe they are doing right, may be saved themselves, so as by fire; but the wood, hay, and stubble which they have industriously put together will be burned.[6]

The passage is substantial enough to accommodate an array of systems of value—economic, moral, social—all with different implications for judging the significance of activity (hence, among other incommensurabilities, the speculator's production of economic value at the expense of moral value, and so forth). Whatever the specific contradictions Clarke finds it necessary to invoke, it is imperative to read dialectically his obsessive desire to cut through all these shades of irresolution and to couple his exhortations to productivity with a clear differentiation between what is productive and what it is not. For the strenuous insistence of such an argument negatively indexes the intensity of the idle threats that it seeks to neutralize. It is a culture-wide anxiety about such dangers that grounds Clarke's demand that unproductivity must serve some higher end, and makes it imperative to imagine a kind of play that would simultaneously perform work.[7]

Even William James, whose lament for the lost calm of the American subject began this investigation, steps into the same snare. In his 1899 lecture "The Gospel of Relaxation," he inveighs against the pathological "eagerness, breathlessness, and anxiety" of American life, championing repose and declaring quite convincingly that "we must change ourselves from a race that admires jerk and snap for their own sakes, and looks down upon low voices and quiet ways as dull, to one that, on the contrary, has calm for its ideal, and for their own sakes loves harmony, dignity, and ease."[8] For all of this dissatisfaction with the prevailing cultural standard, however, James, too, falls back on the hegemonic understanding of the relationship of industry to idleness. Echoing Annie Payson Call in his embrace of "power through repose," he celebrates the calmer, more "efficient" European worker, whose relaxed state of mind is valuable because it is free of "tension and anxiety," thus evading the "surest drags upon steady progress and hindrances to our success" and contributing to intensified productive force.[9] Again, idleness is represented as never truly desirable for its own sake, but rather is assumed subordinate to its other, and praised only as a multiplier of "progress" and individual "success." Hence James, purporting to preach the gospel of relaxation, somehow ends up ultimately delivering a paean to production. He is, however, hardly alone in his perplexity at approaching the limits of productivity.

An Unmotivated Modernity

In contrast to the judgments of those, like Clarke and James and innumerable others, for whom the priority of work over idleness was a given, *Idle Threats* aims to theorize the fundamental arbitrariness of the value accorded to unproductivity, and to document the febrile, if often futile, efforts to fix credible boundaries that would distinguish productive activity from its other. I invoke *arbitrariness* in the semiological sense mobilized by Saussure to highlight the inessentiality of any conceptualization of productivity, and to emphasize the strictly differential grounds of its meaning. Much of Western modernity has been governed by this basic difference pitting *industry* against *idleness*. Yet the abundant and multifaceted nineteenth-century discourse on unproductivity is fascinating for the manifold ways in which it encourages—even necessitates—that this relationship be imagined beyond the seemingly binary terms of productivity and unproductivity. It is not only that unproductivity and idleness occupy a crowded paradigm of related signs, each with its own unstable shadings of meaning: leisure, repose, ease, exhaustion, vacancy, fatigue, and so on. It is also the case that these signs are crucially determined syntagmatically, by the boundless diversity of the discursive contexts that inflect their meaning. The "idleness" of the wealthy urban gentleman, for example, clearly signifies differently than the "idleness" of the indigent and dissolute vagrant. Read at the limits of their intelligibility, some of these discursive contexts call into question the very value of "activity" itself.

It is equally crucial to acknowledge that this differential determination of the meaning of activity extends to its economic value as well. Productive activity, as the source of capitalist surplus, is always calibrated to its unproductive or reproductive opposite. Marx offers a number of ways of imagining economic value as basically differential in character, including the distinction he draws between "necessary" and "surplus" labor-time; it is the relation between the two that determines the degree to which surplus value may be realized.[10] As Kiarina Kordela points out in her penetrating account of such differentiality as the defining feature of what she calls secular modernity, "surplus value is a concept, an idea with no empirical referent." It can only be deduced, she continues, "from the purely quantitative difference between the originally advanced and the resulting amounts of exchange-value."[11] The fact that such economic and symbolic values are "merely" relative or differentially produced does not mean, however, that they do not have real material effects; the systems that produce these categories of value concretely shape the lives of the subjects who inhabit those systems. Surplus-value may be arbitrary, but, as Kordela points out, in modernity it is nevertheless "the cause both of capital and of all things."[12] The value of a sign may be produced "merely" through difference, but that does not mean that its signification, however arbitrary, does not frame our experience of the world it purports to describe. In light of all this, and given that the topic at hand is idleness, it might be helpful to keep in mind not only the principle of arbitrariness but also another Saussurean term for the differential determination of linguistic value: both the meaning and the practitioners of idleness might accurately be characterized as "unmotivated."[13]

In brief, whether we are talking about signs or economic values, the distinction between industry and idleness is arbitrary but nevertheless significant. Often, the arbitrariness of this distinction manifests in unusual contradictions where, say, a flurry of activity deemed "productive" proves, due to its manic lack of focus, incapable of actually producing much that can be said to be "valuable." Or, in even more common instances, activity condemned as "unproductive" is revealed to be in fact profoundly generative of certain kinds of value. Henry David Thoreau, one of the nineteenth-century thinkers to whom one may look most reliably for playful illustrations of the paradoxes of productivity, relates an anecdote that captures both of these aspects. Invited to lend his labor to a potentially lucrative building project undertaken by a neighbor, a "coarse and boisterous money-making fellow" seeking "more money to hoard," Thoreau is set to musing: "If I do this, most will commend me as an industrious and hard-working man; but if I choose to devote myself to certain labors which yield more real profit, though but little money, they may be inclined to look on me as an idler."[14] Thoreau's writing relentlessly foregrounds the arbitrariness of such judgments. The constitutive terms of the industry-versus-idleness binary implode as he shifts them into new contexts, exposing how the most economically "productive" labors might be the most valueless, and how those pastimes judged "idle" can produce the "real profit." As we shall see, Thoreau is just one of many nineteenth-century thinkers who gave voice to such internal disturbances undermining the valuation of activity, drawing attention both to the limits of productivity and to the limitations of the language we use for speaking about it.

The Unworking of "Nineteenth-Century America"

Focusing on the "limits" of productivity helps to strategically fore-ground the fragility and arbitrariness of the boundary drawn between productivity and its supposed other. The "limit" here is understood in something like its mathematical sense, naming the indiscernibility that impedes measurement or evaluation when a system of value is pushed to its extremes. As Patricia Seed points out, "sometimes the limit is reached because no value can be defined," revealing the failure of a system of eval-uation to extend its rational template over that which exceeds the limit—to render what lies beyond the system identical to what is already within the system, and to define values in a manner "that makes them consistent with nearby values."[15] According to this definition, then, the limit marks that point at which the prevailing template for measure falls short, and is destabilized by that which is unmeasurable due to the latter's exteriority to the constituted system.

One can imagine such a limit as a conceptual boundary, like that which cleaves productive activity from unproductive activity, or, analogously, as a geographical border attempting to separate one domain from another. In either case, exactly what happens when the limit is approached is a crucial question. It is certainly the case that straddling such a borderline can make available radical hybrid identities, or new and potentially lib-erating forms of activity; in confronting a limit, however, the system will oftentimes redouble its efforts to colonize and subdue that which stands beyond the boundary, thereby bringing it even more forcefully under the systematic template.[16] Both possibilities are illuminated by the "exchange" theory of limits proposed by Gilles Deleuze and Félix Guattari in *A Thou-sand Plateaus*. They use the notion of the limit to name the last predictable "exchange" possible in a given transaction before a threshold—a point of no return—is crossed. According to this marginalist logic, the limit is the penultimate act that caps a sequence of similar exchanges; when it is exceeded, the prevailing situation must be renegotiated.[17] Beyond the limit is a threshold—the point at which the old system must give way to a new system, where the relative values of the terms must be recalibrated, and the identities of the involved agents redefined: "The limit designates the penultimate marking a necessary rebeginning, and the threshold the ultimate marking an inevitable change."[18] Hence the policing of borders and the reinforcement of limits: once they are exceeded, the status quo is no longer tenable. In terms of border theory, for example, this might be understood as the moment when the fact of hybridity can be observed relentlessly destabilizing the colonial dynamic.[19] In economic terms, it marks the moment when a system of exchange based on predictable values cannot be sustained, precipitating crisis and change.

This theory of limits also may describe a fundamental "economics of everyday life," making comprehensible the meanings of even the most mundane or humble acts, and indicating how they contribute to either stability or change and thereby constitute microlevel negotiations about values and states of being. The helpful examples marshaled by Deleuze and Guattari are worth considering at some length:

> For example, what does an alcoholic call the *last glass*? The alcoholic makes a subjective evaluation of how much he or she can tolerate.... But beyond that limit there lies a threshold that would cause the alcoholic to change assemblage: it would change either the nature of the drinks or the customary places and hours of the drinking. Or worse yet, the alcoholic would enter a suicidal assemblage, or a medical, hospital assemblage, etc.... What counts is the existence of a spontaneous marginal criterion and marginalist evaluation determining the value of the entire series of "glasses." The same goes for having the last word in a domestic-squabble assemblage. Both partners evaluate from the start the volume or density of the last word that would give them the advantage and conclude the discussion, marking the end of an operation period or cycle of the assemblage, allowing it to start all over again. Both calculate their words in accordance with their evaluation of this last word, and the vaguely agreed time for it to come. And beyond the last (penultimate) word there lie still other words, this time final words that would cause them to enter another assemblage, divorce, for example.[20]

Though a marginalist calculation at heart, the observance of the limit thus basically governs not only purely "economic" exchanges, but also those less tangible calculations that determine the stability of all kinds of assemblages. In each case, the parties to an encounter are profoundly aware of how far they can go before the value of their practice can no longer be rendered consistent with the desirable practices that have come before. Whether producing pleasure for the recreational drinker, harmony for the domestic dyad, or affective satiety for the lover, each production must reckon in an understanding of the assemblage and its implicit or explicit limits. This conception of the limit will reverberate throughout much of the analysis that follows. It initially provides a tool for marking out the nebulous zone in which manifold cultural negotiations about the value of activity render productivity and unproductivity complex and sometimes indistinguishable from one another. But, as we shall see, it also focuses attention on the various other kinds of exchanges—crossing geographical, national, historical, and identitarian boundaries—that have been the target of recent pointed interventions in the discipline of American studies.

To rigorously account for the limits of productivity also exposes the limits imposed by the title's other key words: "nineteenth-century" and "America." For the traditional uses of such concepts also follow from a certain productivist bias: they are symptoms of a tendency to fix, master, and act on the objects of thought as products, and in so doing, to reinforce the epistemological stability of the field by deflecting vectors of thought which, in going beyond the limits of convention, threaten to fundamentally alter the disciplinary assemblage. The past couple of decades of work in American studies have done much to puncture the field's established temporal and spatial boundaries, and to "unbundle" (borrowing Wai-Chee Dimock's term) the "American" context so as to reveal its linkages with broader historical and geographical domains. Like the concept of "productivity" itself, then, the operative categories governing the field demand to be relentlessly unworked.

Accordingly, the analysis of productivity benefits from a wide range of interdisciplinary and theoretical optics that make it possible to read "nineteenth-century America" as an unfinished project. John Carlos Rowe, inquiring into the prospects for a "new" American studies, has noted that the discipline's entrenched hostility toward theory tended somewhat disingenuously to downplay the discipline's debt to its philosophical and critical roots in other traditions. As he notes, this policing of disciplinary boundaries was all the more unfortunate given not only the prevailing "fiction of national consensus" typical of traditional approaches, but also the fact that "given its explicitly multicultural and transnational composition and the rapid national legitimation demanded by its revolutionary origins, the United States calls particular, albeit not unique, attention to the fabricated, imaginary qualities of its national coherence." The assimilative model of a single American national identity thus invites the application of ideology critique or poststructuralist wariness about the groundedness of meaning and identity.[21]

Though American studies may traditionally have bristled against "foreign" theoretical tools, such intellectual indifference has thankfully not been reciprocated. Rowe's argument for the urgency of theory is all the more compelling when considered in light of contemporary theoretical interventions (especially the strain of Marxist thought ascendant in contemporary Italy, which will figure consistently in the following pages) in which thinkers of many stripes have turned to American history and cultural production as a complicated experimental theater in which to test ideas about literature, industrial culture, finance capitalism, democracy, and the ontological complexities of the commons.[22] These approaches have already done much to enrich the field by situating its objects in broader political, economic, cultural, and literary contexts. Complementary to radical approaches that stress the complicity of American modernity with the agendas of imperialism, nationalism, and exploitation, they serve as a reminder of the potentials for understanding "America" not as a self-contained given or as a monolithic agent capable of organizing human activity, but as the product of a complex and continuing intersection of historical and intellectual forces within a dynamic global network.

One must persist in acknowledging the exploitative imperialism of the nation, while also insisting on the simultaneity of different orders or registers of social, cultural, and economic organization that contribute to a global capitalist axiomatic. Contemporary global vistas increasingly make it mandatory to recognize, with Deleuze and Guattari, that "the point of departure for ecumenical organization is not a State, even an imperial one; the imperial State is only one part of it, and it constitutes a part of it in its own mode, according to its own order, which consists in capturing everything it can." This process of capture entails not merely the diffusion of a determinate and standardizing force emanating from the imperial center: "it does not proceed by progressive homogenization, or by totalization, but by the taking on of consistency or the consolidation of the diverse as such."[23] The isomorphy of the global capitalist order (predicated on its tendency not to homogenize, but rather to intensify and exploit multiplicity) has today been revealed historically as positioning the state and nation alongside other forms of organization—such as the corporation, perhaps, or other types of affective bonds, social networks, and political movements—all of which, as is shown in the argument below, contribute to governing human activity, forming subjects, and realizing surplus value.

The contemporary diminishment of the nation-state's regulatory influence has revealed how America, in its earlier incarnations too, was an entity always fluid and dynamic in its constitution: a becoming rather than a being, a process rather than a product, a project rather than an object. Such is the persuasive conclusion drawn by Paul Giles, whose efforts to deterritorialize American literature at once acknowledge the force of American nationalism (especially during its heyday from 1865 to 1980) and insist that our "current transnational phase actually has more in common with the so-called early national period, between 1780 and 1860, when national boundaries and habits were much less formed and settled."[24] For it is *this* "America"—a fluid space of unsettled habits and porous borders, of mobilities, traversals, ambiguities, and experimental possibilities for rethinking time and space—that somewhat prophetically rehearses today's exceptional state of global affairs.[25] The American "nation," it seems, was always in some respects postnational.

For all their faults, expedient labels designating "America" and the "nineteenth century" persist in serving an important heuristic and taxonomical function, and for that matter, it would be foolish to think that the problems they raise could be solved merely by pretending to abandon them *tout court*. As arbitrary as they may be, they, too, have produced real historical effects. Thus, the boundaries they produce and the limits they impose must be overcome not by ignoring them, but by critically working through them—or *unworking* them—by embracing the basic principle that "a border always implies . . . a still wider horizon within which the border takes on meaning."[26] As Wai-Chee Dimock has argued, such a conception refuses fixity and universality; it instead insists upon preserving the potentiality of "phenomena as yet emerging, not quite in sight," because still concealed beyond the accustomed (geographical or chronological) limits. The range of such a criticism addresses "a habitat still waiting for its inhabitants, waiting for a humanity that has yet to be born."[27] The invitingly utopian overtones of this appeal suggest the rich upside to rethinking not only the spatial domain of America (as one merely provisional component of a larger planetary set) but also the temporal coordinates of a criticism alert to the ("as-yet") unrealized potential of the infinite experimentation of future time. Dimock's read posits the disciplinary horizon as forever receding—or perhaps better, as forever reopening the limits of the field onto new domains beyond the boundaries we know (and thus, perhaps not coincidentally, justifying the continued existence of the discipline, even as the old "American literature" brand staggers toward obsolescence).

To invoke such an "as-yet" unrealized critical horizon also indicates just how crucial the question of time has been to the "unbundling" of America, and especially to demystifying a "nineteenth-century" America that is often treated as if that historical periodization, too, were self-evident. With this question at the forefront of this inquiry into "American nineteenth-century productivity," one cannot help but note how temporally obsessed these discourses about unproductivity are, how their fixation on idleness makes possible, or in fact necessitates, an experimentation with models of temporality and history that yearn to overthrow and supersede the commonplace of teleological, industrial, linear time. These nineteenth-century experiments—the event of Bartleby's perpetual presence, say, or the temporal stillness of luminist painting—resist productivity by challenging industrial time, and this "untimeliness" is partly responsible for blasting them out of the ossified "nineteenth century" and into relevance for the present. For *their* resistance to the nineteenth century is also *our* "untimeliness," to the extent that we meet them in a common effort to think a different time, a different America, a different kind of activity. In Cesare Casarino's gentle challenge to an earlier Dimock, he writes that Melville, for example, should be read as "neither the timeless genius abstracted from his world nor the timely writer fully belonging to his world but rather a thinker who is at once fully in his as well as in our world and yet nonsynchronous with both. And it is precisely from what Nietzsche called the unhistorical vapors of the untimely that those potentialities emerge that disrupt the status quo of history and of the world."[28] In Casarino's words, so recognizing Melville's "untimeliness" would facilitate reading the literary text less as a "what"—a passive object—than as a "way"—an active means of thinking across time and space.[29]

Among the exemplary nineteenth-century American discourses on unproductivity discussed below, there are certainly those that resist the modernizing time of industrial America by clinging to the past; in their residual ideology they tangle the linear string of industrial time by insisting on natural, aristocratic, or "barbaric" rhythms that hold back from bourgeois productivist measure. Even more interesting in some respects, though, are those that gesture toward an as-yet global realization of their latencies; their dream of an idle world is an imagining of another America altogether. Their impulse to resist capitalist time is not merely nostalgic but also utopian, adumbrating the possibilities of a world beyond work that may still await us. And if they at times seem to dream a "postindustrial" planet indomitable by a strictly American capitalism, they conjure a possible world that, in its challenge to the significance and value of "productivity," is perhaps nearer to us than we might imagine.

In either case, these negotiations at the limits of productivity—like every experience of the limit, as Deleuze and Guattari describe it—are fundamentally oriented toward a possible future. For as the exchange theory of the limit argues, in any transaction, an "evaluation of the limit is there from the start in both groups, and already governs the first 'exchange' between them. . . . [T]he evaluation is essentially *anticipatory*."[30] Whether nostalgically digging in their heels against the imminent emergence of an America wholly governed by the work ethic, or in plunging over the borders into an activity yet to be classified and known, these practices of negotiation at the limits of productivity mark moments of resistance to their present and anticipations of its beyond. Their challenge to "the limits of productivity in nineteenth-century America" demands a planetary and untimely criticism worthy of its object.

The Prehistory of Modern Idleness

It should nevertheless be noted—for example, in the reactions of William James and James Freeman Clarke to the perceived idle threats of the nineteenth century—how the imperative to produce dovetailed with an effort to stabilize productive identities, and often did so through its specific address to a discursive community imagined as national. The unsettled habits and uncertain cultural codes of the period reveal the extent to which, in Priscilla Wald's words, "the changing 'we' of the nation-state makes the very name of any 'us' mean 'something not ourselves,'" and furthermore how this continual misrecognition demands "official stories" that in this case were intended to pacify anxieties about the threat posed by idleness to a national industriousness.[31] William James's exhortation to an "*us . . . here in America*" is interesting not only for its effort to construct a productive national audience, but for revealing how such discourse about productivity invariably expressed a historically and geographically extensive structure of thought with tentacles reaching far outside the American context. James himself avers that industry and idleness are propensities with "which . . . the climate and conditions have had practically nothing at all to do"; they are not products of a natural condition, but rather reflect a social and cultural problematic.[32] It is only through the convergence of a set of specific historical forces that the thinking of such concepts as industry and idleness becomes possible. This project aims to identify those forces, to chart the vectors they pursue in and through discourse, and to genealogically situate unproductivity at the intersection of various and often conflicting value systems equipped with their own specific kinds and intensities of pressure: symbolic, political, and economic. But while it is important to note that only in the nineteenth century could a truly *modern* concept of unproductivity—in all of its contradictoriness—be developed, there are nevertheless many influential precedents upon which nineteenth-century American commentators could depend for vilifying supposedly unproductive activity and combating other idle threats.

Most crucial among these was the sustained attempt in dominant Christian circles to curtail the proclivity toward sloth. Siegfried Wenzel's study *The Sin of Sloth* provides the fullest account of this concept, charting the emergence of *acedia* as a dominant theme from the fourth century onward, and tracing its development through the manifold interventions made by the likes of John Cassian and Thomas Aquinas.[33] Wenzel's study concludes at the end of the Middle Ages, by which time, he argues, the concept of sloth was no longer capable of effectively designating the activity it sought to denigrate. With the exhortation to confession of the Lateran Council of 1215-16, the bindingness of the concept of sloth—the "everyman's vice" identified in some accounts as the primary pathway to the other deadly sins—became increasingly tenuous because it was so widely diffused. By the end of the Middle Ages, Wenzel argues, the concept of sloth was both too complexly theorized and too indiscriminately deployed to retain much of its former moral authority.[34] It seems, in retrospect, that "sloth" had been asked to do too much.

Nevertheless, the proscriptive power of "sloth" did linger, though it surely demanded redefinition due to the early modern rise of mercantilism and the eventual consolidation of the capitalist mode of production. Thus, between the sixteenth and the eighteenth centuries, an uneasy accord between Christian and capitalist ethics emerged, a development most famously explored, of course, by Max Weber in his *Protestant Ethic and the Spirit of Capitalism*. There, Weber explains how the Reformation redefined the relationship of subjects to their work, endowing the latter with a significance in which the economic and moral were ever more closely wedded. According to Lutheran teachings—and especially later, Calvinist, variants—"labor must . . . be performed as if it were an absolute end in itself, a calling."[35] Armed with this idea, Protestantism charged each follower with embracing and executing the tasks before them in the service of religious faith.

This peculiar ethic—not yet a totalizing and saturating economic system, but nevertheless an ethical guidepost for the believer in matters of religious piety—became the centerpiece of Calvinist and Puritan imperatives to simultaneously increase both one's chance of salvation and his capital. This was achieved through a revalorization of worldly activity, for, as Weber describes it, "not leisure and enjoyment, but only activity serves to increase the glory of God, according to the definite manifestations of His will."[36] The increasing pull of this notion removes the comparatively situational and isolated character of Christian ethics and extends these imperatives across the domain of everyday life, such that all activity becomes subordinated to the calling as organizing principle. As the worldly "good works" demanded by Catholicism (enshrined in the sanctification of the industrious Theresa) give way to the more abstract good *work* of the Protestant mind-set, a pair of intertwined tendencies issue forth into early modernity.[37]

Initially, we note a stricter differentiation between active and inactive satisfactions of the calling. Formerly the object of spiritual sanction, contemplation is increasingly deprioritized in favor of worldly exertion; as Weber notes, "inactive contemplation is also valueless, or even directly reprehensible if it is at the expense of one's daily work. For it is less pleasing to God than the active performance of His will in a calling."[38] Physical labor had been an accepted mode of asceticism in the West since at least Cassian's fifth-century writings.[39] But the value of worldly exertion—tendentially emphasizing middle-class, mercantilist endeavor—becomes ever more paramount in the Puritan teachings, reflecting the common cause struck by Calvinism between the calling and economic ambition. Gain comes to serve as a signifier of one's position among the chosen, and of course worldly activity pays better than monastic introversion. The combination of the exhortation to worldly activity and the Puritan condemnation of frivolous expenditure created conditions under which considerable accumulation of capital was not only possible, but unavoidable.[40] So much was this the case that Richard Baxter would negotiate a delicate justification of wealth, characterizing it as a danger to piety only insofar as it creates opportunities for lapsing into idleness. Weber's synthesis notes that "the real moral objection is to relaxation in the security of possession, the enjoyment of wealth with the consequence of idleness and the temptations of the flesh. . . . In fact, it is only because possession involves this danger of relaxation that it is objectionable at all."[41] Meanwhile, the failure to exert oneself in worldly activities is regarded as a lack of grace and an individual pathology. In contrast to Aquinas, where grace tends to be described as collective, the mind-set of Puritanism links activity to a recompense that is explicitly individualized and applicable to all: he that is indisposed to work, should starve.[42] These impulses toward the valorization of worldly activity and the individualization of active duty form the foundations for a truly modern conception of the unproductive. Weber emphasizes as a turning point the moment that the calling becomes a self-sufficient mechanism, and the imperative to produce worldly results is ensconced in a system governed by its own utilitarian logic. Citing Richard Baxter's denigration of "casual and irregular" work, he suggests that it is precisely work's "*systematic, methodical* character which is . . . demanded by worldly asceticism."[43]

The concept of "idleness," increasingly linked in the seventeenth century with its apparent other, "industry," thus comes to signify not only a turning away from spiritual duty but also a shirking of economic responsibility. In the same gesture by which this ethic becomes individualized, it is generalized to apply to all; part and parcel of the Western Enlightenment, it provides a universal template for the calculability and evaluation of activity's value. Yet the universality of this template can only truly be achieved in concert with the unprecedented degree of abstraction of time, space, and money that emerges in the late eighteenth century and is consolidated in the decades to follow. These developments—technological, experiential, intellectual, and economic—would completely recalibrate the terms by which unproductivity could be understood. A modern understanding of space and time, for example, necessarily demanded a newly disciplinary estimation of the powers and limits of bodies, both physical and political; new possibilities for mobility and communication established different standards for activity's speed, location, and scope. And perhaps most importantly, the consolidation of industrial modernity—and the primacy of the wage as the ultimate measure of activity's value—altered not only conceptions of productivity but also the way that subjects ideologically constructed themselves through it. Thus, with the help of the abstraction of equivalence and measure, a modern concept of the unproductive could strip away the training wheels of religious duty and come into its own.

The Production of Idle Men

Without question, the dynamic economic transformation that characterizes the nineteenth century—from the initiation of the first integrated and
mechanized American factory in 1815, to the deployment of rail transportation in the 1830s, to the popularization of the "American system" of
interchangeable parts in manufacturing, to the development of a national
currency in the 1860s, to the Civil War's abolition of inefficient slave labor,
to the mass production of consumer goods, and so on—logically lends
itself to a narrative about intensified productivity. Looking back at the
convergence of these historical tendencies, it is hard not to be struck by
both the explosive potentials of creative praxis and the normalizing tendency that seeks to standardize activity and drive it toward the productive
ends of the industrial capitalist order.

Shadowing all of those developments, however, is a somewhat more
obscure *unproductive* nineteenth century. It commences with the first sal-
vos fired from Rip Van Winkle's fowling piece across the bow of Franklinian and Puritan orthodoxy, and runs, perhaps, until the sounding of the
sweatshop bell that closes the business day and ejects Sister Carrie Meeber
and her kin into the phantasmagoric splendor of the developing turn-of-
the-century leisure economy.[44] In between, innumerable episodes speak to
the fact that the stoking of American productivity and the rationalization
of American life were complicated by a counterhegemonic exploration of
unprecedented potentials released by those very same processes. Though
this narrative of "resistance" to productivity is appealing—and continues to be a popular way of understanding alternative or oppositional
cultures in relationship to a dominant ideology—such a conception still
risks enshrining productivity as the standard, and perhaps inadvertently
denigrating unproductivity as merely an episodic, exceptional, or negative
case. This would perpetuate the error that has now prevailed for centuries.
Unfortunately, this almost automatic misstep continues to handicap most
critical interventions on the topic.[45]

This type of inquiry must, therefore, undertake a much more profound
reconceptualization of the key terms in the binary. The "unproductive"
must be defined not simply as a lack or negation of productivity, but rather
as an ontologically positive value in its own right. For what the concept
most often is made to refer to is not, in fact, a mere negation of productivity, but rather an untold *abundance* of productivities—an infinite mosaic
of creative human endeavor so vast and heterogeneous that it *appears*

unproductive given the limits of the rationalizing templates with which we seek to represent it.[46] For too long, this diffuse field of activity has been derided as "unproductive" when in fact it is the limits of bourgeois thought—and the inherent constraints of any effort to fully rationalize, comprehend, and regulate an activity that exceeds measure and knowledge—that are at fault. Properly considered, the immeasurable force of the so-called "unproductive" is the ultimate horizon of human endeavor, and subtends all local manifestations of productivity: work, labor, and the rest are merely reductionist categories that attempt to manage the infinity of human activity by pressing it into normative molds.[47] The "unproductive" is primary to them all.

Nineteenth-century subjects took advantage of a culture-wide proliferation of discourses and practices beyond the limits of such reductionist categories, experimenting with unproductivity and reimagining themselves through it. The titles of some of the texts discussed here—James's "The Energies of Men," Richard Henry Dana, Sr.'s *The Idle Man*, and so forth—begin to suggest how gender politics framed these as-yet unclassifiable forms of activity; with some exceptions, the emphasis of this work will be largely placed on the way that *men* struggled with, or celebrated the value of, their idle activity. It should be pointed out that the unproductivity of women is every bit as paradoxical and interesting as that of men. Indeed, the unremunerated work of the housewife that shapes women's activity in accordance with domestic ideology epitomizes the neglect or misrecognition of the productivity of the unproductive. In light of the fact that this type of productivity has been well-documented and theorized in extremely compelling ways, I propose to focus instead on new analytical vistas revealed by the linkages between unproductivity and a complicated American "national manhood."[48]

The recent flourishing of critical work on the construction of masculine identity has suggested that—as with the categories of "productivity," "nineteenth-century," and "America" discussed above—a normative "national manhood" was always a highly unstable imaginary edifice. Such a construct tended to assume a certain relationship between the (white) male and his work, the latter typically understood as the exercise of some kind of management of, or mastery over, forces threatening to the purported stability of the mythical masculine paradigm. Dana Nelson notes in his influential study that this abstracted national fraternity was predicated on men's ability to "internalize rational principles of (phobia-inducing) self-management as a precondition of authority for their

(counterphobic) management of others. The occulted space of the managing 'expert' became a democratic as well as a career ideal: a professional
manhood."⁴⁹ The construction of the "male manager" in relation to the
forces of irrationality and disorder that always demand regulation introduces an inherent friction and a nagging paranoia into these "internal-
ized" masculine norms. Far from establishing a stable national abstraction, this process of subjectivation produces an individualized interior
that houses the play of often volatile social forces; it furthermore implies
an ongoing engagement with the possibilities of new social conventions
generated at the limits of normative manhood.⁵⁰

A manhood premised on management and grounded upon practices of
professionalization is always internally troubled by the prospect of other
possible manhoods, producible by experimentation with and translation
of the cultural potentials at hand. In light of the tendency to privilege
such professional identities in masculinity studies—itself arguably representative of another productivist bias in our knowledge of the era⁵¹—*Idle
Threats* seeks to explore exemplary models of manhood that, flourishing
beyond the limits of normative productivity, unraveled the surety of the
linkage between "man" and "management" and opened the question of
productive activity's ultimate value. Recent critical attention to the various manifestations of nineteenth-century bachelordom—and the idle
threats it posed to both to economic and procreative productivity—offers
one route toward expanding this field of inquiry. Vincent Bertolini main-
tains, for example, that the nineteenth-century bachelor, "with no socially
validated practices to call his own . . . exists as a purely conceptual entity
in relation to sexualized nonbachelorhood, and not as a practical (that
is, activity oriented) sexual identity."⁵² The various mysteries presented
by the bachelor—"solitary . . . unmonitorable . . . autonomous"—conjured
"the transgressive triple threat of masturbation, whoremongering, and
that nameless horror—homosexual sex."⁵³ But these various threats coexist with another vague terror, that produced by the prospect of idleness
and economic unproductivity itself. The bachelor's indifference toward
sexual productivity was represented as mirroring a lifestyle preoccupied
not with production, but rather with the "feminine" traits of consumption
and expenditure. As Katherine V. Snyder remarks, "just as bachelors were
imagined as spending their money on the wrong objects or for the wrong
reasons, they were also imagined as channeling, or dissipating, their sexual energy in a variety of nonmarital 'dead ends.'"⁵⁴ Somewhat paradoxically, it might be suggested that an independence not unlike that enjoyed

by the bachelor—freely able to pursue his personal transcendences in the world beyond the marital sphere—would increasingly provide the template for a "male individualism" untroubled by domestic concerns, with this autonomy ultimately better equipping him as a man of business.[55]

Further complicating matters is that the bachelor's apparent hostility toward both types of productivity was merely one, albeit extreme, expression of paradoxes that confronted male identity in much more subtle ways, as in discourses of nineteenth-century sentimentality. Sentimentalism, argues Lori Merish, modeled a specific kind of economic consumption for women readers—that is, a passive "sentimental ownership" in which domestic possessions drove erotic investment and desire—and thus did important cultural work in establishing the appropriateness of a "psychology of the 'family wage,' in which power is exclusively defined as the power of ownership (of labor and property), and in which female economic 'agency' as market subjects (as consumers) is tied to the agency of the male 'breadwinner.'"[56] However, as recent scholarship on this front has contended, the construction by sentimental texts of a relatively passive economic subject—a mere possessor, not a producer, of value—was not limited to only one of the gendered "separate spheres" frequently assumed by past studies of sentimentalism. This sentimental passivity also produced important wrinkles in the surface of an American masculinity based on management and active production. Joseph Fichtelberg's *Critical Fictions* notes the ubiquity and importance of such discourse as a means of "humanizing" the crises of economic development, by mediating "the complex and delicate transition between premarket and market mentalities, between face-to-face and long-distance economic relations . . . through an imperialism of feeling."[57] Performing this important cultural work, the sentimental mode transcended boundaries of gender and genre, he argues, contributing to the embrace of an economic passivity that was far more widespread than more gender-specific accounts have realized. Ultimately, the resulting passive subjectivities proved oddly suited to more advanced types of white-collar management, a model of corporate masculinity that again seems to complicate the normative professionalism of the "national manhood" described by Nelson. The active practices of rational mastery and control so central to Nelson's conception are here subordinated to an affect of passive reactivity, "a subtle form of yielding in which the actor responded to his milieu," as Fichtelberg describes it. "That capacity," he writes, "originally the hallmark of feminine sensibility, was gradually transferred, through a massive cultural experiment, from the privacy of domestic life to the conflicts of international trade, and thence to a domestic market where men came to adapt the 'feminine characteristics' of transparency and compromise."[58] Assuming a stance of passivity in order to be creative, this economic subject depends less upon his own productive force than upon his ability to harness and redirect economic energies that originate outside of himself.[59]

The figure of the bachelor and the affective work of male sentimentality suggestively begin to illustrate how the uncertainties of masculine identity were bound up in the conceptual tangle determining the value of productivity. The chapters that follow, addressing themselves to both documentary and theoretical concerns, pursue some additional ways in which the unproductive broadened and destabilized the repertoire of possibilities for masculine subjectivation. They attempt to provide organizing rubrics—the disciplinarity of time and the poetics of space, the creative power of artistic repose, the energy of the body, the utility of speculative thought—that further draw out some of the hidden "patterns" sculpted by discourses about unproductivity. Some of what these patterns trace will feel familiar, though hopefully recast by new optics; other components of the design will demand thinking far beyond the usual limits typically imposed on studies of the period. Certainly, a handful of literary texts are so deliberate in their treatments of unproductivity that they simply cannot be avoided: "Bartleby, the Scrivener," *The Idle Man*, *Sister Carrie*. However, the claim that the problem of unproductivity creates a disturbance felt across the field of cultural production—and indeed beyond the traditional spatial and temporal boundaries of "nineteenth-century America"—may only be sustained if those works enter into new juxtapositions with other texts and practices that often confront unproductivity indirectly, symptomatically, or from unexpected quarters. Hence, these works are here considered alongside treatments of aesthetics and landscape painting in chapter 2, of governmental administration and city planning in chapter 3, of theories of physiology and political economy in chapter 4, and of philosophy in chapter 5.

Though it will be clear that the problem of unproductivity insinuated itself all throughout various aesthetic, geographical, physiological, and philosophical imaginaries, the character of all of these debates is fundamentally economic. The study of political economy—including the Marxist theory of circulation, Simmel's philosophy of money, and the efforts of twentieth-century economists to explain the mystery of that unmeasurable productivity they termed "the residual"—thus helps to illustrate patterns within the discourse about unproductivity and, hopefully, to explain them in a fashion that illuminates more generally the conditions of Western modernity, and especially the capitalist mode of production that, despite its ongoing internal transformations, persists in defining the value of our activity to this day.

Our contemporary culture often appears to have neared perfection in striking the most efficient equilibrium between industry and its other; the fluidity and flexibility of the postmodern economy certainly makes possible an unprecedented exploitation of economic value produced through supposedly unproductive activity. It is perhaps easy to imagine our nineteenth-century precursors as being comparatively clumsier in their handling of the limits of productivity, but we should keep in mind that those limits posed a conceptual, economic, and intellectual problem to them that no longer troubles us in exactly the same way. To future generations, this "problem" may be all but unimaginable, so thoroughly has the principle of production saturated contemporary lived experience and come to define an age in which, theoretically, every minute of lived human time can be made to pay. It is not only that we can "send a fax from the beach," as that advertisement for AT&T, now somewhat striking in its quaintness, promised in the 1990s; it is not even that the boundaries between work time and free time have been rendered all but entirely porous by the creep of "working vacations," casual Fridays, and pocket-sized devices that take the office anywhere. It is also the case that the very pleasures we take in living today function like work—as when we consume a constant flow of spectacular images and thus produce a surplus in the "attention economy," or when the credit lines we maintain accrue interest and thus produce value for others even as we sleep.[60] Our restive dreams of a genuine respite from production occupy us during waking hours too, but in the global factory without walls, such idle fantasies remain just that.

Our task, then, is to dignify the unproductive ambivalences of the nineteenth century, and to struggle to read them against teleology, that is, to avoid imagining them as the primitive miscues of a people who have yet to figure out their inevitable fate. Generously, we might even regard them as a prophylactic against that fate, a prophetic recognition of the direction toward which the prevailing cultural tendencies were pointing, and a seizure of opportunities to jar and reorient the progressive course of productivity. Such a notion of reverse causality—in which the cultural phenomena of the past react to developments latent or threatened but not yet realized—reveals the nineteenth-century debate as an uncomfortable anticipation of our own contemporary age, in which no real exterior to productivity can be said to exist any longer. Nineteenth-century American unproductivity might then be recognized—to adopt and revise Levinas's earlier formulation about indolence—as truly a holding back against a certain kind of future. In our time, there may no longer be any such holding back. And so it goes for this introduction, too. For it is long past time to dispense with the preliminaries, to overcome our procrastination, and to get on with the task at hand.

1

The Bartleby Industry
and Bartleby's Idleness

Bah! Bartleby!

Despite being perhaps the single most profound work about idleness in the whole of American literature, Melville's "Bartleby" is also, ironically, among the tales in that tradition that have been most badly overworked. Suspecting that "Bartleby" has been done to death, one initially recoils from the duty of critically rewriting this scrivener's tale once more. Yet the tensions of this contradictory position—of being compelled to rework the text and simultaneously preferring not to—may only be discharged by a renewed engagement with its inscrutability, its inevitability; one can inquire into the history of neither American literature nor American productivity without confronting, at least for a few pages, the problems that the story persists in raising.

To begin this work by confronting "Bartleby" already complicates any inquiry into the question of idleness. For doing so entails hazarding a small contribution to the proliferation of criticism that Dan McCall, seizing on this paradox, has termed the "Bartleby Industry."[1] The critical machinery of that uncommonly productive industry has long strained to disentangle the tale's various mysteries, paradoxes, and ambivalences; innumerable such critical ventures seem to contradict, overwhelm, and undercut each other, most of them refusing to work together. Often, then, the highly productive application of all this "industry" appears to draw us further from the possibility of getting anything substantial or definitive done. The exegetical task is never complete. And especially when it comes to "Bartleby," the considerable energies of criticism seem hopelessly diffused. Precisely because of the excess of productive energy it attempts to marshal, the Bartleby Industry thus risks exposing the unproductivity that lies at its very heart. And yet to say something important about the encounter between nineteenth-century American culture and the powers of unproductivity, it is through this industry that one must push. It is perhaps a matter of kicking poor old Bartleby's corpse around one more time, firm in the conviction that some reflex from this apparently catatonic hulk will confirm the presence, there, of life.

Though Bartleby is deservedly one of the most widely beloved of nineteenth-century idlers, he is certainly not alone among his contemporaries. The implications of the story's obsession with unproductivity become clearer when "Bartleby" is juxtaposed with a previously undiscovered source text, from 1846: Robert Grant White's *Law and Laziness; or, Students at Law of Leisure*.[2] Borrowing both from White's cast of characters and from episodes in his narrative, Melville's 1853 story renews the earlier tale's concerns and conducts an exceptionally sustained and subtle inquiry into just what nineteenth-century idleness is and what it means. Founded itself on these questions, "Bartleby" explores how the problem of unproductive activity constitutes a limit for the imperatives of the work ethic and the jurisdiction of Enlightenment certainty; it demonstrates how the economic intangibility of idleness unworks the geometric rationality of modern time and space and demystifies the specious autonomy of the modern subject.[3] Reconsidering "Bartleby" in this light makes possible a new understanding of the unusual significance—even productivity—of the unproductive. Enter Bartleby, that "motionless young man . . . pallidly neat, pitiably respectable, incurably forlorn!"—who, starting in upon his tenure as a legal scrivener, embodies the growing pains of this transitional period in the history of unproductivity.[4]

Law and Laziness

Much of the enigma of Bartleby—and of his legendary obduracy in the face of his employer's demands to either work or leave the law office in which he has taken up residence—results from the inability of his employer, the story's narrator, to step outside of the Enlightenment standpoint that restricts him to a "normative accounting of character," in the words of Thomas Augst.[5] It is from within the work ethic and its subtending systems of rational calculation that the narrator reports, thereby binding our own comprehension, as readers, of Bartleby. The story wastes little time in alerting us to this condition and furthermore indicating its inadequacy. Particularly striking is the narrator's proud introductory claim to embody two Cartesian motifs, those of "method" and "prudence" (14):[6] the reportage is poised uncomfortably between the two, the tension between them making visible the limitations of this rationalist approach. Methodologically, the narrator apes Descartes in strenuously imposing an evidentiary standard that excludes such doubtful information as secondary commentary and installs the self as the ultimate mediator of certainty: "I believe that no materials exist, for a full and satisfactory biography of this man. . . . Bartleby is one of those beings of whom nothing is ascertainable, except from the original sources, and, in his case, those are very small. What my own astonished eyes saw of Bartleby, that is all I know of him, except, indeed, one vague report, which will appear in the sequel" (13). When the attorney's attempts to understand Bartleby grow desperate, however, cracks in this soberly methodical persona appear: doubt prevails, hearsay is admitted, and the classical epistemological privilege accorded the narrator's "own astonished eyes" eventually yields. Equivocation about his own reason mounts over the course of the story, culminating in the serious doubts that inaugurate the concluding "sequel" passage: "Yet here I hardly know whether I should divulge one little item of rumor, which came to my ear a few months after the scrivener's decease. Upon what basis it rested, I could never ascertain; and hence, how true it is I cannot tell" (45). The rumor—of Bartleby's one-time employment at the Dead Letter Office and consequent emotional trauma—is nevertheless admitted into evidence; as an explanation of Bartleby's behavior, it is suggestive but hardly conclusive.[7] It is nonetheless the best that the methodical narrator can do to make Bartleby "ascertainable" and thus to unfold the scrivener's mystery. Where method fails, prudence compensates; this is a modest diminution of certainty. For "prudence"—which in Cartesian times referred to the ability to negotiate the coexistence of opposed tendencies in one object or situation—is a means of embracing doubt and turning it to advantage, rather than seeking to vanquish it, in the manner of method.[8] It is as if, in the face of Bartleby's challenge to the sensible, "cool tranquility" of the law office, the attorney lapses from Enlightenment reason into baroque doubt (14). Thus do the paradoxes and ambivalences of the story begin to accumulate.[9]

The narrator's Enlightenment character finds further expression, as Marvin Hunt has suggested, in his insistence on using biographical conventions to equip Bartleby with a fixed, individualized identity, as well as in his devotion to the law as a calculating, instrumental system of order.[10] The former impulse has been perpetuated by the critical tendency to understand Bartleby's recalcitrance as merely the fickle whim of a disturbed psychology, the bitter revenge of a downwardly mobile bureaucrat, or the class hate of an inflamed proletarian—in each case resorting to an individualized explanation, the biographical imperative of which runs up against the same interpretive paralysis of the flummoxed narrator.[11] We come closer to an adequate explanation by resisting the temptation to reproduce the narrator's avowed standpoint on the matter of the scrivener's personality and by following the narrative clues that indicate ways of understanding Bartleby by *depersonalizing* him.[12] Hunt, for example, argues that over the course of the story Bartleby increasingly functions as less an individual than a mere "symbolic presence."[13] A recent text of political philosophy reaches a similar conclusion, taking Bartleby to embody a doomed strategy of oppositional sovereignty: "Bartleby in his pure passivity and his refusal of any particulars presents us with a figure of generic being, being as such, being and nothing more."[14]

However intangible Bartleby's presence may be, it nevertheless has concrete ramifications for his office mates and their workplace. According to some readers, for example, the story traces the narrator's growth through exposure to self-knowledge: the apparition of Bartleby forces him to change himself. It is precisely because Bartleby wields some real, transformative power that the attorney is provoked to tactics of containment: "His faith in a reasonable universe at stake, the lawyer deliberately and repeatedly triggers Bartleby's negative responses; he cannot do otherwise because he cannot leave the mystery alone."[15] Nevertheless, there is certainly cause for skepticism about any such growth narratives, since the narrator does not, in terms of first principles, change all that much: his repeated confrontations with Bartleby, as James Wilson notes, are marked by a cyclical recurrence of the same behavior. Whenever Bartleby refuses his entreaties, the attorney is at first stunned, then retreats into self-defense, then conjures up a rationalization on the basis of a cost-benefit analysis.[16] The impact of Bartleby is momentary if recurrent, repeatedly recuperated in a dialectic driven by reasoned self-interest.

Moreover, the text indicates that Bartleby's impersonal force, rather than transforming the narrator, merely makes manifest something that was latent in him all along. The latter's careful self-inventory at the story's outset attests to his methodical sobriety and pragmatic prudence, the cool tranquility he so values, and his essentially conservative and "eminently safe" character (14). But as his description continues, the attorney goes on to disclose certain proclivities regarding exertion and ease that subtly adumbrate the existing fault lines along which this safe and sober character will later be dangerously jarred: "I am a man who, from his youth upwards, has been filled with a profound conviction that the easiest way of life is the best," he explains. "Hence, though I belong to a profession proverbially energetic and nervous, even to turbulence, at times, yet nothing of that sort have I ever suffered to invade my peace" (14). Indeed, the turbulence that upsets this law office will stem not from the feverishness typical of the legal profession, but rather from Bartleby's inert passivity, which troubles the détente between Enlightenment reason and the narrator's own inherent penchant for unproductivity—his position in the self-described and doubly negative grey area of the "not unemployed" (14).[17]

Like the narrator's subjectivity, the tale itself pivots on this ambivalent relation between the rational and the irrational, between productivity and unproductivity. Once having introduced the foreign element of Bartleby into the machinery of the office, the attorney takes to judging his existing staff—the two scriveners, Turkey and Nippers, and an office boy, Ginger Nut—in turn, by their own unproductivities. In this process of investigation, to which much of the story is dedicated, he attempts to tease out the inner ambivalence that inheres in each of them, as in himself.[18] And the contradictions unearthed in each character are reproduced at the level of the office as a whole, which is organized so that alternative currents of productivity and unproductivity compensate for each other. Bartleby's force is single-handedly to disrupt these equilibria.

Depicting the manifold incarnations of unproductivity that saddle this office, the tale thus pits the irrationality of the unproductive (Bartleby's weird passivity, the narrator's own apparent propensities) against the systemic, methodical character of enlightened existence (the work ethic, reason, and the law), in the process revealing the unexpected power of the former and the fallibility of the latter. In exploring this binary, Melville builds on the precedent set in the title of White's 1846 text: *Law and Laziness; or, Students at Law of Leisure*. This story about unproductivity, which sketches an office full of legal wannabes intoxicated by the idleness of Edgar Bulwer Lytton's *Pelham* (1828), raises a similar question about what happens when law and laziness collide; more significantly, it serves as a crucial source from which Melville, writing "Bartleby" seven years later, evidently draws some of his conception and characters.[19]

"There is no place like a law-office for making a fashionable acquaintance, and doing the least work with the greatest ease," White writes, introducing a cast of characters likely somewhat familiar to us. While in Melville's story, it is Bartleby who speaks with a "flute-like tone" (22),

White describes an office boy who likewise plays a flute until "he is out of breath," and then "eats gingerbread under the lid of his desk"[20]—suggesting that the umbilical connection between the two texts might be traced in the character of Ginger Nut. Apparently acting on the precedent of White's distracted office boy, Ginger Nut litters his desk with snacks; we are told his nickname pertains to the small cakes of gingerbread that are a favorite around the office. Melville echoes White's title in describing Ginger Nut as a "student at law," adding that, "to this quick-witted youth, the whole noble science of the law was contained in a nut-shell" (18). Ginger Nut thus most clearly imports the problematic of *Students at Law of Leisure* into "Bartleby"; he signals—in a nutshell—that Melville's story grounds itself in the same troubled relationship of the law with unproductivity.

Sketch two of *Law and Laziness* consolidates the relationship between these texts, and further belies Melville's disingenuous invocation at the beginning of "Bartleby" of "an interesting and somewhat singular set of men, of whom, as yet, nothing, that I know of, has ever been written—I mean, the law-copyists or scriveners" (13). For in a rare interval when the law students of White's text are (uncharacteristically) diligently at work, "only the scrivener is idle": "Resting his head upon his hand, and lulled by the never ceasing sound of busy life rising from the street, he slumbers by fits, and dreams of studying the long summer morning in a country school house; hears the brook tumble over its rocks near the door and the trees rustle. Then he wakes, by fits, to a dim perception of the objects around; and has a vague sense of the daily drudgery by which he earns his bread."[21] That Melville speculates, in turn, on the biography of this dreamily idle scrivener is perhaps less interesting than the way in which he does so. For while White will largely content himself with illustrating the oppositions that separate law from laziness and rationality from the unreasonable— suggesting that the natural primacy of the former will in any case be triumphantly restored[22]—Melville depicts the situation of the student at law of leisure with considerably more complexity. For him, the contrary terms of law and laziness are palpably intertwined and inseparable, at the level not only of narrative and character but also of concept. In each case, activity resists classification: the characters occupy the odd ground of being "not unemployed" and yet not quite productive either. So when Bartleby's impersonal force penetrates into the delicate relationships that hold the office together, thereby illuminating for the narrator the manifold unproductivities that abound there, he furthermore threatens to hollow out the authority of the law itself, in all of its orderliness, calculability, measurability, and predictability.

Unmoored from the law, the attorney is drawn into a vortex of uncertainty and fear: "I trembled to think that my contact with the scrivener had already and seriously affected me in a mental way," he frets, as his own activity becomes increasingly contradictory and passionate under Bartleby's influence (31). He balances his desire to flee Bartleby with a longing to stay near him; he equivocates between hostility and sympathy; he hastens to "dismiss Bartleby the better to defer the dismissal," as Ann Smock explains, "rushing lethargically, hurrying to delay."[23] He seems betrayed not only by the law, but with it, by his own will as well. In one attempt to provoke Bartleby to remove himself from the premises, the lawyer proclaims the beauty of his own "doctrine of assumptions"—a strategy in which, by giving Bartleby no quarter, by refusing to even entertain the notion that Bartleby could refuse, the attorney hopes to assume his tormentor out of existence. The invocation of such a doctrine recasts the law in economic terms (given the reputation of economics as the ultimate science of assumption); Bartleby's obstinacy predictably perverts the rationality of this system as well, violating the sanctity of the work contract by riddling it with "the unheard-of exemptions" that formed its "tacit stipulations" (26). The arrangement is made ridiculous (as are the juridical exemptions Bartleby later enjoys in the Tombs, where he is allowed to walk the grounds freely like no other prisoner may) by having as its reason for survival precisely the exception that renders it meaningless. Thus: a prison stay characterized by freedom of movement, a work contract stipulating that the employee may elect not to perform tasks as he pleases.[24] The perversion of this system of assumptions, and the imperiling of the very certainties that ground both law and economics, induce in the narrator a budding doubt about his own "reason" and the system of "justice" that it serves (22).

The perverse logics unleashed by Bartleby's arrival are experienced by the lawyer as nothing less than the severing of the connection between will and action. This is clearest in the scene of Bartleby's second refusal, when all the office staff have assembled to proofread a document that the scrivener has copied in quadruplicate. Bartleby prefers not to participate, of course, but in balking at the attorney's request, opts for a strange formulation: "What is wanted?" he mildly calls from behind the screen that demarcates his corner of the office. It is a charged question, its passive construction disqualifying the attorney or anyone else from serving as an individualized willing agent: Bartleby's formulation impersonalizes desire. The attorney manages only to further exacerbate the situation with his hasty rejoinder, which deflects the thrust of the query by handling it as a matter of assumption and not one of will. His matter-of-fact doctrine writes his own agency out of the equation: "The copies, the copies . . ." he replies. "We are going to examine them" (21). We are going to examine the copies, but nobody—and this holds for each member of the attorney's office staff—can claim to *want* to do so. We note that Turkey's bland submission to authority reduces him to merely parroting what he imagines to be the boss's desire; of Nippers, we have already been told that his personality is in part defined by the fact that "he knew not what he wanted" (17).[25] Ginger Nut, who will at least hazard a tentative opinion of Bartleby's intransigence ("I think, sir, he's a little luny"), undermines the force of his own judgment by delivering it through a grin (22).

Thus occurs a breakdown of the basic coordinates that connect desire and agency. Bartleby's question charges the attorney and his staff with being estranged from their desire, and indicts them for compensating for that estrangement by engaging in pursuits to which he himself would prefer not to stoop. He apparently has a point, judging the effect of his question by the intensity of the narrator's subsequent ruminations: "It is not seldom the case that, when a man is browbeaten in some unprecedented and violently unreasonable way, he begins to stagger in his own plainest faith," he muses. "He begins, as it were, vaguely to surmise that, wonderful as it may be, all the justice and all the reason is on the other side" (22).

In light of the way that the unproductive interpenetrates the system of law—in the process revealing how the systemic and methodological is always predicated on its potential destabilization by the singular and unreasonable—the suggestive title of White's story might be interpreted with "Bartleby" in mind. Thus, "law and laziness" must be read not as an opposition of the two terms, but rather as an equation in which the former presupposes the latter and is unthinkable without it. Reconsideration of White's subtitle, *Students at Law of Leisure*, buoys this interpretation: a less awkward variant ("students of law at leisure") would differentiate between the two activities, but here the second term neatly coincides with the first—these are leisurely students of law who study the regnant law of leisure. The narrator, finding himself unexpectedly stranded at this dangerous intersection where law and laziness coincide, attempts vainly to combat the play in his beloved systems of rationality—his economic assumptions, his method, his law. At the same time, however, he must come to grips with an unproductive impulse that is revealed as profoundly his own.

The "Residual": Leisure without Measure

Though it is Bartleby's uncommon listlessness in the story's latter movements that usually draws the most sustained critical attention, it is necessary to notice how initial descriptions of the scrivener attribute to him an equally uncommon productivity. Remember how, at first, he "did an extraordinary quantity of writing": "As if long famishing for something to copy, he seemed to gorge himself on [the narrator's] documents. There was no pause for digestion" (19). Despite Bartleby's apparently extreme dedication—and subsequent reference to his "incessant industry" and "unexampled diligence" (25, 32)—something lingers that discomfits the attorney. "I should have been quite delighted with his application," he confides, "had he been cheerfully industrious. But he wrote on silently, palely, mechanically" (19–20). Even at his most diligent, Bartleby fails to please his employer—a logical consequence, perhaps, of the attorney's confused desires, his own troubled relationship to industry, and his expectation that Bartleby perform what is ultimately a contradictory task. He explains that his aims in hiring the scrivener were twofold: to infuse the office with easy calm (for Bartleby's sedate aspect seemed to promise a palliative for the turbulent tendencies of his colleagues) and also to attend to business industriously on the not-uncommon if "trivial occasions" that would demand his services, at which times he would be expected to see to "any trifling thing . . . without the least delay" (20, 19, 20). One suspects that no employee could flourish under the demand to be both a sedative and a catalyst, both calming and invigorating.

Bartleby's response to either demand is equally extreme—he applies himself with comparable dedication to both productivity and unproductivity. His initial display of industry and his subsequent apathy occupy his time entirely. Whether copying documents or merely standing in a vacant reverie, he is a "perpetual sentry" in the office—always there, and unavoidable (23). Furthermore, his pallor, his cheerlessness, and his sheer indifference all provoke the attorney to liken his "perpetual occupancy" to that of a "ghost": he is an "apparition" and an "intolerable incubus" (38). Bartleby's quiet vigil resonates, during the phases of his "employment" by the narrator, through all the office's functioning, upsetting meetings with clients, disrupting workplace bonds, challenging authority, and resulting in proceedings to which Turkey diplomatically refers at one point as "quite out of the common" (22).[26] Such is the power that Bartleby embodies, a power that is not just the individualized force of a memorable personality, but a ghostly force that exceeds the merely human form within which readers and the narrator attempt to contain it. Whether he is diligently working (and nevertheless being judged somehow unsatisfactory) or absolutely idle (and nevertheless exerting an influence throughout the office), Bartleby embodies the shadowy presence of the not-quite-productive in all work. This force was latent in his office mates before his arrival, and it persists in producing anxiety long after Bartleby's eventual death: among its effects are the meditations that provoke the narrator, at least "a few months" after the fact, to pen his rather uncertain account. If the story is one of class struggle, this represents the crowning triumph of Bartleby's strategy: ultimately it is the attorney—the boss man—who is himself compelled to sit down and write. Bartleby forces him to do the work of a scrivener.

Like the powerful specter of Bartleby, the ambiguous productivity of the unproductive has proven a haunting phantom unascertainable by economic theory. Despite modern capitalism's tireless efforts to understand the relationship between productive and unproductive activity (and, whether through the scientific management of labor or the development of the consumerist "leisure economy," to turn it to profit), the basic indeterminacy of these categories has presented a chronic problem for economic and cultural thought.[27] The application of ever-more-subtle rationalized schemas to the problem has, in many respects, rendered the specter of the unproductive only more mysterious, reproducing the incomprehension that troubles Melville's narrator.

An instructive episode in the history of these efforts is the reaction to Wassily Leontief's postwar development of unprecedentedly nuanced techniques for analyzing the relationship between resource investment and capital realization. The Leontief model, however, generated considerable bafflement for midcentury economists, as vast percentages of economic growth turned out to be simply inexplicable in quantitative terms—sometimes resulting in miscalculations of up to 50 percent.[28] Economists finally explained this haunting difference, which they christened the "residual," to be the consequence of apparently extra-economic, qualitative factors: the unexplained productivity, they found, arose from the efforts of self-interested actors to improve their own capacity through investments in themselves. Activities that had been classified as "unproductive" in the direct sense of the word—education and training, improvements in physical capacity, and augmented facility in exploiting professional opportunities—were nonetheless discovered to intensify productive force, via what Gary Becker called "the imbedding of resources in people."[29] Essentially, this theory of "human capital" sought to resolve the problem of the nebulous residual, and thus to explain the productivity of the unproductive through an adjustment to the rubrics of normative accounting, recasting the category of "consumption" as one of "investment."[30]

The implications of the theory of human capital opened up fresh questions for the definition of human productivity, and the efforts of neoliberal economics to account for it via categories of labor time and the capitalist firm. "There can be no doubt whatsoever," comments Theodore Schultz, "that the concept of a labor force, or of man-hours worked, fails to take into account the improvements in the capabilities of man," and that "theories of firm behavior ... almost invariably *ignore the effect of the productive process itself on worker productivity.*"[31] For the most part, however, human capital theory insisted on stressing the self-investment of the individualized worker, describing such investment in the quantitative terms of wages and opportunity costs rather than via broader qualitative or social categories.[32] The theory, sharing in the individualist prejudice that afflicts the narrator and critics of "Bartleby," thus runs up against similar interpretive limits. Human capital, such as that generated by nonspecific worker training, for example, produces value that tends to circulate beyond the calculability of the individual firm, denuding the hermetic entrepreneurial environment.[33]

This idea is developed further in Fritz Machlup's comprehensive three-volume work *Knowledge: Its Creation, Distribution, and Economic Significance.*[34] There, he defines three categories of knowledge capital, ranging from that capital embodied in physical or material instantiations, to that which has a specific human embodiment, to that which he defines as "nonmaterial nonhuman capital," which "consists entirely of knowledge, embodied neither in persons nor in material things." He goes on to claim that "this is a recently invented concept; technological progress as a lever of productivity had been relegated to the residual of the production function, was then promoted to the rank of an independent variable ... and has finally been elevated to the stately class of capital, neither physical nor human."[35] The nonmaterial, nonhuman aspect of this capital refers not to its origin but instead to the way it cannot be exhaustively localized in specific material, human, or entrepreneurial contexts. Nevertheless, like the "very ghost" described by the narrator of "Bartleby," it is "always there," haunting the economic categories that may only imperfectly measure it and eluding exploitation by any one boss (25, 26). Nonproprietary and nonexclusive, such capital circulates freely in a composite, shifting field of economic externalities; in a contemporary theoretical vocabulary it would be called "social capital."[36]

Attempts by the discipline of economics to devise more refined means for quantifying the productivity of such seemingly intangible inputs—thereby corralling them within the limits of the preexistent economic models—have failed to acknowledge the extent to which the difficulty of quantification is symptomatic of undertheorized complexities in the very concept of production. An intriguing footnote to Larry S. Sjaastad's contribution to the landmark *Journal of Political Economy* issue on "investment in human beings" alludes to one particular obstacle impeding such quantification—the "value of leisure": "The value of leisure is . . . neglected when comparing earnings. If the individual labor supply is not backward bending, smaller earnings will necessarily be accompanied by larger amounts of leisure time, which should not be valued at zero. Thus one should look at hours of work as well as earnings. There remains the value to impute to an hour's leisure. While an imputation probably can not be accurately made, this omission should be borne in mind."[37] To bear this question in mind is to be haunted by the ghost of the unproductive. For what Sjaastad seeks simultaneously to exclude and to explain threatens—like the enigma of Bartleby hanging around the office—to destabilize the rationality of the entire system that quantifies economic value by way of the treacherous distinction between "productive" and "unproductive" activity.

This is a problem inherent to the capitalist mode of production. As Antonio Negri argues, the form of economic value founded on measurable labor reveals itself, by the twentieth century, to be unsustainable. "The distinctions between 'productive labor' and 'unproductive labor,' between 'production' and 'circulation,' between 'simple labor' and 'complex labor' are all toppled," he notes.[38] Yet this historical crisis is, as Marx indicates in his *Grundrisse* of 1858, implicit all along as the logical consequence of capital's ineluctable tendency to render productive even that activity which is not immediately recognizable as labor: "The accumulation of knowledge and of skill, of the general productive forces of the social brain, is thus absorbed into capital . . . and hence appears as an attribute of capital, and more specifically of *fixed capital*, in so far as it enters into the production process as a means of production proper."[39] This, despite—or because of—its resistance to quantitative measure. Ultimately, Marx anticipates the bourgeois political economists of the twentieth century, speculating that

> an increase of free time . . . reacts back upon the productive power of labour as itself the greatest productive power. . . . [I]t can be regarded as the production of *fixed capital*, this fixed capital being man himself. It goes without saying, by the way, that direct labour time itself cannot remain in the abstract antithesis to free time in which it appears from the perspective of bourgeois economy. . . . Free time—which is both idle time and time for higher activity—has naturally transformed its possessor into a different subject, and he then enters into the direct production process as this different subject. This process is then both discipline, as regards the human being in the process of becoming; and, at the same time, practice.[40]

As discipline and as practice, then, "free time" functions productively; its value manifests in the productive power embodied in the human being as fixed capital, but also directly in the material processes whereby subjects produce themselves. Though recent analyses, like those of Negri and Paolo Virno, have suggested that these dual functions tend toward total overlap in so-called late capitalism, it is possible to discern in the nineteenth-century context points of productive tension between them, points where their immediate translation is yet impeded and crisis threatens. Amid the economic consolidation of nineteenth-century America, the productivity of this ostensibly "free" time is the site of considerable contestation, among the stakes of which is control over the definition of productive activity itself.

Space: Indulgent Confinements and Convenient Retreats

It is certainly the case that the internal crisis of capitalist measurement that reaches full maturation in the twentieth century posed a set of similar problems for nineteenth-century onlookers. The widespread effort to increase productivity was facilitated by an emergent sense of space and time generated by technological development and the coalescence of Enlightenment rationality, and the creeping hegemony of economic gain as the prevailing value system. Within these spatio-temporal coordinates, as Foucault's analysis of disciplinary institutions and modern power describes, modern institutions and networks of power micromanage human activity with an eye toward intensifying not only its productive capacity but also its receptivity to various kinds of authority: "Discipline increases the forces of the body (in economic terms of utility) and diminishes these same forces (in political terms of obedience). . . . [D]isciplinary coercion establishes in the body the constricting link between an increased aptitude and an increased domination."[41] As the body becomes the object of scientific, medical, and economic knowledge, as well as the site upon which social power is enacted, it is understood as being defined by sets of spatial and temporal coordinates that may be managed for maximum disciplinary impact. The treatment of unproductivity in "Bartleby" cannot be properly understood without being contextualized amid these nascent understandings of the relationship of economic value to time and space.

As has been widely acknowledged in the aftermath of Foucault's inquiries, it is characteristic of modern or disciplinary societies that they enclose bodies in various types of institutional spaces capable of augmenting productivity. Because such managerial techniques are based on a generalizable model—typically translatable from site to site—the spatial inducements to proper activity in the prison greatly resemble those of the school, which resemble those of the factory, and so on. That "Bartleby" registers this modern condition is clear in the devices that foreground the similarity between the workplace where Bartleby lives and the prison in which he dies.[42] These uncanny entrapments have led Leo Marx to designate the story's ubiquitous walls as its "controlling symbols"—the monotonous monoliths that loom outside the office windows, the partitions and screens that divide the office (and that the narrator so carefully delineates at the story's inception), and the very idea that Bartleby's is "A Story of *Wall* Street." And yet, where Marx sees this story as "a parable of walls, the walls which hem in the meditative artist and for that matter every reflective man," we might rather insist that these walls are as much historical walls as they are constraints on the romantic imagination; they reflect the social imperative of applying instrumental technique to the organization of space for the disciplinary end of productivity.[43]

The setting of the story on Wall Street foregrounds the dovetailing of spatial rationality with the imperatives of the economy; it reflects a moment in which New York's financial district was being refashioned to better symbolize its growing significance as a center of economic activity. This refashioning was directly and materially dedicated to the principle of productivity. Long dominated by Greek revival structures, the area began to incorporate new designs based on Italian precedents, hewing to the notion that the "monolithic grandeur" of Florentine and Roman palazzo designs not only conveyed the sober power of the economic agent, but also offered the additional benefit of being highly efficient structures, capable of dealing with the increased premium on office space. Inaugurated in the Phenix Bank building of 1849, and at its most influential in the Bank of the Republic building at the corner of Wall Street and Broadway, the new style was "constructed with a view to economy," and was based upon expandable plans much more responsive to the practical needs of changing tenants than the old structures, which had emphasized classically spectacular external appearances. Internally, the new bank buildings introduced the fashion of placing the main banking enterprises at the structure's rear, so as to open up rental spaces for other tenants, among which prominently figured insurance brokers and lawyers.[44]

The tale's description of Bartleby's habitat indexes some of these changes—we might recall how the "small side-window" near Bartleby's workspace "originally had afforded a lateral view of certain grimy backyards and bricks, but . . . owing to subsequent erections, commanded at present no view at all" (19). As the rationalization of Wall Street space via these new erections ensued, the views from inside the law office—suggestively described by the narrator as "deficient in what landscape painters call 'life'" (14)—are limited only to the dead walls of Bartleby's vacant reveries. His apparently rather low estimation of these surroundings is inimical to the spirit of Wall Street at midcentury, however, as vocal converts lauded the instrumentalization of space as a boon to moral health, order, and industriousness, an approbation that echoed in locales considerably more remote from the metropolis as well. Consider the commentary of the architectural historian J. S. Gibbons, writing in 1857 under the thrall of Wall Street's architectural reorganization:

> Communities thrive in proportion as this organization is effected. They prosper not only in material substance but in education and morals. Anyone who has traveled among our country villages, out of the immediate influence of cities, has occasionally been struck by the neglect of natural advantages, the lack of energy, the rudeness of life and character, and the almost savage features of the common people. But on visiting the same

place after an interval of a few years, he has seen a total change: a larger
population, a better class of building, an air of thrifty growth and a manifest increase of comfort. The old lethargy has disappeared; a new life has
been fused into everything; even the countenances of the people are soft-
ened; a less brutal and more intelligent spirit beams from their eyes. A
bank has been the starting point of their new career.[45]

Though Gibbons's effusions reflect the overarching midcentury doctrine
of spatial instrumentality, it should be noted that at the same time, for
the man possessed of a certain degree of leisure, it was precisely the lack
of rational organization that made retreat from the city so inviting. This
helps to explain why time and again the narrator of "Bartleby" seeks to
resolve his condition (in fact, both his own and that of Bartleby) by invoking the pleasures of natural retreat, rejecting the "unwholesome" atmosphere of the office and urging his underling to seek "wholesome exercise
in the open air" (39, 32), imagining the salubriousness of removing him to
"some convenient retreat" (32), and finally—somewhat ludicrously—finding in the Tombs rudimentary elements of landscape: "It is not so sad a
place as one might think. Look, there is the sky, and here is the grass"
(43).[46] The lawyer, cracking under the stress of his unusual responsibilities
and the insoluble contradictions of his work environment, himself seeks
quiescence in a drive "through the suburbs in my rockaway. . . . In fact,
I almost lived in my rockaway for the time" (42).[47] To *almost live*—that is
the promise of bourgeois leisure to this character, whose reputation and
prosperity grant him VIP access to the pastoral, and hence to a clear alternative to the office's unresolved tensions . . . *almost*.

As for Bartleby, other than the sad strands of prison grass, the green he
accesses is merely that of the disciplinary screen that encloses his workspace—what Leo Marx refers to as a "chemical means of protection"[48]
that partitions off his habitat from the hubbub of the other scriveners,
in the meantime enabling the attorney to work unperturbed by the pres-
sures of a too excessive society. Thus does the disciplinary reality of Bartleby's green screen resonate with the mystifications implicit in the rural
retreat—the green of nature, sponged clean of the traces of work, is an
ideological necessity, a means of coping with work while leaving unmodi-
fied the structures proper to it. Bartleby, of course, regards the lawyer's
encouragements with indifference. He knows, it seems, that for him it is
hardly a matter of fleeing—there is nowhere left to go, the confining enclosures of discipline will seek to domesticate him regardless of whether they

are those of the office or the prison (or a dry-goods shop, for that mat-ter—there would be "too much confinement about that," he says [41]). No overt attempt on his part to break out of the disciplinary mechanism is made. Nevertheless, Bartleby's unusual effectivity necessarily overcomes this disciplinary space, and troubles its functioning from within.

The explanation for Bartleby's effectivity resides in Foucault's own description of the disciplinary measures of enclosure employed by a plague-stricken seventeenth-century town: "Each family will have made its own provisions; but, for bread and wine, small wooden canals are set up between the street and the interior of the houses, thus allowing each person to receive his ration without communicating with the suppliers and other residents; meat, fish and herbs will be hoisted up into the houses with pulleys and baskets."[49] With the enclosures in place, all that remains is to prevent the contamination from spreading to or from the "interiors," whether between the residents or to those who supply them. Above all, a kind of *communication* must be impeded—in the sense that we asso-ciate the term with communicable disease—but also in the spatial sense designating the way that adjoining rooms are thought to communicate with each other. When Foucault later discusses the surveilling function of disciplinary enclosure, and the way it produces a knowledge about the confined subject, he returns to this idea: "[the confined individual] is the object of information," he says, "never a subject in *communication*."[50]

Despite enclosure, Bartleby's effectivity diffuses itself through the office via communication, through the contagion of his circulating "pref-erences" and that unavoidable, infectious word "prefer," which is involun-tarily picked up by Turkey, Nippers, and even the attorney himself. Ann Smock has likened this spread of Bartleby's pathology to the communica-tion of an illness—though here this communication conveys the creativity of life rather than death. "Everything in this story transpires in such a way as to suggest not so much that communication is impossible, as that its impossibility comprises and endlessly sustains it," she notes: the "prefer" of Bartleby is a sign communicating a force.[51] In that one innocuous word, then, Bartleby's ambiguous preferences circulate, as it were, above the law, permeating and penetrating the enclosures and partitions of discipline, and in so doing, inducing the subjects inhabiting those confinements to produce themselves and their preferences in accordance with the force of Bartleby's unproductivity.

Time: The History of Idleness

As is the case for space, so, too, does negotiation over the productive use of time form a central preoccupation of "Bartleby"; we might begin to explore this facet of the tale by focusing on Melville's description of Bartleby's eventual removal from the office to the Tombs: "The poor scrivener, when told that he must be conducted to the Tombs, offered not the slightest obstacle, but in his pale unmoving way, silently acquiesced. Some of the compassionate and curious bystanders joined the party; and headed by one of the constables arm in arm with Bartleby, the silent procession filed its way through all the noise, and heat, and joy of the roaring thoroughfares at noon" (42). The model for this procession appears to be another episode in White's *Law and Laziness*, in which two of the students at law, thoroughly besotted, are transported to "the Tombs, where, laid out upon the floor, they "sle[ep] with a deep and childlike slumber." It is significant that Melville, however, has shifted the temporal coordinates of this transport. Where *Law and Laziness* describes a "procession of the night police . . . a funeral march in the broad moonlight and frosty air," Bartleby is herded to jail at midday, at which time, according to traditional superstition, the "noonday demon" of sloth appears.[52] That Melville indeed had the noonday demon in mind is further suggested by similarities between Bartleby's reveries and a description of the phenomenon attributed to the fourth-century monk Evagrius: "The demon of acedia, also called the 'noonday demon,' . . . makes the sun appear sluggish and immobile, as if the day had fifty hours. Then he causes the monk continually to look at the windows and forces him to step out of his cell and to gaze at the sun to see how far it still is from the ninth hour."[53] The tale's emphasis on "twelve o'clock, meridian" throughout reinforces this connection.

This is but one indication of the way in which "Bartleby," the story—in marked contrast to Bartleby, the scrivener—evinces a rigorous consciousness of time throughout. The narrating attorney is constantly, even distractingly, defining actions by measuring their temporal relations with each other. Surely this apparently automatic impulse to peg events to abstract temporal markers is another facet of the attorney's disciplinary rationality:[54] to be ascertainable, modern activity must be abstracted, measured, and calibrated to what E. P. Thompson has called "purposive" time.[55] As Foucault, too, notes, it can thereby be made productive: "One must seek to intensify the use of the slightest moment, as if time, in its very fragmentation, were inexhaustible or as if, at least by an ever more detailed internal arrangement, one could tend towards an ideal point at which one maintained maximum speed and maximum efficiency."[56] The narrator's careful fixation on time actually seems a somewhat excessive protest against the unproductivity with which his office is riddled—the surfeit of wasted, idle moments, the distraction, overindulgence, and confusion that reign there; it is as if he fantasizes that a sufficient tightening of the temporal grid might contain the idiosyncratic unproductivities of his employees and himself. Far from achieving "an ideal point" fusing speed and efficiency, however, the lawyer rather endures constant confrontation with failure, bungling, and waste. Speaking of the bizarre way in which the eccentricities of Nippers and Turkey complement each other, the narrator offhandedly refers to the office's prevailing conditions as "a good natural arrangement, under the circumstances" (18). The ostensible adequacy of the arrangement conceals just how perversely "undesirable" are the circumstances: an office of employees with unavoidable tendencies toward unproductivity, supervised by a boss who, by his own admission, knows all too well the seductions of ease.

Much of the comical thrust of the story's opening movement proceeds from descriptions of this "good natural arrangement" and the relentless relays of productive and unproductive time it organizes. Each scrivener functions as an exchangeable half of the copying machinery of the office, such that their respective penchants for production and dissipation are yoked together into equilibrium: "I never had to do with their eccentricities at one time," the lawyer explains. "Their fits relieved each other like guards. When Nippers' was on, Turkey's was off; and *vice versa*" (18). In the case of Nippers, it is indigestion and frustrated ambition that produce in him a counterproductive "nervous testiness and grinning irritability" in the morning (16). Turkey, in contrast, is at his wildest in the afternoon, as the narrator explains in an illuminating descriptive passage:

> In the morning, one might say, his face was of a fine florid hue, but after twelve o'clock, meridian—his dinner hour—it blazed like a grate full of Christmas coals; and continued blazing—but, as it were, with a gradual wane—till six o'clock, P.M. or thereabouts, after which I saw no more of the proprietor of the face, which gaining its meridian with the sun, seemed to set with it, to rise, culminate, and decline the following day, with the like regularity and undiminished glory. There are many singular coincidences I have known in the course of my life, not the least among which was the fact, that exactly when Turkey displayed his fullest beams from his

red and radiant countenance, just then, too, at that critical moment, began the daily period when I considered his business capacities as seriously disturbed for the remainder of the twenty-four hours. (15)

Yet this "singular coincidence" is hardly coincidental, as we learn shortly thereafter: the obstreperous unproductivity of Turkey's afternoon exertions stems from his indulgences at the dinner hour—the "critical moment" when his morning trustworthiness lapses into insolence. But it is not that he is "absolutely idle" after noon, as the narrator cautions us: "Far from it. The difficulty was, he was apt to be altogether too energetic. There was a strange, inflamed, flurried, flighty recklessness of activity about him" (15). Thus, with this appearance of the noonday demon, is the very definition of unproductivity once more complicated, cast not as mere idleness but rather as a surplus of energy that is just as detrimental to the rational regularity of the office.

Turkey's daily arc across the office sky is notable here for its regularity: it is not only like clockwork but seems, in its faultless predictability, to observe the even more dependable rhythms of nature. It is nevertheless the workday by which the narrator measures Turkey's exertions and excesses, tracing them from the morning to the dinner break, then on to the adjournment of daily labor at 6:00 p.m.—after which time Turkey embarks on activities that, however intriguing we might justly suppose them to be, are considered by the lawyer entirely inconsequential. Of the temporal markers the narrator deploys, the most decisive—the "critical moment" to which he repeatedly alludes—is that of "twelve o'clock, meridian." At high noon, Turkey's daily showdown with unproductivity occurs, and it is the precise temporal point orbited by the Turkey–Nippers production assemblage; its significance builds further in Melville's use of the phrase "twelve o'clock, meridian" no fewer than seven times in the passage devoted to the office's "natural arrangement."

Though things work well enough in this fashion, given the apparently unalterable "circumstances" of production, Bartleby's arrival further complicates the delicate temporal balance observed in the office. As the narrator begins to pay more vigilant attention to the scrivener's ways, he finds that the noontime transition means little to Bartleby: "I observed that he never went to dinner; indeed that he never went anywhere. . . . He was a perpetual sentry in the corner" (23). Later, the narrator reiterates this theme: "*he was always there;*—first in the morning, continually through the day, and the last at night" (26, italics in original). These circumstances initially salve the narrator's concern for production, for Bartleby's industriousness at the outset is all the more impressive for observing none of the usual temporal demarcations of the workday. Remember: "At first Bartleby did an extraordinary quantity of writing. As if long famishing for something to copy, he seemed to gorge himself on my documents. There was no pause for digestion. He ran a day and night line, copying by sunlight and by candle-light" (19).

Instead of yielding to the idle threats of the dinner hour, Bartleby feasts on documents without pause; the language of the passage directs our attention to the many ways in which the office is organized around its inhabitants' literal and figurative appetites. Bartleby's insatiable hunger for documents, Nippers's indigestion, Turkey's overindulgences at noontime, and of course the alimentary sign that defines Ginger Nut—these defining regimes of consumption are inextricably wedded to the characters' workplace personas, to their capacities to produce. The hermetic regulation of the workday gives way, and thus the reproductive sphere of consumption finds entry into the productive realm.

The boundaries between work time and idle time, between production and reproduction, are rendered even fuzzier by the events of the fateful Sunday morning when the attorney, pursuing a whim, stops by his quarters and is astonished to find that Bartleby's vigil continues through the weekends as well. Refused entry by the scrivener, the lawyer mulls over the implications of his weekend tenancy: "Think of it. Of a Sunday, Wall-street is as deserted as Petra; and every night of every day it is an emptiness. This building, too, which of week-days hums with industry and life, at nightfall echoes with sheer vacancy, and all through Sunday is forlorn" (27). The description of the financial district's Sunday aspect helps to further define Bartleby's vacant unproductivity, for he is himself described as "forlorn" in our first encounter with him (in his perpetual presence in the attorney's office, he smuggles the emptiness of the day of rest into every moment of the work week). It furthermore draws an association between the ancient carved-stone city of Petra with the vacancy of unproductive time—conjuring the image of the desert, with its idle expanses of both space and time conventionally thought hostile to production and duty.[57] When there are no mortgages to process and no title-deeds to notarize, Wall Street becomes a mere wasteland. But when challenged by the attorney at the office's threshold, Bartleby suggestively responds that he—despite the hour and the day—is "deeply engaged just then, and—prefer[s] not admitting [his employer] *at present*" (26, emphasis added). Bartleby's famous preferences are refined and intensified by the invocation of his "presentness," which invocation he utters repeatedly as an integral part of his formula: asked to provide some sense of his biography shortly thereafter, he replies, "*at present* I prefer to give no answer," and, just prior to his fateful involuntary evacuation from the office, he uses it to stave off any kind of progress or transition whatsoever, stating, "*at present* I would prefer not to make any change at all" (30, 41, emphasis added).

It would be too glib to suggest that "making change" falls outside the "tacit stipulations" of Bartleby's job description were it not that his indifference to time explicitly confounds the linkage between time and money. Codified in the writings of Ben Franklin, this equation derives from the thoroughgoing abstraction of activity that marks the self-realization of Weber's spirit of capitalism. Though concern about time had long been primary in Puritan ideology, it was Franklin, as E. P. Thompson points out, who unleashed temporality from its theological trappings only to suture it to exchange value.[58] Weber's analysis notes the change of inflection that occurs during this important transition: for the Puritan ethos, "waste of time is . . . the first and in principle the deadliest of sins. . . . Loss of time through sociability, idle talk, luxury, even more sleep than is necessary for health . . . is worthy of absolute moral condemnation." Crucially, however, this condemnation does not arise from a perceived equivalence between time and money; calls for time's "redemption" instead follow from the belief that time "is infinitely valuable, and that 'every hour lost is lost to labour for the glory of God.'"[59] Franklin, however, cuts loose the transcendent anchor of this conception, instead understanding time as a finite resource materially bound to specific quantities of currency. He argues not only that "*time* is money" but also that money value is a function of abstracted time, a pledge against future values: "Remember, that *credit* is money. . . . Remember, that money is of the prolific, generating nature."[60] Since all activity is bound to the time-money nexus established in credit, moral virtue, previously the ground *for* time management, is now itself produced *by* the management of time. "The most trifling actions that affect a man's credit are to be regarded," Franklin cautions. "The sound of your hammer at five in the morning, or eight at night, heard by a creditor, makes him easy six months longer; but if he sees you at a billiard-table, or hears your voice at a tavern, when you should be at work, he sends for his money the next day. . . . [Diligent labor] makes you appear a careful as well as an honest man, and that still increases your credit."[61] Honesty, punctuality, industry, frugality, and other virtues are virtues to Franklin only because they assure credit, and thus, as Weber puts it, "the *appearance* of honesty . . . would suffice, and an unnecessary surplus of this virtue would evidently appear . . . as unproductive waste."[62]

Bartleby baffles the narrator in part because the time-money-virtue nexus is of so little concern to him: practically speaking, this is due to the calibration of scriveners' pay to piecework and not to an hourly wage. But the story's vigilant awareness of the relationship between activity and time suggests a disturbance that is somewhat more profound than this residue of the preindustrial economy. The narrative reaches a turning point when the lawyer, resorting to extreme measures, attempts to eject Bartleby from the office with an oddly laconic statement of fact: "The time has come; you must quit this place; I am sorry for you; here is money; but you must go" (33). This particular concatenation of time and money is much more convoluted, however, than that assumed by the simple equivalence drawn by Franklin between the two. In the lawyer's unusual formulation, the relationship between time and money is predicated upon "quitting" instead of working, it is mediated by sympathy ("I am sorry for you"), and it demands, instead of a fixed task with a concrete object, an indefinite and intransitive movement ("you must go"). Further complicating what should be the relatively simple transaction equating wage to activity, the lawyer calculates Bartleby's pay, and—his virtue appearing as unproductive waste indeed—presents Bartleby with an extra twenty dollars, left behind "under a weight on the table" (33). It is if money's own fleeting properties might allow it, no longer hindered by the pretended stability of the office, to remove itself into the dissipation of circulation. Perhaps the narrator optimistically imagines that it might take Bartleby with it.

Nevertheless, even the narrator's complex equation does not compute—he remains burdened with Bartleby and with the constant haunting reminder of Bartleby's indifference to the modern ratio that defines activity through the calibration of time to money. There is no modern economic rationality, he seems to conclude, that can accommodate this employee who yearns for no weekends, hungers for no dinners, and furthermore refuses any change. His ghostly presence—and his temporal present-ness—exceed the impoverished modern calculus that deems concrete activity meaningless unless it satisfies the measurable, quantifiable standards of economic productivity. It is this immeasurable activity that is economically misrecognized as the "unproductive."

Modern disciplinary regulation imposes a geometric structure that effectively "empties space and time"; this regime's indifference to concrete activity renders the latter meaningless unless it meets the norms of "productivity"—that is, the measurable, quantifiable standards of economic production.[63] This logic thus performs a subtraction from the total activity of social production—the multiple activities that generate the ontological horizon of human life. Arguing for the autonomy and specific effectivity of the superstructures, Louis Althusser proposes that such "unproductive" activity might be imagined as something like an infinite "microscopic dust" of contingent, personal, political, and ethical actions, only some of which are deemed "productive" and therefore admissible to the apparent historical continuity forged by the factors of Power: "The forms of the superstructures are indeed the cause of an infinity of events, but not all these events are *historical* . . . only those of them that the said 'factors' *retain, select* from among the others, in short, *produce as such.*"[64]

Unable to represent the productivity of the unproductive, then, the geometry of capitalist time and space nevertheless presupposes that it exists; the unproductive is that substrate comprising all the undifferentiated activity that, outside of measure and remuneration, generates the lives of subjects and their ontological horizon. Industrial (and industrious) modernity is defined by the specific spatio-temporal mechanisms through which a fraction of this generative force—not yet quite production, certainly not pure idleness—is disciplined. The result is a normative model of individualized experience. Thus does Foucault add to the well-known litany of modern technologies ("agronomical, industrial, economic") that of discipline, which ensures order, efficiency, and productivity and should be considered "a very real technology, that of *individuals.*"[65]

To the extent, however, that capitalist discipline forges individuals through the imposition of measure, it risks crisis when that geometric order confronts its limits. It is not only that Bartleby, by ignoring the requisite time-discipline of the workplace, frustrates the system of capitalist value and nevertheless still produces real effects in the lives of his colleagues (demonstrating what Negri would call a "productivity of the system that is not reproduction of command").[66] It is also—and perhaps even more crucially for our understanding of his function in the story— that his unique productivity of the unproductive contests the assumption of individuality that is enshrined in disciplinary ideology. Such is the ideology that has here been traced not only in the bourgeois myth of autonomously self-interested economic actors but also in the critical and narrative tendency that attempts to contain Bartleby's force within the limits of individuality and biography. Bartleby thwarts the imposition of such disciplinary matrices, and more: he peels them back to reveal a collective network of indeterminate activity extending beyond the impoverishing structures of the capitalist workplace. As the narrative implicates various characters for their various unproductivities—the lawyer's love of ease, Turkey's weakness for drink, Nippers's diseased ambition—it reveals how the activity of each of these disciplined subjects exceeds the templates of mere productivity. They share in a fundamentally hybrid constitution, each erasing the line between work and idleness.

Chief among the beauties of Melville's tale are those moments in which the narrator timidly recognizes that it is their collective unproductivity, and not their alienated stake in serving the law, that unites the office staff together in sympathy. This is why the quick dismissal of "Bartleby" in Hardt and Negri's *Empire* is so unsatisfying: it fails to acknowledge that Bartleby's refusal is hardly an empty heroism (a "kind of social suicide," as they put it), but rather the articulation of a collective sentiment that exceeds the individual and persists despite the scrivener's seeming martyrdom.[67] Hardt and Negri here inadvertently follow the long tradition of individualizing Bartleby's activity—just as capital would—and this, in defiance of Melville's text itself, which, as we have seen, carefully depicts Bartleby's indefinable activity as part of a larger, impersonal, and collective social force. Far from being merely an enigmatic local hassle for capital, Bartleby and what he embodies are not extinguishable once and for all at the Tombs.

Viewed through the lens of Bartleby's productive unproductivity, the narrative offers up an alternate resolution, which finally addresses the story's engagement with time, its contestation of individuality, and its challenge to the laws of economic value. Throughout the narrative, the lawyer consistently defers the task of dealing with Bartleby and what he stands for, quite reasonably, it would seem, putting it off to a later time: "My business hurried me. I concluded to forget the matter for the present, reserving it for my future leisure" (21). Later, "Once more business hurried me. I determined again to postpone the consideration of this dilemma to my future leisure" (22). He holds in abeyance the real questions raised by Bartleby—concerning the collective praxis that is the work of life—due to the relentless rhythms of the office. Late in the story, however, and in a state of passion provoked by Bartleby's redoubled indocility, a signal transition occurs. The lawyer proposes that Bartleby quit the office and come to live with him, and "remain there till we can conclude upon some convenient arrangement for you at *our* leisure . . . *Come, let us start now, right away*," he implores (41, emphasis added). This sympathetic gesture makes the previously deferred promise of a future leisure an imperative of the present. In that moment, the leisure to which the narrator refers is disclosed as something that must be shared: it is *our leisure*. And in the recognition of that shared sympathy there glimmers forth the collective reward reserved for the true student at law of leisure.

As White puts it in *Law and Laziness*: "In the fierce scramble for wealth, fame, or respectability, in which we are all taking part, the idle man is hustled about, elbowed out of the way, and trampled on. . . . It is a god-send then, for an idle man to find, in this great city, a fellow idler, who sympathizes with him in doing nothing."[68] It is in the spirit of this sympathy that we hereby dispense with the task of confronting "Bartleby" and endeavor more fully, in chapter 2, to track, in the refined habitats of early American painting and aesthetics, this leisurely species: the idle man.

2

Repose

*The Expression and Experience
of the Circulatory Sublime*

> What is called improvement . . . generally destroys Nature's beauty
> without substituting that of Art. This is a regret rather than a com-
> plaint; such is the road society has to tread; it may lead to refinement
> in the end, but the traveller who sees the place of rest close at hand,
> dislikes the road that has so many unnecessary windings.
>   —Thomas Cole, "Essay on American Scenery," 1836

Though the supposed hostility of nature to utilitarian progress
is an ideological formation that continues to be relevant to us today, it can
be difficult to conceive of the unique burdens that "nature" bore in the
nineteenth century. The capacious concept housed some very different,
and often contradictory, imaginings of a national destiny and a leisured
manhood. The foregoing excerpt from Thomas Cole's "Essay on American Scenery" suggests some of the complexity of the relationship between
nature, art, and the history of industrious "progress" in the first half of the
nineteenth century, giving voice to a rather common apprehension suffered by those whose aesthetic sensibility was to be an obstacle to smooth
travels upon the road to improvement. His words prototypically convey a
sense of loss that was variously mingled in other contexts with stridency,
weariness, and, sometimes, resignation. Despite his singular influence on
other painters, critics, and cultural observers, Cole's hopeful allusion to
a refined state of rest at the end of improvement's tortuous road would
not—at least on his terms—be widely realized.

Cole's particular investment in nature as a site of both spiritual salvation and potential liberation from the encroaching imperatives of utility

and gain nevertheless made a signal contribution to the history of nineteenth-century unproductivity. Inveighing against a society whose spirit "is to contrive but not to enjoy—toiling to produce more toil—accumulating in order to aggrandize," shuddering at the prospect of that "meager utilitarianism . . . ready to absorb every feeling and sentiment," and cowering at the likelihood that "what is sometimes called improvement in its march makes us fear that the bright and tender flowers of the imagination shall all be crushed beneath its iron tramp," Cole sought an antidote in a nature conceived chiefly as a place of rest, a detour nestled alongside the deepening ruts of the road to improvement.[1] For the aesthetically inclined, that road was both metaphorical and literal, as is clear in the very mobility of Cole, touring natural beauty along the newly opened Erie Canal, or of William Dunlap, confessing "some taste for the picturesque and more for rambling," and of all those others—Church, Bierstadt, Heade—who took advantage of the improving technologies of modern travel as they cantered across western plains and upon equatorial volcanoes in pursuit of nature's elusive truths. Their art was enabled only by the increasing rationalization of genteel tourism, geographical mobility, aesthetic technique, and economic circulation, all of which engendered new possibilities for experiencing and representing states of rest. Such idle men thus depended upon the road of improvement at the same time that they invoked repose as its antithesis.[2]

But what was the character of this promised rest, at once so "close at hand" and yet the object of such strain? Many of its paradoxes were bundled into the concept of "repose," which enjoyed increasing prominence alongside the budding respectability of American landscape painting, and which possessed no small appeal to the aesthetes and others who feverishly redefined it during this period. Despite its ubiquity, "repose"— understood both as an experience of tranquility and as a specifically aesthetic expression of harmony—is nevertheless not nearly as transparent and unproblematic a concept as might be assumed from the apparent confidence of those who used it.[3] Further, the prominence of the concept of repose was not merely a secondary by-product of the American landscape painting with which it chiefly came to be associated: as we shall see, in the exemplary writings of Cole, the art theory of Washington Allston, and the works of midcentury luminist painting, the pursuit of repose shaped the prevailing conventions of American landscape painting. Moreover, it is clear that the concept lent itself often and easily to translation into other fields, becoming a fundamental means of organizing refined life for worldly types of various persuasions.[4] We shall therefore resist attributing to Cole sole responsibility for repose's rise, acknowledging, however, his singular role in marking out the clearing in which the concept could flourish.

As Cole's essay appeared in 1836, traffic along the road of improvement had quickened considerably on the strength of the railroad's 1832 debut; that acceleration likewise intensified the stirrings of those who sought to understand and retard the seemingly ineluctable flow of progress. A premonition of this tendency had already been registered in the early 1820s by Richard Henry Dana, Sr., in his aptly titled journal, the *Idle Man*. The journal's six issues featured writing by Dana (as well as his compatriot Washington Allston); its titular figure was intended as the archetype of the "man of fine feeling," whose aspirations to refinement and worldly erudition faced suffocation beneath mounting utilitarian hustle and bustle. That the *Idle Man* recognized this quandary as both aesthetic and economic is made clear by the preface, in which Dana mildly mopes about both his need for money and the "motive to industry" it engenders; the preface weighs the merits of the difficult exertions of a writing project aimed at meeting those ends.[5] Having thus acknowledged the contradictoriness of its dual impulses toward refinement and economic self-preservation, the *Idle Man* goes on (in a piece triflingly entitled "Musings") to further invoke the horrors of "improvement." Anticipating Cole by a decade and a half, Dana, too, imagines "improvement" as a thoroughfare directed only toward vulgar gains. "Must we for ever travel the straightforward, turnpike road of business, and not be left to take the way that winds round the meadows, and leads us sociably by the doors of retired farms?" he queries. "Must all we do and all we think about have reference to the useful, while that alone is considered useful which is tangible, present gain?"[6] In Dana's description, the culture's indifference to the merits of rest has cost it the rewards of being able to "sit awhile to cool and rest ourselves in the shade of some shut-in valley, with its talking rills, and fresh and silent water plants," or to "pass over the free and lit hill-tops, catching views of the broad, open country."[7] Enjoying such a contemplative rapture, he who rests is visited by the spiritual force of Nature, and he thereby may defy the corruptions ensnaring his fellow men and clear the ground for a new becoming: "When such an one [the 'man of fine feeling'] turns away from men, and is left alone in silent communion with nature and his own thoughts, and there are no bonds on the movements of the feelings . . . he feels his spirit opening upon a new existence—becoming as broad as the sun and the air—as various as the earth over which it spreads itself, and touched with that love which God has imaged in all he has formed."[8] Nature, properly enjoyed in a state of rest, is thus the romantic sanctuary in which spiritual rebirth may blossom; it is simultaneously, and crucially, viewed by Dana as the decentering antidote to the encroaching world of self-interest and utility.

Cole's "American Scenery" essay exercises these same themes, though enriching its opposition of nature to improvement with the overt argument that it is "Art" that compensates for nature's subjection—the substitutive effect of art is that of reproducing natural beauty all the while that improvement eviscerates it.[9] The allure of this conceit is as palpable as its danger, embodying as it does the nineteenth century's "ideological art religion"—a phenomenon diagnosed by Hegel and later critiqued by Adorno, who was ever-wary, in his *Aesthetic Theory* as elsewhere, of "the satisfaction in a reconciliation symbolically achieved in the artwork."[10] Adorno indicts that "religion" for effacing the gap between natural and aesthetic beauty, assuming the reproducibility of natural effects in the artwork, and, especially, for obscuring not only the historical mediation that enables the appearance of that reproduction, but also the material reality of nature's annihilation.[11] The artwork offers itself as an antidote to improvement to the same extent that it marches along with improvement's iron tramp, for the natural beauty it purports to convey only becomes beautiful when it is socially necessary to recognize it as such. "What appears untamed in nature and remote from history, belongs— polemically speaking—to a historical phase in which the social web is so densely woven that the living fear death by suffocation," he argues. "Times in which nature confronts man overpoweringly allow no room for natural beauty. . . . Natural beauty, purportedly ahistorical, is at its core historical."[12] The circulation of the concept of repose in the historical context of the early nineteenth century facilitates this dubious translation from natural to art beauty; it is a cognate that bridges two languages of divine truth. "Repose," often sloppily defined and inconsistently deployed, nevertheless succeeds in this by designating, often in the same utterance, two different things: the *experience* of surrendering to the tranquility of natural beauty, and the *expression* of such tranquility through the formal harmoniousness of the artwork. Though clearly related, the two meanings are nonetheless not sleekly interchangeable—one identifying an experiential phenomenon or situation of reception, the other denoting a formal principle. In the reduction of one to the other without remainder, the two meanings converge, the boundary between natural beauty and art beauty is blurred, and the "ideological art religion" is vindicated.[13]

In this respect, the treatment of "repose" mirrors that accorded the "sublime": at once a quality of objects and phenomena, the concept often also suggests a subjective experience. Indeed, Barbara Novak has argued that it is under the sign of repose, as a mode of aesthetic and spiritual contemplation, that American artists recalibrated the sublime in order to make it appropriate to their sense of the specific spaces, subjectivities, and mythologies of America, in the process abjuring many of the conventions typical of European landscape representation. While in the early nineteenth century the traditional, Burkean version of the sublime continued to flourish (especially in the often-stormy canvases of the Hudson River school), it was increasingly complemented by a new sublimity, predicated upon a quietly contemplative stance toward natural beauty and imbued with the prospect of Christian revelation.[14] Novak interprets Cole's "American Scenery" as making the incipient gesture away from the traditional sublime and toward this more contemplative strain. The transition is especially apparent in the germinal passage where Cole, himself reposing amid the lakes of New Hampshire's Franconia Notch, reports: "I was overwhelmed with an emotion of the sublime, such as I have rarely felt. It was not that the jagged precipices were lofty, that the encircling woods were of the dimmest shade, or that the waters were profoundly deep; but that over all, rocks, wood, and water, brooded the spirit of repose, and the silent energy of nature stirred the soul to its inmost depths."[15] It is curious that Cole simultaneously encounters, upon the playground of nature's "silent energy," both the sublimity of repose and the features of its Gothic progenitor. "It was not"—he insists—"that the jagged precipices were lofty," the woods daunting, or the waters frightening. In short, Cole's was avowedly not an experience of the traditional sublime, though it very well could have been, given that the features of that sublime are recorded here in profusion. What are we to make of this insistence?

Cole confronts this vista with not only a respect for nature's diversity, but also a claustrophobia felt at the encroachment of the concept of sublimity itself, a concept that in its ubiquity had veered dangerously into the territory of cliché. To Cole, traditional Gothic sublimity is everywhere— not just at Franconia Notch, but *everywhere*: the concept is so blunted by overuse that one understands Cole's desire to avoid rehearsing its praises yet again. Become "traditional," sublimity is no longer sublime enough. As Nathaniel Parker Willis astutely complained at around the same time, "the sublime is so well imitated in our day, that one is less surprised than he would suppose when nature produces the reality."[16] The achievement of Cole, then, is not only to announce the existence of contemplative sublimity, but to do so in proximity to, in resistance to, and despite the facile draw of, the trappings of the traditional sublime. He experiences the sublime in the midst of the towering peaks, the gloomy forest, and the enveloping aquatic depths that inspired Salvator and all the others. But his experience of silence and tranquility negates the effect of those characteristics, and he champions instead the sublimity of repose.

Cole thus broadens the protocols for experiencing nature, while illuminating the traditional sublime's rather sad fate in the second quarter of the nineteenth century, as it is dulled by its appropriation by the juggernaut of progress. The vocabulary of the sublime, as Leo Marx's analysis in *The Machine in the Garden* demonstrates, was with increasing frequency being deployed as the ideological tool of headfirst improvement.[17] Diagnosing the emergence of what he calls the "technological sublime," Marx notes the proliferation of discourse about the potential of progress to rend time and space, to suddenly transform experience, and to reconfigure identity. "No stock phrase in the entire lexicon of progress," he writes, "appears more often than the 'annihilation of space and time.'"[18] Nature's divinity is thus supplanted ever more by the promises of the industrial epoch, masquerading in the cloak of nature's old theatricality; God's hand, meaningfully arraying the sublime elements of nature, is wrestled down by the hand of man, clutching the throttle. A representative statement of this transition appears in Tocqueville: "The wide air and deep waters, the tall mountains, the outstretched plains and the earth's deep caverns, are become parcel of his [man's] domain and yield freely of their treasures to his researches and toils. The terrible ocean . . . conveys . . . [him] submissively. . . . He has almost annihilated space and time."[19] Not only does the language of traditional sublimity lend itself in this fashion to the celebration of industrial and technological progress, but in the transition it simultaneously loses its allure. The ever-cavalier Nathaniel Parker Willis, for example, seems troubled to stifle a yawn as he holds forth on his first train ride, in 1834. What began at "a pace that made my hair sensibly tighten, and hold on with apprehension" is rendered comfortably mundane even before the subsequent sentence can unfold: "Thirty miles in the hour is pleasant going when one is a little accustomed to it, it gives one such a pleasant contempt for time and distance."[20]

In this context, Cole's "discovery" of repose and the contemplative sublime appears as a strategic intervention into the definition of sublimity itself, a preservation of nature's importance against the corrosion of a Gothic sensibility that had been tainted by its complicity with technological development. Presenting this newly sanctified contemplative stance alongside the elements of the traditional sublime, Cole heightens the contrast between the two, in their proximity rendering more acute their basic difference—his brooding repose inhabits a province of rest, tranquility, and silence *amid* the persistent power and terror of the old sublime. He thereby recasts the conventional opposition of nature to improvement as one of two competing experiences of sublimity. As the traditional conception of the sublime is supplanted by its quieter, contemplative cousin, a new significance for the experience of repose is inaugurated.

The Ethic of Compositional Harmony: Washington Allston

> Even ghosts and hurricanes become at last familiar; and books grow old, like those who read them.
> —Washington Allston, "The Hypochondriac," 1821

> Grandeur in any of its moods, but especially in that of extent, startles, excites—and then fatigues, depresses. For the occasional scene nothing can be better—for the constant view nothing worse.
> —Edgar Allan Poe, "The Domain of Arnheim," 1847

While the efforts of Dana and Cole largely considered repose as the contemplative experience of natural or aesthetic phenomena, the work of Washington Allston illustrates the transition by which repose becomes a category of art theory, a specific problem of composition. Allston, too, spent considerable time wrestling with the character of sublimity; his painting as well as his elaborate theory of art probe the question with greater depth than Cole achieved, though not without a corresponding increase in the murkiness of his concepts. And while Allston would reach conclusions similar to Cole's, his efforts further illuminate the stakes of the discourse of repose as a political and, especially, economic intervention.

Allston's preoccupation with these questions is signaled by his 1818 work *Elijah in the Desert* (figure 1), which depicts the blind prophet Elijah

Figure 1. Washington Allston, American (1779–1843), *Elijah in the Desert*, 1818. Oil on canvas. 125.09 x 184.78 cm (49 ¼ x 72 ¾ in). Museum of Fine Arts, Boston. Gift of Mrs. Samuel and Miss Alice Hooper. 70.1. Photograph © 2012 Museum of Fine Arts, Boston.

bowed in a state of exasperated contemplation. He is surrounded by a gloomy landscape distinguished by its detailed depiction of a rheumatic tree in the foreground; its crooked extremities direct the gaze to the mountain, evergreens, and waterfall at right. Notable for its attempt to fuse the conventions of both landscape and historical painting, *Elijah in the Desert* also significantly portrays coexistent sublimities, at least in the interpretation of William Ware, who, writing just after Allston's death, was plainly familiar with Cole's treatment of sublimity.[21] Ware, prefacing his account with reference to Allston's "love for the silent, the solitary, the contemplative," and peppering it with hyperbolic comparisons of Allston to Titian and his ilk, regards *Elijah* as "a landscape of a most sublime, impressive character," going on to reproduce Cole's formula of the contemplative sublime existing in contrast to—and in defiance of—traditional sublimity: "Melancholy, dark, and terrific, almost, as are all the features of the scene, a strange calm broods over it all; as of an ocean, now overhung by black, threatening clouds, dead and motionless, but the sure precursors of change and storm. . . . The sublime, after all, is better expressed in the calmness, repose, silence, of the Elijah, than in the tempests of Poussin, or Vernet, Wilson, or Salvator Rosa."[22] Contemporary commentators such as Ware were largely content with paintings, such as *Elijah in the Desert*, that were capable of representing the contemplative experience—often with the additional trappings of dreamy reverie—at the level of content. Ware avers that Allston's works ably describe "the breathless silence and deep rest of a mid-summer day, when not a leaf moves and the shadows fall dark and heavy upon the face of the clear water, which repeats every object near it as in a mirror; the cow on the bank, half-asleep, lazily chewing the cud and flapping away the flies from her side; and the only sound to break the silence, the sleepy drone of the locust; while a warm, misty atmosphere, through which you just catch the roots of the neighboring village, wraps all things in its purplish folds."[23] Margaret Fuller also was struck by this effect, writing about Allston's work that "a certain bland delicacy enfolds all these creations as an atmosphere." In it, there "is no effort, they have floated across the painter's heaven on the golden clouds of phantasy."[24]

For all this approbation, both Ware and Fuller want to imagine Allston's facility with formally representing repose as an outgrowth of his own ease at *achieving* repose, a wishful claim belied not only by various records of Allston's own critical self-examination, but also by the analysis of David Bjelajac, who describes how Allston created this impression of effortlessness only through considerable technical strain. Those "misty" atmospherics, so convincing to Ware in their verisimilitude, in fact result from the glazing techniques Allston picked up during an 1817 visit to the Louvre. The diffuse color and ethereal richness of pieces like 1819's important *Moonlit Landscape* depend upon this quality, their translucent veils of color removing the very "appearance of paint" and mystifying Allston's considerable effort.[25] Fuller's somewhat backhanded compliment to Allston's effect of repose thus mischaracterizes the connection between Allston's figural paintings and his ethical standpoint. His figures, she observes, "are almost all in repose": "[These pictures] tell us the painter's ideal of character. A graceful repose, with a fitness for moderate action. A capacity of emotion, with a habit of reverie. Not one of these beings is in a state of *epanchement*, not one is, or perhaps could be, thrown off its equipoise. They are, even the softest, characterized by entire though unconscious self-possession."[26] It is understandable that such an interpretation of Allston's works as expressions of the painter's sensibility should emerge, given the way that his own writings themselves conflated ethical and aesthetic issues: indeed, he treated the question of idleness in his tract on aesthetics, and the problem of harmony in a short story about restless activity. By no great coincidence, one place in which this confusion emerges is in Dana's *Idle Man,* to which Allston contributed (Allston and Dana were entwined by not only their collegial relationship but also by Allston's marriage into the Dana family). As with Dana, for whom the very publication of the *Idle Man* was partly an exercise in unfortunate economic necessity, Allston was highly sensitive to the way that the dictates of economic exchange increasingly threatened his artistic and ethical sensibilities; such is repeatedly suggested by his correspondence, including an early letter to Robert Rogers, in which he acknowledged that "it is my greatest misfortune to be too lazy."[27] Despite this "misfortune," Allston was reputedly the first American painter to have subsisted entirely on the monetary rewards of his art—a status most likely earned at the cost of intensifying what he already experienced as an uncomfortable contradiction.

A trifling short story entitled "The Hypochondriac," appearing in the *Idle Man* in 1821, narrativizes his personal pursuit of a balance between the danger of sheer relaxation and the fatigue brought on by a condition in which his desires "seemed to have resolved themselves into a general passion for *doing.*"[28] It begins with a confession: "I could be moderate in nothing. Not content with being employed, I must always be *busy*; and business, as everyone knows, if long continued, must end in fatigue, and fatigue in disgust, and disgust in change, if that be practicable,—which unfortunately was my case."[29] Swayed by the belief that his disgusted disposition would benefit from the adoption of a fresh form of activity, the narrator takes up writing history (and subsequently abandons it out of frustration at being able to produce nothing terribly original), and then, since "it is natural for a mind suddenly disgusted with mechanic toil to seek relief from its opposite," tries his hand at poetry.[30] As might be expected from the piece's self-deprecating tone, every attempt by the narrator to alleviate his ennui only serves somewhat comically to perpetuate it. He therefore commences, upon torturing his "brains for another pursuit," to obviate activity altogether, reasoning that "in fortune I have a competence,—why not be as independent in mind? There are thousands in the world whose sole object in life is to attain the means of living without toil; and what is any literary pursuit but a series of mental labor, ay, and oftentimes more wearying to the spirits than that of the body. Upon the whole, I came to the conclusion, that it was a very foolish thing to do any thing. So I seriously set about trying to do nothing."[31] After a week of this idle pursuit—a week during which the passage of time stumbled to a disagreeable crawl—the narrator concludes that "a toad in the heart of a tree lives a more comfortable life than a nothing-doing man," and embarks on a new regimen of strictly trivial and amusing endeavors, steeled by his newfound belief in "something being better than nothing."[32] Reeling through the amusements of light reading and cigar smoking, Allston's narrator encounters only further dissatisfactions, until the society of men provided by a local tavern convinces him to take the world as his study "for the sake of his health."[33] Careering from one extreme to the next, the story's "hypochondriac" is perhaps not as deluded about his condition as Allston's title makes him out to be, for he is afflicted with what, in another context, Allston diagnoses as a disruption of the natural equilibrium between activity and idleness, a disruption that "we call . . . disease."[34]

If "The Hypochondriac" charts the quest for equilibrium between sheer idleness and excessive activity as a problem of personal economic disposition, Allston's *Lectures on Art* (comprising five essays written during the 1830s) effectively recast it as an aesthetic quandary as well. It is a most curious and irritating text, replete with its share of spongily idealist grappling, through which, however, glimmer numerous moments—as confused as they are confusing—in which the problem of idleness emerges as central, notably in the improbable coda to the *Lectures*' "Introductory Discourse." The appearance of that problematic as the concluding flourish of this most salient piece not only indicates how resolving the question of idleness and activity is fundamental to Allston's attempt at a comprehensive theory of art, but further that that theory demands to be redeemed as not merely a transcendent glorification of the spiritual, but also as the product of, and an intervention into, a set of historical and material concerns.

The stage is set for this discussion of idleness early in the piece, when Allston makes an initial allusion to the divine balance between rest and activity, between utility and pleasure: "It pleased our Creator, when he endowed us with appetites and functions by which to sustain the economy of life, at the same time to annex to their exercise a sense of pleasure; hence our daily food, and the daily alternation of repose and action, are no less grateful than imperative."[35] The invocation of this polar balance between economy and pleasure recalls the lesson of "The Hypochondriac," but here the condition is complicated by Allston's definition of idleness as itself a form of activity, one of the myriad ways—"physical, intellectual, and moral"—in which man's endeavor strives toward the realization of the "Sovereign Principle of Harmony." The pursuit of a harmonious state is driven by yearning for completion and fullness, and the achievement of Allstonian harmony is described in the language of the sublime: in harmony "what we call self has no part . . . any personal considerations, or any conscious advantage to the individual" are overcome.[36]

Yet the state of complete harmony remains forever beyond human activity's reach; the harmony of the whole may be posited only negatively, in the confused and unsatisfying attempts of the human mind to attain it: "Now, as the condition of Harmony, so far as we can know it through its effect, is that of *impletion*, where nothing can be added or taken away, it is evident that such a condition can never be realized by the mind in itself. And yet the desire to this end is as evidently implied in that incessant, yet unsatisfying activity, which under all circumstances, is an imperative, universal law of our nature."[37] All activity—even that which seems most idle—is therefore circumscribed by this "imperative, universal law." The mind aims at "neither rest nor action," taken in isolation, "for in a state of rest it desires action, and in a state of action, rest." And thus in Allston's conception neither a pure idleness nor pure activity is possible; it is rather the resolution of their dialectical tension in a state of harmonious equilibrium that is to be sought. Echoing "The Hypochondriac," Allston chides those who repose in merely sinful idleness. "We never find," he asserts, "that any one individual has been contented with doing nothing. Some, indeed . . . have conceived of idleness as a kind of synonyme with happiness; but a short experience has never failed to prove it no less remote from that desirable state.[38] Even the business of doing nothing, then, is charged with some sort of productive end, and neither could "the veriest idler, who passes a whole day in whittling a stick, if he could be brought to look into himself, deny it": "So far from having no object, he would and must acknowledge that he was in fact hoping to relieve himself of an oppressive portion of time by whittling away its minutes and hours. Here we have an extreme instance of that which constitutes the real business of life, from the most idle to the most industrious; namely, to attain to a *satisfying state*."[39] The idler seeks to approach harmony by killing time, attempting to cast off its "oppressive" yoke. Though Allston stops short of crediting this ignominious time-killing with achieving harmony (for, by definition, harmony as the sovereign principle is unattainable by the human mind), he nevertheless tellingly fails to indict it as any more trivial than activity of other sorts. Falling short of the sovereign state, it meanwhile attains the same kind of satisfaction—of harmonizing the material world with man—afforded by Beauty.[40] The activity of art, then, is revealed as only a substitutive satisfaction, its beauty indicating infinite harmony, but capable of realizing only a material approximation of it.

That unsatisfying conclusion is the apex of one long critical moan expressing Allston's contentment with the transcendent panacea expected of the next world. Things become quite a bit more intriguing, however, when Allston complements the foregoing concepts with that of sublimity. Then the confines of the subject are prised open (the sublime "is not in man: for the emotion excited has an outward tendency; the mind can not contain it"),[41] as is the hermetic unity of Allston's argument, which, unfolding in the flash of sparks generated by its contradictory frictions, threatens to internally combust. The tension surfaces as Allston perseveres in celebrating a traditional notion of sublimity, despite hedging that definition with a couple of significant exceptions.

The first hedge is Allston's admission that sublime effects needn't *directly* involve the Infinite Idea: "A sublime effect is often powerfully felt in many instances where this Idea could not truly be predicated of the apparent object. In such cases, however, some kind of resemblance, or, at least, a seeming analogy to an infinite attribute, is nevertheless essential. It must appear to us, for the time, either limitless, indefinite, or in some other way beyond the grasp of the mind."[42] Thus, among the usual litany of those traditionally sublime phenomena originating in divine provenance—the Vesuvian crater, the agitated sea—Allston includes, for example, the contemplation of Newton's conjecture about the existence of stars so removed from the sun that their light has yet failed to reach Earth. He posits, therefore, a sublime effect—the radical disruption of time and space relations—that is apparently *analogous to* that provoked by the Infinite Idea. It is attained through the material labor of thought, the conjuring of an idea by man (here, admittedly, a man who happens to be Newton). The integrity of the traditional sublime is further weakened by Allston's acknowledgment of the possible coexistence of simultaneous effects of sublimity and beauty—the possibility of a satisfying beauty inhering in (though subordinate to) the overawing effect of sublime emotion. The sublime includes "within its sphere, and subdue[s] to its condition, an indefinite variety of objects, with their distinctive conditions; and among them we find that of the Beautiful."[43]

These two caveats provoke the conclusion that a moderate, material harmony—such as the achievement in the artwork of a beautiful whole—can aspire to effects analogous to those of the infinite, and thereby very well attain sublimity. Influenced by his study of the old masters, Allston argues that such a whole, driven by Harmony's "mysterious power," presupposes two conditions—the individual artistic treatment of each individual part, and "secondly, the uniting of the parts by such an interdependence that they shall appear to us as essential, one to another, and all to each. When this is done, the result is a whole."[44] Composition, then, aims to produce the intense effect of the whole, an effect potentially analogous to sublimity. This effect of aesthetic unity pushes Beauty to its most extreme degree, but does not, according to Allston, attain sublimity.

It is here that Allston's "love for the silent, the solitary, the contemplative" proves the undoing of his aesthetic categories. For all his efforts to preserve the traditional—instantaneous and overwhelming—character of the sublime, Allston finds himself without a proper concept for the effect produced by a perfectly composed whole. Beauty again? Of course. But in discussing the composition of a Claude landscape and the power of "perfect unity" its lines generate, Allston's language suggests something more: the painting's spell acts "upon us with a vague sense of limitless expanse, yet so continuous, so gentle, so imperceptible in its remotest gradations, as scarcely to be felt, till, combining with unity, we find the feeling embodied in the complete image of intellectual repose,—fulness and rest."[45] Fulness—*impletion*—is achieved, and with it an effect Allston describes in terms appropriate to not only the discourse of repose but also that of the contemplative sublime: "We have stood before some fine picture, though with a sense of pleasure, yet for many minutes in a manner abstracted,—silently passing through all its harmonious transitions without the movement of a muscle, and hardly conscious of action, till we have suddenly found ourselves returning on our steps. Then it was,—as if we had no eyes till then,— that the magic Whole poured in upon us, and vouched for its truth in an outbreak of rapture."[46] The silent fulness of rapture emerges in the form of a sublimity that Allston will nevertheless refuse to name. That the experience of this perfect whole partakes of the language of the contemplative sublime is impossible to deny—no longer are we merely on the plane of Beauty, with its comprehensible and containable harmonies. *Instead, the harmony of beauty envelops the viewer in the experience and the expression of the contemplative sublime.* Moving, like the prophet Elijah, from blindness to revelation while surrounded by a quiet chorus of truth, one is to reproduce in this contemplative rapture Elijah's experience of sublimity, which "was the still, small voice that shook the Prophet on Horeb; though small to his ear, it was more than his imagination could contain."[47]

That the Whole *pours* in upon us, just as the truth does upon Elijah's desert meditation—cascading down Horeb in the form of a waterfall to the right—is fitting: the waterfall elsewhere appears as a signal emblem of the contemplative. In it, the two sublimes coexist, and—as Cole noted—incessant movement fuses with complete stillness: "the same object at once presents to the mind the beautiful, but apparently incongruous idea, of fixedness and motion—a single existence in which we perceive unceasing change and everlasting duration."[48] Allston discovers in the quiet sublimity of Elijah's waterfall a harmony that would embody not only the rhythms of human activity, but also those of the work of art. In either, harmony attains, despite Allston's labored conceptual efforts, a sublimity predicated on the achievement of rest.

Industrious Affect and Sublime Circulation in Marx

> The sublime has become normal.
> —Antonio Negri, "Value and Affect," 1999

Allston's description of sublime experience before Claude's landscapes not only hints that the harmony of contemplative sublimity is attainable through the unified beauty of the perfectly composed work, but furthermore that that condition is the product of a heightened spatio-temporal awareness. The linear rhythm of passing minutes is violated by sudden rupture, time and space are recalibrated, readjusted, and even . . . *annihilated*? As such, Allston's inadvertent theory of sublimity partakes in the regnant obsession, so prominent in the 1830s, with the manipulation of time. Allston's conception is, however, rather conservative: for him the annihilation of time effected by the pseudosublime instant must heel itself, like everything else in his theory, to the sovereign principle of harmony. In other words, harmony serves for Allston as a tempering element, a means of containing the rampant disintegration of the aesthetic whole. In his discussion of "Variety," we can discern that this account of time and the dialectic of rest and movement has a significance that is both aesthetic and social.

As always, everything in moderation for Allston. Though he considers variety ("difference, yet with relation to a common end") as an essential aesthetic principle, its realization is fraught with the risk of dangerous excess: "Indirectly, from our disgust of monotony, we infer the necessity of variety," he argues. "But variety, when carried to excess, results in weariness. Some limitation, therefore, seems no less needed."[49] The differences attendant to variety must be properly managed in order to profit the aesthetic whole, and greatness is realized in those compositional triumphs that most ably effect this negotiation and thereby combine the extreme of variety with perfect unity.

There is in Allston's zeal for the proper ordering of particulars a bit of the spirit of the age. The experience of variety itself was a function of technological developments and expanded economic democracy; no longer the province of the elite, variety in manufactures would be experienced as an unprecedented diversification of material reality—a visible and palpable representation of the "progress" so characteristic of this period. As such, the shocks and upheavals with which unmitigated variety threatened the unity of the artwork borrow some of their force from the experiences endured (or enjoyed) by Allston and his contemporaries as a consequence of the emerging consumerist phantasmagoria. The celebration of variety mirrors an experience of modern life in which diversity and novelty have become broadly available—the expansion of travel and mass manufacturing beckon, inviting exploration of new worlds of experience. Frolicking amid the potentials of a world that is both shrinking and becoming more cluttered, Allston's narrator in "The Hypochondriac," having pledged himself to the diversion of light, amusing reading, breathtakingly chronicles the subsequent implosion of time and space: "month after month pass[ed] away like days, and as for days,—I almost fancied that I could see the sun move. How comfortable, thought I, thus to travel over the world in my closet!" Predictably, Allston's hypochondriac soon finds that the allure of that unprecedented variety begins to pale: "The ease with which I thus circumnavigated the globe, and conversed with all its varieties of inhabitants, expanded my benevolence. . . . But alas! . . . Though I was still curious, there were no longer curiosities."[50]

The painter confronting the problem of variety regards it as a compositional puzzle to be harmoniously solved and brought to balance. Nowhere does Allston make this so manifest as in his discussion of Paolo Veronese's *Marriage at Cana*, which he regards as the extreme case of compositional harmony triumphing over the propensity of particulars to scatter and diffuse themselves: in Veronese's mesmerizing work, more than one hundred figures jostle each other, contained in the bottom two-thirds of a space 32 feet long by 22 feet high. Allston's analysis celebrates the painting for producing a unique experience of time and space. Variety, he says, prevails "to such an extent, that an hour's travel will hardly conduct us through all its parts; yet we feel no weariness throughout this journey, nay, we are quite unconscious of the time it has taken."[51] Travel— a primary figure, as we have seen, of technological sublimity—provides the metaphor for viewing the painting, and it is a travel that compresses duration to the point of its incomprehensibility. That this travel has an *economic* character as well is suggested by the following passage, where movement in the absence of duration becomes a dance among exchangeable forms mingling in the constant seduction of novelty:

> Literally the eye may be said to *dance* through the picture, scarcely lighting on one part before it is drawn to another, and another, and another, as by a kind of witching; while the subtle interlocking of each successive novelty leaves it no choice, but, seducing it onward, still keeps it in motion, till the giddy sense seems to call on the Imagination to join in the revel; and every poetic temperament answers to the call, bringing visions of its own, that mingle with the painted crowd, exchanging forms, and giving them voice, like the creatures of a dream.[52]

Veronese's painting, at the extreme of compositional harmony, reconfigures time in a movement that appears, like Elijah's waterfall, as atemporal stasis coexisting with absolute movement. The negation of time—the appearance of impletion, rest, and stillness—is achieved at the expense of the feverish pother of the particulars, and simultaneously depends on their variety for its effect. It relies upon, just as much as it defies, the pageant of "novelty" that flaunts its appeal as if from behind the reflective sheen of a shop window, seducing the imagination to mingle promiscuously in an orgy of *exchange*. The completed totality of Veronese's painting achieves rest by overcoming the temporal character of incessant circulation and the exchange it facilitates.

Veronese's *Marriage* proceeds by uniting those disparate moments of exchange; Allston's analysis does so by wedding the vocabulary of art to that of the consumer economy. It is therefore not cause for surprise that the relation between the appearance of harmony and the sublimity of progress was of concern to another social observer at midcentury: Karl Marx. Writing ten years after Allston's death, Marx's depiction of the vigorous energy of exchange addresses the same tendencies that Allston indirectly diagnosed in their incunabular stage: what appeared to Allston as the defining characteristic of the aesthetic whole would be realized in the tendency of the capitalist economy toward impletion. Informed by the maturation of those tendencies in the genesis of the global capitalist economy, Marx's work likewise seizes upon the spatio-temporal character of circulation as an explanation of the sublimity of everyday life.

For Marx, the monetary crisis of 1857, which began with a bank collapse in New York and thereafter spread to the European capitals and inaugurated a worldwide slump, provided evidence of the newly totalizing character of capital. The crisis was the first of its kind, no longer tethered to the cycles of agrarian production but rather immanent to the system of self-reproducing and incessant instances of capitalized exchange. Cut adrift from any natural ground, the crisis of 1857 announces the reconstitution of the mode of production around the sublime fungibility of the monetary abstraction: in Sergio Bologna's words, Marx is overawed by his intellectual encounter with "the first complete form of a modern monetary system."[53]

In describing the emergence of this complete monetary system constituted by abstract exchange, it is not entirely surprising that Marx, too, invokes the reassurance of nature as an antidote, as a site that is external, or at least anterior, to the system of exchange. The discussion of the monetary system laid out early in the *Grundrisse* uses the notion of the "natural" to establish the concreteness of production upon which the edifice of capitalist exploitation is built. It is, for example, the "natural form of the product," its "natural value," that is abstracted into exchange and circulation.[54] The natural appears in the *Grundrisse* as the realm of use value in opposition to that of exchange; its opposite number is depicted via all the monstrous trappings of the Burkean sublime. "The exchange relation," he notes, "establishes itself as *a power external to and independent of* the producers. What originally appeared as a means to promote production becomes a relation *alien to the producers.*" Entering exchange, the natural product of man's labor "is *abandoned to the mercy of external conditions,*" and—as for the producers—they "are subsumed under social production; social production *exists outside them as their fate.*"[55] The increasingly inevitable subsumption of individual producers and their products under the alien jurisdiction of the exchange economy looms as would a volcanic explosion or a stormy sea—an external and uncontrollable force capable of encompassing, determining, and overwhelming the natural product of man's activity.

We have seen that the language of traditional, terrifying sublimity is ever more common by midcentury as the means for describing the immeasurable force of the social transformation then under way. Marx's depiction of the hegemony of the exchange economy, however, goes further, situating that sublimity firmly in a habitat that is strictly material—the completed economic totality in which diverse acts of exchange, different from each other in content and potentially far removed from each other by the broadening reach of communications and transportation, form a unified system. Capitalist circulation, he argues, consists not of "isolated acts of exchange"—that is, individuated particulars—"but a circle of exchange, a totality of the same, in constant flux, proceeding more or less over the entire surface of society; a system of acts of exchange."[56] Further, the intensification of circulation—buoyed by the expansion of railroads, the telegraph, and later by a national currency—is a prerequisite of capitalist sublimity, the ground of what is no longer merely an instrumental economic mechanism but rather a saturating *social experience*: "Circulation, because a totality of the social process, is also the first form in which the social relation appears as something independent of the individuals, but not only as, say, in a coin or in exchange value, but extending to the whole of the social movement itself."[57] Saturating the social whole in a tendential movement girdled only by its own productive horizons, this circulatory network thus appears to the enmeshed, individual producer as an infinite and incomprehensible phenomenon. But though Marx avers that "at first sight, circulation appears as a *simply infinite* process [whereby] the commodity is exchanged for money, money is exchanged for the commodity, and this is repeated endlessly," he will also insist that the circulatory process "reveals other phenomena as well; the phenomena of completion, or, the return of the point of departure into itself."[58] The capitalist social whole, while aspiring toward infinity, is nevertheless drawn back to totality—it describes a completed process, a returning upon its own steps. It is in this that the system of monetary circulation fulfills itself, and in so doing, recalls Allston's viewing of Claude's landscapes. Remember: "We have stood before some fine picture . . . silently passing through all its harmonious transitions without the movement of a muscle, and hardly conscious of action, till we have suddenly found ourselves returning on our steps. Then it was,—as if we had no eyes till then,—that the magic Whole poured in upon us, and vouched for its truth in an outbreak of rapture."[59] With the prospect of a completed circuit of circulation, harmony is achieved, the dangerous propensities of the particulars are neutralized, and the apparent stability of the whole is produced.

What is achieved by the artwork is mirrored in the economic system. The appearance of restful harmony, the seeming attainment of equilibrium, obfuscates the actual character of incessant and totalizing exchange. All the seemingly equivalent exchanges, ostensibly embodying harmonious fair play among multitudinous economic interests, are in fact instances of inequivalence and contradiction—that is, moments of exploitation. Their apparent harmony is in fact the façade concealing an economic violence.

In the *Grundrisse*, this is explained as follows: money serves, simultaneously and contradictorily, three different functions. It is at once the measure of value and the medium of exchange, and in these instances it is possible, at least theoretically, to imagine it functioning harmoniously. Money is the mediation that enables participants in exchange relationships to establish and swap quantities of value. But money's third function—as the material representative of wealth—intervenes to disrupt this seeming equilibrium, for it makes no sense to a capitalist to exchange money for money in equivalent amounts (unless his aim is to cease being a capitalist). The harmonious cycle of "Money-Commodity-Commodity-Money, which we drew from the analysis of circulation, would then appear to be merely an arbitrary and senseless abstraction, roughly as if one wanted to describe the life cycle as Death-Life-Death," Marx smirks.[60] The capitalist's aim is thus to always exchange money for greater quantities of money, to realize greater quantities of price and profit. Thus results, according to Marx, an inevitable tension in circulation equivalents. The apparent harmonization of these equivalents in the supposedly free and fair percolation of mutually gratifying exchanges is a fundamental mystification by which the economic system operates. The seeming rational harmony of the system of economic circulation in fact conceals the greed that drives it.

The previous sentence, for all its appearance as a mere polemical stab, in fact enables us to follow this detour into political economy back to the place of rest, and to the question of what constitutes and characterizes repose. In Marx, such an affect as that of repose must be understood as the product of an economic context. That much is made clear by his discussion, in the *Grundrisse*'s "Chapter on Money," of greed, the existence of which presupposes the existence of totalizing capitalist circulation. That is to say, greediness for Marx is a *product* of the experience of totalizing economic relationships, and not the natural motor producing those relationships. Such a conception of greed not only rescues us from the mystifying misapprehension of greed as a natural quality of man, with the capitalist system as its logical and natural extension, but it also explains how emotional states—miserliness, hedonism, and, as I would argue, repose—themselves are determined by the material experience of basic economic conditions. "[G]reed itself is the product of a definite social development, not natural, as opposed to historical," Marx asserts.[61] He goes on to explain more fully that "when the aim of labour is not a particular product standing in a particular relation to the particular needs of the individual, but money, wealth in its general form, then firstly, the individual's industriousness knows no bounds; it is indifferent to its particularity, and takes on every form which serves the purpose; it is ingenious in the creation of new objects for a social need, etc."[62] In spreading the objects of industry throughout the social, capital thus produces—in the tireless exertions it demands—the affective relationship between men and money, generating the very impulses that fuel the system. Among those impulses is that of industriousness, geared toward augmenting material wealth and realizing gain.[63] It is thus the historical totalization of circulation that generates the saturating ideology of industriousness: "General industriousness is possible only where every act of labour produces general wealth, not a particular form of it; where therefore the individual's reward, too, is money. Otherwise, only particular forms of industry are possible."[64]

That same totalization of circulation is what makes repose emerge as an important affective phenomenon in this period of intense capitalist accumulation. The experience of repose, its expression, the very feeling of enjoying and valorizing it, are traceable to the economic conditions that render it an absolute necessity. Of course, repose—in its putative resistance to improvement, donning all the utopian garb Dana, Allston, and Cole can stitch together—may be realized only in amputated form. Increasingly the product of capitalist economic relations, repose persists in aligning itself with them even as it seeks to negate them. The ideology of repose ultimately serves to efface the appearance of society's actual radical disequilibrium. In that fickle harmony—dignified by Allston as the goal of all activity, artistic and otherwise—industriousness and repose join forces under the command of the advanced system of economic exchange.

The Luminist Intensification

> We are never tired, so long as we can see far enough.
> —Ralph Waldo Emerson, "Nature," 1836

The sway of repose—complete with its complicated relationship to nature and history, its sincere celebration of nature's placidity, and its ideological calming of the new era's economic commotion—reaches its apotheosis in the landscape painting of midcentury, and particularly in that mode of painting now referred to in some quarters as "luminist." Straining toward the quietude of the contemplative to an extent unmatched by any other visual art of the time, these works may do so only by enveloping and muffling in their tranquil mists the fervent crises of midcentury.

Luminism was first dignified as a movement only in the middle of the twentieth century, and one senses that the lateness of this "discovery," credited to the historian John Baur, has intensified the attempt to properly define what luminism is. Baur used the word for the first time in 1954 to designate the minor trend in mid-nineteenth-century American landscape painting toward exaggerated atmospheric and light effects; numerous critics have since attempted to refine and augment his initial insight.[65] Noting the shift away from the regnant conventions of the early Hudson River school and its generally European formal approach to representing nature, he remarked in many respects the same historical transition that alters the character of the sublime. Though other critics have convincingly demonstrated that luminism is a characteristic of works, not of artists (and that, therefore, paintings of a luminist quality are to be found not only in America, and not only during the style's midcentury heyday), the primary characteristics tend to be associated with the names of Martin Johnson Heade, Sanford Robinson Gifford, Fitz Hugh Lane, and John Frederick Kensett.[66]

This ongoing definitional exertion has defined luminism in part by the effect of repose, reanimating a critical tradition dating back to Tuckerman, who gushed, upon viewing a painting by Kensett, "what sublime repose." This restful quality in luminism mobilizes the contemplative, transcendent sublimity identified by Cole and Allston, producing a harmony that is at once passive and active: as Barbara Novak has claimed, luminism's "silence, in the repose of inaction, represents not a void but a palpable space, *in which everything happens while nothing does.*"[67] In mixed-breed paintings such as the marine landscapes of the 1860s, this effect of repose is often achieved through explicit contrast with the transcendent sublimity of the older tradition; such is the case especially in works by Heade and Lane, including the latter's *Ships and an Approaching Storm off Owl's Head, Maine*. There, the tranquil repose of ships in placid water dominates the foreground, while a building churn of clouds and darkness, promising imminent disruption, mounts in the distance. The severity of Lane's horizon neatly distinguishes the two sublime modes: beneath it, barely agitated water is subtly strafed by two white bands, the mildest of contrasts being provided by the gauzily illuminated side and reflection of the central vessel's hull. This restful horizontality, however, is contrasted above, by the active perpendiculars of the ship's masts and a primary thunderhead at the painting's center. Rest is implied in a temporal caesura, marking the presence of the proverbial calm that precedes a stormy disruption. A similar treatment of this quiet instant may be found in Heade's *Thunderstorm on Narragansett Bay* (1868, figure 2), in which the image—and the two sublime modes—are split two ways: once bilaterally, and again at the horizon, which is intersected by a stab of lightning that effectively helps to designate the sublime spaces of the painting. At front and left, the cavalier pace of the retreating fishermen and the absolute reflective stillness of the painting's foregrounded inlet are suggestive of harmonic completion.

These and other, purer, manifestations of the luminist paradigm further achieve their sublime quietude and inaction by invoking infinity. This is apparent in the compression of immense scales into relatively tiny paintings, their unbroken horizon alluding to the vast space beyond the painting's perimeter, in which restful horizontality perseveres. Such an expansive effect is intensified through techniques for creating a suffusing and overwhelming light—a tendency discernible as early as Allston's *Moonlit Landscape* of 1819—often using colors of such great visual intensity that their ethereal effect threatens to overwhelm all merely material, terrestrial clutter. Water heightens the preceding effects, in glassy expanses, freed of any claustrophobic Claudean framing, that create reflective doublings and the infinite shimmerings of cut crystal, the "sublimity of a shoreless ocean un-islanded by the recorded deeds of man," to quote the sentiments of Cole, for whom any landscape lacking water is defective.[68]

Perhaps the most effective feature of luminism in this regard is its strict reliance on horizontality, the works being structured, as Novak has demonstrated, in a series of horizontal steps; in the passage from one to the

Figure 2. Martin Johnson Heade, American (1819–1904), *Thunderstorm on Narragansett Bay*, 1868. Oil on canvas. 32 ⅛ x 54 ¾ in. Amon Carter Museum of American Art, Fort Worth, Texas.

next the eye is egged on into the apparently infinite distance. That technique, along with the distended horizontal framing of most luminist works (often as much as twice as wide as they are tall), follows from the teaching that "the horizontal is indicative of a universal law of nature, that of a general subsistence and repose of inanimate matter" (the perpendicular, needing the horizontal as its ground, suggests the tension of "power and action").[69] Finally, the tendency in luminism is to eschew that implicitly political indulgence of much American landscape painting in which an elevated spectatorial position—that which Albert Boime has labeled the "magisterial gaze"—asserted the dominance of man over the natural surroundings.[70] Luminism, by contrast, generally relegated the viewer to a horizontal equality with the setting, further establishing by this common altitude the certainty of seducing the viewer into the painting, of making the experience of nature intuitive, rather than cognitive or instrumental. In this way, according to Powell, "the plane of a luminist canvas extends towards the viewer to encompass his presence in the conceptualized space of the landscape itself."[71]

Large blocks of light and water, cleaved by dramatic and seemingly infinite horizons, shooting in both directions toward the limits of comprehension—such are the raw materials of the contemplative sublime as

Figure 3. John Frederick Kensett (1816–1872), *Eaton's Neck, Long Island*, 1872. Oil on canvas, 18 x 36 in (45.7 x 91.4 cm). Gift of Thomas Kensett, 1874 (74.29). Image copyright © The Metropolitan Museum of Art / Art Resource, NY.

realized in luminist composition. The luminist mode, at the peak of its maturity, sought compositional repose in greatly abstracted masses and relatively blunt symmetries:[72] such is the case in those works of Kensett and Heade that, as in Kensett's *Eaton's Neck, Long Island* (1872, figure 3), use a curved shoreline to propel the gaze into the space and light that are the works' primary concern. In *Eaton's Neck*, the three moderate masses of the painting's lower half (the sea, its curved perimeter of white sand, and the dense, dark outcropping at right) are aligned to propel the gaze outward, into the central nexus from which the piece's dominant subject—the open, open sky—radiates. With the greater abstraction of these masses, harmony is achieved almost by fiat in the still balance of land mass against air. The painting's simplicity is such as to suggest its militancy against not only activity, but also variety, in all their forms.[73]

The effect of these harmonies, symmetries, and inertias should not be underestimated. In contrast to the sublime or picturesque firepower behind the Hudson River school's meticulous virtuosity or the programmatic enclosure of a Claudean landscape, luminism's achievement of repose resounds like a silenced revolver. In this effect is revealed the kinship between such painting and the transcendentalist sensibility of, for example, Emerson, for whom it was the "tranquil landscape" that, in some of his most famous passages, enabled the ego to be transcended and the self to align itself with the natural whole.[74] Yet there remains something suspicious about such repose, and especially the ostensible immediacy attributed to it not only by Emerson but also by critics like Novak, who described it as "impl[ying] presence through the sense of thereness rather than through activity."[75] We must address not only the "presence" of luminist unity, but also the absence that it suggests and conceals. Among the speedy conveyances, hectic utilitarianism, and budding communications of a period in which the economic character of America was consolidated, the appearance of such an unprecedented, stultifying harmony appears incongruous, unless we insist on repose's simultaneous debt to, and attempted defiance of, the budding logic of exchange. Luminist repose, masquerading under its apparent promise of unity, is a site for the symbolic unification of an inharmonious social whole. There, the fundamental antagonism of the exchange system is defused by way of the very horizontality and abstraction that typify it—its inequivalent exchanges are flattened and made smoothly tranquil in the instantiation of luminist harmony. That luminism could attain such repose is therefore not merely a function of the communion with nature that it encouraged and supposedly provided. For luminism's "nature," like that of Claude and Cole and the Hudson River school, was a production of culture, its beauty a product of historical determination, its harmony the negative of society's dissonances.

Technically speaking, the effects sought by luminism depend on a stable of specific strategies, crucial among them those which mystified the production of the work, especially that elimination of the "labor trail" by luminism's characteristic concealment of the painter's stroke. It is this divergence from Hudson River school technique—which sought to foreground the adroitness of the artist by impressing upon the viewer the extent of his labors—that makes plausible luminism's approach to the beneficent salvation of transcendence. The mediation of the artist is obscured, and God's hand intervenes to wield the brush, his radiance deftly conveyed in luminism's incomparable illumination. So unrepentant was this apparently unmediated realism that James Jackson Jarves was provoked to comment that "to such an extent is literalness carried, that the majority of works are quite divested of human association."[76] This abolition of signs indicating a material painterly mediation is complemented by the seeming abatement of the ceaseless motion of the worldly, as the concealment of the painter's presence eliminates the temporal relativism by which one stroke might be assumed, by some interval, to follow the last.[77] The stoppage of time, then, necessitates a fundamental mystification of the labor process: the fetishistic concealment of the stroke obscures the traces of the product's production, and occasions its phantom objectivity.

It is this clandestinity of the luminist artist that ensures his craft's successful execution, a mystification that furthermore requires the disguising of these works' geometric rationality. Luminism's emphasis on horizontal symmetry, marked by slight diagonals and occasional vertical stabilizers, was drawn on a long-developed tradition—where transcendentalist intuition fails, the painter's handbook provides the key.[78] The embrace of geometric form was compatible with faith in a certain type of compositional license that prevailed among American landscape painters—Cole, Allston, and others endorsed the painter's agency in selecting parts to recombine into natural-looking wholes. Cole, in an 1825 letter to his patron Robert Gilmore, argued that "the most lovely and perfect parts of nature may be brought together, and combined in a whole, that shall surpass in beauty and effect any picture painted from a single view."[79] Of course, this logic contradicts the unmediated order of a nature that seems to merely await its adequate representation. It instead dictates that the agency of the artist in collecting various parts and articulating them with one another in a coherent unity be accorded a value almost divine. In this respect, landscape painting might be said to mirror that early-nineteenth-century development in commodity manufacturing that came to be called the "American System," which increasingly supplanted organic, fully formed wholes with systems of interchangeable parts.[80] The concurrence of these aesthetic and economic strategies of production suggests the broad experience of rationalized approaches to the problem of harmony—that is, of creating functioning wholes out of diverse particulars.

Luminism's attempt to convey infinite, eternal harmonies—all the while keeping the manipulation of its method behind the scenes—is indisputable. For while its contemplative repose supplies, as we have seen, a kind of antidote to the juggernaut of improvement, it simultaneously and deceivingly creates the impression of a harmony that prevails despite the emergent industrial conditions. Martin Johnson Heade's work acutely exemplifies this impulse, simultaneously utopian and ideological, to invoke rest as a supreme value. Heade, a manically restless traveler energized by the mobility of a shrinking globe, was nevertheless a paradigmatic figure of luminist repose.[81] His work includes landscapes from along the eastern seaboard, as well as Latin America and elsewhere, but despite being bolstered by advancements in transportation and communication,

it is curiously virtually devoid of instances in which such industrious figures as the railroad appear.

This is all the more peculiar, given, for example, the relatively common
representation of locomotive travel in American landscape painting generally. While the literature on this point is broad and thorough, a brief
consideration of one of the more famous railroad paintings, Jasper Cropsey's *Starrucca Viaduct, Pennsylvania* (1865, figure 4) is instructive.[82] In
Cropsey's painting, the lush Susquehanna River valley is invaded by the
appearance not only of the locomotive itself, but also of the awe-inspiring
man-made viaduct—which, built in 1848, stretching to more than 1,200
feet in length, and comprising seventeen arches some 114 feet high, epitomizes the burgeoning incursion of industry into the natural picturesque.
But in addition to reflecting the dialectic of nature and culture in an
emblematic instance, the painting is further interesting for the unusual
appearance of two foreground figures whose appearance is highly suggestive. These observers of industrial progress are, significantly, out of place
in American landscape painting—they are neither the well-heeled aesthetes of Asher B. Durand's *Kindred Spirits* (which, painted in 1849, depicts
Thomas Cole and William Cullen Bryant discoursing over a Catskills
vista), nor are they the cultured connoisseurs of Italian light effects whose
gaze devolves upon Mount Mansfield, in Sanford Gifford's 1858 painting
of the same name. Instead, the onlookers in *Starrucca Viaduct* are suspi-
ciously derelict: the standing figure slouches slightly forward, the sleeve of
his unstructured coat patched at the elbow. His companion reclines on the
ground, lazily propped on an elbow as if only recently jarred awake from
a nap. One dog, wearily and barely upright, is complemented by another,
which nearly melts into the rock in its sleepy indolence. Even the smolder-
ing fire nearby burns in wan indifference.

There is no suggestion of why these men repose here—no boat pulled up
to a nearby shore to index their activity (a prop by which the Native American in Cropsey's 1868 *Dawn of Morning, Lake George* is dignified), no rifles
for hunting or instruments for trail blazing or wicker baskets abundant
with bottles of wine. There is only the faint implication that the arrival of
these men—tramps, by all outward appearances—on the scene of American painting is coincident with that of the chugging locomotive in the distance. They are therefore interesting not only for the dubious distinction of
being among the first Industrial Age slackers represented as merely chill-
ing out in an American landscape painting (a distinction shared, perhaps,
with the foreground figure in George Inness's *Lackawanna Valley*, ca. 1855),

Figure 4. Jasper Francis Cropsey, American (1823–1900), *Starrucca Viaduct, Pennsylvania*, 1865. Oil on canvas, 22 ⅜ x 36 ⅜ in (56.8 x 92.4 cm). Toledo Museum of Art, Toledo, Ohio. Purchased with funds from the Florence Scott Libbey Bequest in Memory of her Father, Maurice A. Scott. 1947.58. Photo Credit: Photography Incorporated, Toledo.

but likewise for marking a historical juncture in which conjoined notions of industry and idleness are being renegotiated due to the developing forces of production. At Starrucca Viaduct, the river valley is not the only threshold being crossed. Just as the wafting steam of the train is kin with the bank of natural clouds that frame the work's right-hand perimeter, these two fore-grounded idlers adopt a stance—as the observers of landscape—that echoes but is nevertheless distinct from the posturing of the idle rich more commonly represented in such paintings. Their idle behaviors, effecting a satiric straddling of the class divide, are meaningfully transgressive in not only the ideological context of industrialism but also that of the conventional treat-ment of landscape. In both contexts, their unproductive presence tweaks the relationship between nature and culture, as well as that between idleness and activity.

Similarly exceptional is Martin Johnson Heade's *Lynn Meadows* paint-ing of 1863 (figure 5)—his only painting featuring a locomotive motif—which makes a similar point by very different means. It is typically severe in its horizontal conception, its width attenuated to two and half times

Figure 5. Martin Johnson Heade, American (1819–1904), *Lynn Meadows*, 1863. Yale University Art Gallery. Gift of Arnold H. Nichols, B.A. 1920.

its height; three-fifths of the painting is devoted to a sky empty save for a few swelling smoky clouds, in purplish and orange hues, creeping from the left side. But those drifting bodies are complemented to the right by the steam spout of a locomotive, barely discernible as it reaches the right-hand frame of the image. Upon closer inspection, it becomes clear that the railroad in fact is constitutive of the painting's horizon; though the train itself is almost invisible, its track—raised above the marsh by a rickety set of stanchions, neatly cleaves the painting, abruptly closing off the serpentine meander of the marsh. Not only does the balance of the composition get redrawn around it, but the implication, as Theodore Stebbins has argued, is of the transformation of an entire way of life: the railroad's causeway regulates the free movement that would have given a natural rhythm to the painting's setting—the movement of not only clamdiggers diving after the swamp's yield, but also that of the tides that made their endeavor possible.[83]

That the rail's appearance was felt as an intrusion into Heade's luminist universe is evident not only from its imposition, common to other paintings of the period, upon the scene's serene bliss, but also from the fact that Heade would not paint a train again. The train, moving along its road of improvement, afflicted Heade's tranquil atmosphere with such severe strain that it simply could not be accommodated there. Its disappearance is typical of Heade's works, which tend to describe, as Sarah Burns has noted, "a static world that lingered in an increasingly distant and irrelevant past while real agriculture was being transformed by expansion, technology, and capitalism."[84] There is nonetheless the sense that Heade's works dangerously negotiate between these two worlds—but not only with the overt presence of the railroad to mark the contrast. For his landscapes took as their primary setting these marshlands, productive of hay and thereby of great value to the traditional modes of living that prospered upon them, but not readily lending themselves to other valuable uses—to the improvements of "real" agriculture. In painting some 120 marsh paintings, Heade generated the most extreme effects of contemplative sublimity—the paintings' indefatigable horizontality and their geometrically precise processions of haystacks leading the eye to vertiginous depths realize fully the principles of luminist composition. And just as the lands they document would remain an obstacle to the march of agricultural progress, as a painterly subject they would seem just as infertile.

"Almost by definition, a painting of a marsh could not be picturesque," Stebbins says, quoting one unattributed judge as saying that "as scenic features they are monotonous and uninteresting in the extreme because of their lack of relief and uniformity of appearance."[85] This monotony of effect—perhaps achieved by the complete elimination of tension, and especially that strain between industry and idle land so common to the period—is however, precisely what elevates these paintings. They represent not the fermenting dialectic of productive technology and idle wilderness, but rather a point at which these two have already met, consummating their frozen checkmate in a repose both expressive and experiential.

Utility, Superfluity: The Paradox of American Painting

> THE IDLE MAN;—a very quiet and unpretending name for a man in a passion.
>
> —Richard Henry Dana, Sr., *Idle Man*, 1821

Heade's marshlands, as spaces that are not quite "productive," and not quite purely "idle," rather aptly analogize the condition of American art in the early nineteenth century. A key concern for the American art elite was that of combating the prejudices that disparaged American painting—its overshadowing by the European greats, its purported lack of indigenous tradition, its outclassing by the other arts. As in the marsh, something was germinating in American painting. The question was whether it was good only for feeding to the animals.

To conclude that painting was without real utility was logical for those eastern elites who, steeped in a Puritan ethic, thought highly of preoccupying themselves with grander concerns. Consider the appeals of one eighteenth-century exemplar, John Durand, who in 1768 published a short advertisement in the *New York Journal*, seeking to market his portrait paintings "at as cheap rates as any person in America." He addresses "such gentlemen and ladies as have thought but little upon this subject and might only regard painting as a superfluous ornament," insisting that "history painting, besides being extremely ornamental has many important uses," among them those of provoking interest in history, providing "lively and perfect ideas" of historical scenes, and triggering memory of same. Paintings, he argued, could "have an effect, the very same in kind (but stronger) than a fine historical description of the same passage would have upon a judicious reader."[86] Others echoed Durand's appeal, elevating the public's estimation of painting and contrasting it to mere ornamental frippery, as is demonstrated by an 1816 chronicle of Benjamin West's visit to decayed Rome. There, his travels "confirmed him in the wisdom of those strict religious principles which denied the utility of art when solely employed as the medium of amusement: and impelled him to attempt what could be done to approximate the uses of the pencil to those of the pen, in order to render painting, indeed, the sister of eloquence and poetry."[87]

The niggling suspicion of art's superfluity was likely ensconced even more solidly in the puritanical mind by the common appearance in the early nineteenth century of itinerant painters. Trafficking in portraits and profile cuttings—as they apparently did in other slack schemes and cunning cons—they moved from town to town scrounging whatever existence would be made available to them. One practitioner of this "art" was James Guild, who left a memoir of his exploits, very few of which might have burnished painting's reputation as an upright and useful trade. Consider this extract:

> I put up at a tavern and told a Young Lady if she would wash my shirt, I would draw her likeness. Now then I was to execute my skill in painting. I operated once on her but it looked so like a wretch I throwed it away and tried again. The poor Girl sat nipped up so prim and look so smiling it makes me smile when I think of while I was daubing on paint on a piece of paper, it could not be called painting, for it looked more like a strangle cat than it did like her. However I told her it looked like her and she believed it, but I cut her profile and she had a profile if not a likeness.[88]

In contrast, the field of painting which was esteemed the most useful was history painting, which, as Durand asserts above, earned some modest social merit; by the 1820s, numerous painters would claim to work in the "Grand Historical Style." John Trumbull, whose paintings decorate the Capitol rotunda, memorably played upon this value in an early letter to Thomas Jefferson seeking the commission. Proclaiming his desire to use history painting to commemorate the revolution in the service of the state, he avers: "I am fully sensible that the profession, as it is generally practiced, is frivolous, little useful to society, and unworthy of a man who has talents for more serious pursuits." Nevertheless, when it came to his own historical works, he added the following disclaimer: "I flattered myself that by devoting a few years of life to this object, I did not make an absolute waste of time, or squander uselessly, talents from which my country might justly demand more valuable services; and I feel some honest pride in the prospect of accomplishing a work, such as had never been done before, and in which it was not easy that I should have a rival."[89] History painting succeeded in projecting an aura of usefulness despite remaining largely unremunerative to the artists in economic terms.[90] The promise of better-paid work opened a schism between the social utility of the Grand Historical Style and "mere" landscape painting, especially as the latter was associated with panorama exhibitions that attained a degree of mass popularity and generated heftier monetary rewards. Such is apparent in the tone—whether bred of envy or genuine contempt—taken by the *National Advocate* upon reporting John Vanderlyn's leaving "the higher department of historical painting" for the "more humble, though more profitable, pursuit of painting cities and landscapes" in the second decade of the nineteenth century.[91]

This schism between the "higher" aims of historical painting and the purported profit-orientation of other painting suggests that, in the period leading up to 1820 or so, it was possible to conceive of two opposed systems of artistic value. In the proclaimed intent of history painting to educate, inform, and interpellate its viewers into a national mythology, the proof of painting's significance is found in its capacity to produce something other than monetary reward—it was thought indispensable for the creation of *citizens*. Nevertheless, despite its dogged mobilization of those faithful to the history painting tradition, the distinction between history painting's use values and the exchange value of painting for profit was a rather tenuous one. Even the most pious among history painters sought adequate recompense; even the *National Advocate*, so convinced of the humility of the panorama painter, would go on to encourage Vanderlyn's talent in the direction of historical subjects, insisting that such works "would not only be highly national and popular, but exceedingly profitable" as well.[92]

As we have seen, budding anxiety over the intensifying dictatorship of exchange rattled those who, at least publicly, sought to situate art in loftier realms. Asher Durand, for example, responded to the market's perceived desecration of aesthetic ideals by considering the corruption of artistic endeavor a more serious offense than the commodification of other forms of activity—those that one would more properly consider "work." Counterposing the exchangeability of artworks to that of other commodities, he regards the former as an intensified version of the latter: "It is better to make shoes, or dig potatoes, or follow any other honest calling to secure a livelihood, than seek the pursuit of Art for the sake of gain. For whoever presumes to embrace her with the predominant motive of pecuniary reward, or any worldly distinction, will assuredly find but a bundle of reeds in his arms."[93] As Durand's plaint about the "degradation of Art" and its perversion "to the servility of a mere trade" unfolds, it becomes even more specific, lamenting—at a moment uncoincidentally contemporaneous with the ascendancy of luminist landscape conventions—art's "prostitution by means of color, strong effects and skillful manipulation, solely for the sensuous gratification of the eye."[94] The increasing desperation of such objections reflects the actual triumph of the pursuit of gain as painting's motivation; the milk—along with the color—had already been spilt. The hegemony of market forces and mere "sensuous gratifications" was paradoxically, though fittingly, announced by the color, effects, and manipulation of luminist composition.

Durand's expostulations further suggest that something other than the merely economic exchangeability of landscape imagery is at stake here; by this point, the *social* utility of landscape is no longer contestable—it is a utility that stems not only directly from the pursuit of gain, but also indirectly from the more intangible economics of taste and distinction. To recognize nature as picturesque means to have attained the cultivation necessary to experience nature as a repository for aesthetic and moral value; such recognition, as Adorno insisted above, is a historically specific development. The techniques of nineteenth-century observers for making such evaluations needed to be produced, and not merely assumed. That said, it is precisely the ease with which art consumers of the time deployed those techniques—their *naturalization* in Kenneth John Meyers's terms— that lent credence to the idea that a divine ordination of nature lay behind the strokes of the painter's brush. According to Meyers, landscape painting achieves this effect by the 1820s—validating, with the sanctity of its representations, the leisure time invested in learning to enjoy them.[95] As the ability to appreciate natural landscapes came to signal refinement, those works proved their social and moral utility, and increasingly earned the right to coexist as equal to history painting, while requiring that their value as a class marker be preserved in defiance of the democratizing tendencies of the market.

Landscape painting thereafter could serve as a vehicle for the circulation of symbolic representations of class and national identity; it is such circulation that provokes W. J. T. Mitchell to make a suggestive analogy: "As a medium for expressing value, it [landscape] has a semiotic structure rather like that of money, functioning as a special sort of commodity that plays a unique symbolic role in the system of exchange-value. Like money, landscape is good for nothing as a use value, while serving as a theoretically limitless symbol of value at some other level."[96] However, to dismiss use value in such a hasty fashion is to underestimate the productive power of both landscape and money. With regard to money, we have already seen how, despite its status as "a special sort of commodity" (or in fact because of that very status), the medium itself becomes productive. The exchange system and its thrumming circulatory network produce affects of greed and industriousness, and, in this context, produce the repose associated with landscape as well. If landscape is to get its due in Mitchell's analogy, it must be regarded as not only a vehicle for the circulation of meaning, but as itself meaningful in producing affects, subjects, and culture: it is in this capacity that landscape embodies a use value. Its production is a production of a kind of life.

In this respect, it is helpful to recall once more the advocacy of Thomas Cole, Richard Dana, and the *Idle Man*. There, Dana inveighed against the primacy of utility, but not without subtly transforming its very meaning: "Must all we do and all we think about have reference to the useful, while that alone is considered useful which is tangible, present gain?"[97] The implication is that, against the allure of exchange—at once so seductive to artists yet so purportedly disrespectful of art—there remains a more intangible form of productivity. Its utility contributes to the production of the social; Dana eagerly recognizes in it the utopian promise of refinement, aesthetic feeling, and freedom from the realm of gain and mandatory industry. His vision is, in short, of an aesthetic praxis capable of transforming the way the world is lived. As a consequence of the refined man's disavowal of gain in favor of contemplation, "the ordinary acts which spring from the good will of social life, take up their dwelling within him and mingle with his sentiment, forming a little society in his mind, going on in harmony with its generous enterprises, its friendly labors, and tasteful pursuits."[98] Aesthetic endeavor, governed by nature and experienced in repose, promises a self-determined society of goodwill, a society predicated on harmony and the friendliness of a labor that knows no alienation.

Dana exhorted the American man of refinement to describe out of that potential the contours of a new society; today, it is clear that that provocative impulse survives only in latency, except in a cultural elite become embarrassing in proportion to its impotence, and in the lingering tendency of our contemporary culture to equate aesthetic pursuits with inconsequentiality. Yet, in the resistance to improvement, in the appeal to harmony, in the light of luminist virtue, it becomes clear that landscape painting in the American nineteenth century was experienced as producing something more than a stereotype of classy refinement or a bad reputation for the arts: it was also producing the prototype for a revolutionary kind of citizen, an "idle man" who would be governed by the necessity of repose.

3

The Line of Productiveness

Fear at the Frontiers

> It is not strange that the steadily moving wave of immigration,
> which has gone westward uninterruptedly for a hundred years,
> should have gathered an impetus that is now carrying it beyond the
> line of productiveness; but it has reached its outposts, and should be
> warned to halt, and not encouraged to go farther.
>
> —William B. Hazen, *Our Barren Lands,* 1875

The sentiments expressed in *Our Barren Lands*, a cautionary 1875 pamphlet written by General William B. Hazen, give vent not just to his discomfort with the headlong rush to settle the West, but also to a more widespread apprehension about the threat posed to productivity by the modes of life characteristic of the nation's geographical and economic frontiers. Though eastern men of refinement had gravitated to the limits of market culture for an assurance of natural harmony in repose, others who confronted the western and southern boundaries of capitalist productivity posed the question of the value of activity there with no small amount of trepidation. Hazen's particular plea to mind the western "line of productiveness" responded to what he saw as a reckless plan for expansion, initiated and marketed by the Northern Pacific Railway, into a region whose desiccated terrain would be hostile to profitable development. But the line of productiveness he drew demarcated not only a geographical boundary, but also a conceptual one—those wishing to operate beyond it he regarded as dupes or con artists, seduced by open land, blinded by the lust for gain, and unable to understand that productiveness had its limits.[1]

Hazen gave voice to a persistent suspicion that frontier lands offered safe harbor to unproductivity, an attitude that only began to unravel at the end of the period investigated by this study. His contribution to an

1866 government report detailing a tour in the region argued that "the country has little value. . . . No amount of railroad schemes of colonization, or government encouragement can ever make more of it," and in so doing opened questions that may, in fact, remain open to some debate today.[2] But he nevertheless also keenly apprehended how the frontier was ultimately an imaginary construction, subject to the influence of opinion-makers who in many cases lacked direct experience of either its potentials or its exigencies. Writing with dismay in 1875 about "that magic power, the Press," he noted that through its influence, "suddenly . . . these 'bad lands,' 'sandy plains,' 'wasted deserts,' '*el llano estacado*,' 'basins of salt,' 'black hills,' and so on, [had become as] fruitful as the Vale of Cashmere."[3] To Hazen, upon such "wasted deserts" only further "unproductiveness" could blossom.

The aspersions cast by Hazen upon the lands of the trans-Missouri region was in keeping with the prevailing inclination to imagine such tracts—and, in fact, most lands beyond the expanding horizons of settlement—as "wastes" and "deserts."[4] Since Stephen H. Long's Great Plains expedition in the 1820s, and his labeling of Nebraska, Kansas, and Colorado as the "Great American Desert" on the resulting map, commentators on the prairie landscape frequently had recourse to the motif.[5] One chapter (entitled "The American Desert") of Horace Greeley's influential 1856 travel account, for example, proposes that station 18 of the Pike's Peak Express Co. might compete with "any other scene on our continent for desolation."[6] Similarly unimpressed was the newspaper correspondent John F. Finerty, who dramatically described the soil of the region as resembling "the surface of a non-atmospheric planet, hard, repulsive, sterile," and acknowledged that "it made one's heart sick to look at the place."[7] A similar and related convention likened the prairie landscape to the sea, the two spaces boasting in common the lack of both population and visual relief. Given this context, it becomes easier to understand Hazen's alarm at the relentless drive to develop this space, where arid ravines, sandy gullies, and sublime tracts of seeming emptiness threatened to disperse and evaporate the productive energies of westward immigration's onrushing "wave."[8]

Depicting this boundary as both geographical and imaginary, Hazen's characterization of the frontier as a "line of *productiveness*" thus frames the problem of western wastelands as one of political economy as well. The frontier functions in his discourse as a threshold between civilization and nature, between the familiar and the unknown, and between productivity and unproductivity. It marks a boundary between modes of production, distinguishing between the coalescing model of eastern capitalist production and the perseverance of western tribal organization; a similar conceptual boundary tended to delimit the persisting cultural logics of the wage regime in the American South.[9] To Hazen, the hybrid constitution of such a frontier was a temptation to unproductivity and an alternative to the industrious subjectivities increasingly valorized as part of an American national identity. The unknown forces that lay beyond the line of productiveness promised—and often, apparently, delivered—a break from the conventional, the fixed, and the certain, and thereby generated a palpable foreboding about the infinite potential opened up by such exceptional activity. Accounts like Hazen's affirm the hegemonic force of productive subjectivity by projecting qualms about unproductivity onto the other spaces, races, and practices that lurked beyond the border. In their insistent policing of those geographic, economic, and ideological exteriors, they register the fragility of the concept of productivity in the face of displacements internal to the capitalist system of value itself.

Forty years prior to Hazen's campaign, Washington Irving had provocatively articulated a similar account of the relationship between activity and subjectivity at the frontier. His chronicle of a tour with American rangers in the Oklahoma territory describes the inhabitants of frontier space as follows: "There was a sprinkling of trappers, hunters, half-breeds, creoles, negroes of every hue; and all that other rabble rout of nondescript beings that keep about the frontier, between civilised and savage life; as those equivocal birds the bats hover about the confines of light and darkness."[10] This mysterious frontier mélange, "equivocal" in its identity and "hovering" at the very threshold of reason and civilization, seems to resist representation; its "nondescript beings" defy more specific labels and are made to trouble racial, occupational, and even species boundaries. But while the texts of this period generally seem hesitant in their approach to this indeterminacy of activity—thought to characterize both the land and those who inhabited, explored, and settled it—the case of Irving is exemplary in illustrating how this indeterminacy was the object not only of anxiety but also of a powerful yearning as well. As we shall see, Hazen's careful mapping of the "line of productiveness," like Irving's depiction of the nondescript identities of frontier inhabitants, expresses deep and widespread ambivalences about unproductivity that were generated at the nation's economic, imaginary, and ideological frontiers.[11]

Nondescript Beings: The Native and the Freedman

Given the ubiquity of heroic narratives depicting rugged frontier exploits, consumed with great relish by readers of eastern magazines, it would seem to take nothing short of a willful misrecognition of the data to characterize the frontier as an idle one.[12] Nevertheless, despite the convention that time and again stressed the incomparable virility and strength demanded by settlement—and which is prevalent in texts ranging from Crévecoeur's *Letters from an American Farmer* (1782) to Hamlin Garland's *Main-Travelled Roads* (1893) and beyond—a fundamental misrecognition of frontier motivations and imperatives persisted in the East.[13]

According to one viewpoint, the frontiersman's flight from the institutions and regulations of the East discloses his fundamental irresponsibility. "The class of pioneers cannot live in regular society," Yale College president Timothy Dwight alleged. "They are too idle, too talkative, too passionate, too prodigal, and too shiftless to acquire either property or character. They are impatient of the restraints of law, religion, and morality, and grumble about the taxes by which the Rulers, Ministers, and Schoolmasters are supported."[14] Dwight's conceptual net weaves idleness together with an unruly passion, an indifference toward renunciation, a shiftless disregard for structure, and a resentful impatience with the institutions of civil society. Though his diagnosis presents the pathology of idleness as part of a complex of other inherent subjective weaknesses, many credited the frontier itself with having converted otherwise good men into idlers.[15] This is in part represented as resulting from exposure to the land itself—which, in accounts of its sublimity, is often described as rendering self-interested activity impossible—as well as from mingling with the natives and other inhabitants already entrenched at the frontier: Irving's half-breeds, creoles, negroes, and savages of all hues.

Representations of the supposed idleness of the Native American population are symptomatic of this attitude; several enduring conventions cement that association in literary texts, government discourse, western painting, and photography. Careful consideration of the specificity of Native American "production" is eschewed in favor of a handful of well-worn formulas, each of which indicts what is seen as an endemic state of sheer passivity and inactivity. Horace Greeley's assessment was among the more vituperative, bluntly describing the native as "squalid and conceited, proud and worthless, lazy and lousy," and arguing that they "will strut out or drink out their miserable existence, and at length afford the world a sensible relief by dying out of it."[16] Though much of the discourse concerning Native American idleness manages to be more subtle than Greeley's condemnations, he partakes in a common poetics of immaturity, naivete, and irresponsibility typical of descriptions of natives as underdeveloped "children of nature."[17] Thus do many representations portray the Native American in a state of idleness thought to reflect absolute incomprehension at the incursion of industrial ways of life. An 1868 Muybridge photograph described by Mick Gidley, for example, features a quartet of Indians who "simply sit, all of them looking at the camera, unsmiling, with nothing, apparently, to do. It is impossible to determine why they were included at all."[18]

Of course this representational "inclusion" of native (in-) activity is simultaneously an exclusion, doing the important cultural work of affirming industrious subjectivity through negation, while naturalizing eastern expansion over the frontier tracts. As William Cronon points out, John Mix Stanley's *Oregon City on the Willamette River* (figure 6) makes this exclusion pretty explicit, depicting its natives helplessly on the margins as the progressive westward march of order, industry, and cleared land leaves them behind and bereft. Here, as in other works seeking to capture the dynamic dialectical energy of the transition from nature to civilization, the natives are afforded only the opportunity to look on passively. Cronon argues that at that point, "any natives who appear in landscapes like this one serve only as reminders of the world they have lost. More and more, representations of pastoral progress will omit them altogether."[19] The Native American is thereby rendered subject to a logic of *erasure* that, according to Cronon, is enacted in precisely the same gesture that brings the native into representation to begin with. Depicted as an object of nostalgia, the native recedes into a nature safely consigned to the past, only to be reintroduced, in Susan Hegeman's words, "by precluding the possibility of action, of connection to the landscape, of participation in history."[20]

The purported idleness of the native is therefore symbolically secured though representational formulas that seek to sever his connection to the land, enforcing the Jeffersonian freehold philosophy that dictates that the value of land depends on it being roused from idleness and harnessed for stable cultivation. The righteousness of this activity was at once the foundation for and the consequence of the expansion of material and agrarian productive capability; the land was to be honored by the righteous overcoming and eradication of any "blot or mixture" presented by either the persistence of the archaic or the unwanted erection of new transcendent

Figure 6. John Mix Stanley (1814–1872), *Oregon City on the Willamette River,* ca. 1850–52. Oil on canvas, 26 ½ x 40 in. Amon Carter Museum of American Art, Fort Worth, Texas.

structures.[21] The implications of this ideology are legible not only in those depictions of Native Americans that reduce them to stoic foils for industrious progress, but also, despite a very different representational strategy, in conventional portrayals of natives engaged in warfare and hunting. Though these paintings would appear, at first glance, to grant at least some modicum of agency to the native (albeit an agency only of an anachronistic and "savage" variety), they nevertheless raise doubts about the effectiveness of that agency. Judged from the standpoint of a dominant ideology for which control, development, and cultivation of land were tantamount to entitlement, the activity of the roving, transient brave on horseback fails to measure up. The representation of these energetic pursuits rather emphasizes the natives' nomadism, the apparent transience of their existence, and their static, nonteleological relationship to an unimproved land.[22] It also purports to establish a seeming visual proof of the intransigent insistence of these impediments to progress, consequently intensifying the productive vigor of those credited with their obliteration.

The tracing of these lines of productiveness was thus instrumental to managing the geographic imaginary of the western frontier, and that tracing likewise delimited the South, a region in some ways even more economically recalcitrant than the West. Confronted there with the persistence of the slave mode of production, the ideology of capitalist productivity was manifest in various attempts to accommodate, regulate, represent, and evaluate the activity of slaves prior to the Civil War and of freedmen after it, as is palpable in debates regarding the economic inefficiency of the slavery model and the purported passivity of the slave population during the emancipation. But nowhere is the fixation on southern idleness more transparent than in the Reconstruction-era efforts of the United States government to instill the former slave with the discipline of work—defined as real, remunerative, contract labor.[23]

Following upon Frederick Douglass's definition of freedom as "appropriating my own body to my use," abolitionists had long argued for the desirability of contract labor on the grounds that it guaranteed the fundamental right of individuals to dispose over the body's useful potentials as they saw fit.[24] Unlike the ossified structures of the slavery mode, contract labor was viewed by its advocates to achieve horizontal fluidity in transactions of labor-power, hewing to Francis Amasa Walker's argument that men "transact their affairs like particles of some fine dry powder absolutely destitute of cohesion."[25] That prospect, however, was precisely what provoked anxiety at the prospect of slave emancipation—free movement and disposition over the energies of the body appeared as the threat of freedmen transacting their affairs like the sands of the idle desert, dissipating in drifts of "some fine dry powder" over the line of unproductiveness.

Seeking a principle of "cohesion" capable of managing this freed activity, the government's Freedman's Bureau campaigned to cultivate in these emergent capitalist agents a faith in contract labor, as well as respect and desire for the fruits of that labor. One Freedman's Bureau text, Helen E. Brown's *John Freeman and His Family*, achieved this through direct contrast between the work ethic required of contract labor and the panoply of "old, lazy, filthy habits of the slave-quarters" thought to persist in freedmen.[26] The text stridently insists that the basis of freedom is the very specific form of methodical activity recognizable as economically remunerative *work*. To be free, it counsels, "is not to be let loose like the wild hogs in the woods, to root along in the bogs and just pick up a living as we can. . . . [E]very freeman, black and white, works for a living."[27] But to the extent that the old days of the slave economy are here invoked, they serve primarily as a means of leveraging a new code of conduct in the transitional subjects of the Reconstruction present. These texts ultimately disavow any role for the African American in past history, and to the extent that they imagine their task to be one of creating industrious subjects almost from scratch, they are all the more bluntly transparent in their curious contradictions.

In one case, for example, the narrative recounts how a government representative addresses newly freed slaves, informing them that no idlers need apply: "Freemen must not be lazy. Those who don't want to work hard better go back to their plantations and to their masters, if they are to be found."[28] This coincidence of laziness and slavery must have been a surprising twist for those unacquainted with the plantation as a realm of ease. Complicating this apparent reversal, the narrative takes great pains to condemn a character named Prince, who at one point is found abusing his freedom by "lounging" with his pipe under a tree, and whose intransigence regarding the new mode of production provokes his wife to exasperation: "I ain't going to be tied to your lazy, mean niggers, no how," she proclaims.[29] This freedman's wife has been loosed from the bondage of slavery, only to be re-"tied" by new chains of laziness that undermine both the emergence of a new racial identity and a personal success now understood as individuated (as the character named Lieutenant Hall declares, "If we allow idlers in the camp they will not only cause disturbance to us, but they will stand in the way of their own prosperity").[30]

John Freeman's paean to racial uplift through industry is matched in its intensity, and in its contradictions, by another period text, *Plain Counsels for Freedmen*, penned by Clinton Bowen Fisk, assistant commissioner in the Freedman's Bureau. *Plain Counsels* provides just what it promises, decocting from the narrative approach of *John Freeman and His Family* an unambiguous litany of exhortations reflecting mostly the ethical bottom line of financial advancement.[31] The promise of moral altitude is replaced by the specter of financial ruin, deliberately summed up in the Franklinian decree that "*You cannot afford to be idle*": "Time is money. Every day you lose sets you back two or three days. Shake off sloth, then, rise early, roll up your sleeves, and quit yourself like a man. . . . Idleness destroys a man's health, weakens him, shortens his life, makes him feel mean, and sends him on a short road to ruin."[32] The palpable shift from the moral to the economic register coincides with the effort of *Plain Counsels* to contain the freedman's potential idleness through an industrious consciousness of space and time. The idle freedman's potential ruin is seen as stemming from his inability to translate his labor into a temporally meaningful form: "Time is money." Moreover, the rewards of labor, be they the consumerist plenty elsewhere promised by *John Freeman* or the alluring prospect of disposable leisure hours, are tempered by this same disciplinary temporality. The freed slave is duly reminded that he can neither "afford to smoke fine cigars" nor "afford to drink any kind of spiritous or malt liquors." And, as for dancing: "You have no time to spend in kicking up your heels. I speak of *time*, not of the right or wrong of dancing. . . . It may be dull, hard work, for awhile, to sit down and study your book, while Peter Puff is hopping around the ball-room like a monkey, with Betty Simple, but it will become easy after awhile, and it will pay richly in the end."[33] Not only does the passage displace questions of morality onto those of time, it redoubles this gesture by presenting hard work in the present as an investment with, "in the end," a future dividend to be realized.

In a similar vein, the freedman is advised to "spend all [his] spare time at home," and thus, the temporal configuration of activity is coupled with a spatial reorganization as well.[34] The "home" becomes a symbolic enclave that stabilizes the freedman and his activity within the prevailing paradigm by providing a practical disincentive to geographical mobility. Acquisition of a home serves as not only the promise, but also the proof, of having transcended idleness, and therefore having laudably made the transition into the capitalist system of value.

Stress on the home as a signifier and guarantor of industrious citizenship is not restricted to the audience addressed by Clinton Bowen Fisk. A similar implication prevails in the cautionary *Sloth and Thrift; or, the Causes and Correctives of Social Inequality* (1847), the narrative of which is motivated by the distinction between the families Williams and Mosely, and especially their divergent dispositions toward labor.[35] The story opens with a description of the decrepit Mosely house, whose residents have irresponsibly overslept, allowing the hogs to run wild through a broken fence and ruin the garden. In stark contrast to the neighboring Williams home, where fresh fruit and flowers compete for attention with round-faced children and a sparkling kitchen, the Mosely domicile, indifferent to time and order, is a vision of simple slackness: "Before the late hour of their supper arrived, Mrs. Mosely had achieved her family washing, and her clothes, after having passed through the process deemed necessary, were drippingly displayed on bush and fence, with many a stain which Mrs. Mosely asserted would not come out, and many a rent which had not been repaired. These were fully exhibited to all who chose to gaze."[36] Meanwhile, the Mosely and Williams men provide their own study in distinction. In his time off, as we are told, Mosely "insisted upon celebrating his *freedom*": "And the next morning Williams was alone at the work-bench, and when he afterwards met Mosely, he was sorry to see every indication of a *merry* evening, followed (although not included in the stipulation) by a sorry morning. . . . The aim of Mosely was *pleasure*. The rule of Williams was *duty*, yet, surely, Williams found more pleasure, while quietly pursuing the path of duty, than Mosely enjoyed while sacrificing duty to gratification."[37]

Driven by this prominent binary severing and then reuniting duty and pleasure, the moralizing narrative embarks upon a grisly punishment of its idle subjects. Chapter 7 inaugurates the Moselys' precipitous decline; the death of their child Jen is soon thereafter followed by the expiration of other Mosely offspring. Finally, and perhaps most damningly, the remaining Moselys are condemned to homelessness. This last wound is pointedly salted by the text's homily that "blessed are the families who, dispersed and settled abroad, have still the *old home* to serve as a rallying point and refuge."[38]

The value of the well-kept and presentable home as a visual index of industriousness is resuscitated in Fisk's *Plain Counsels*. The point is made without ambiguity in the competing descriptions of the homes of "Dick Slack" and "Thrifty Paul," which so recall the above descriptions of sloth and thrift that one almost imagines the homeless Moselys familiarly finding temporary lodging in Dick Slack's guest room: "Have you ever seen Dick Slack's home? Let me describe it. It stands on a bare lot. The fence is down, and much of it, to tell the truth, has been used for kindling. The pigs root around his door and sleep under his house. No flower blooms about his dwelling, no green plot of grass spreads its charms before your eyes. His house is innocent of paint or whitewash, and from one window the crown of an old hat sticks out, from another a pillow!"[39] Dick Slack's idleness is confirmed by his home's unsightly visual aspect (figure 7). By means of a formula not uncommon on both the western and the southern frontiers, the state of the subject here explicitly mirrors the state of his land. "Dick is like his house," we are told with epistemological confidence. "See him standing there, motionless as a post, half bent, with his hands in his pockets. Oh, Dick, stir yourself!"[40] The tone of moral authority here reinforces the way this discourse uses visual and conceptual means to wed marginal subjects— the Native American, the freedman, the outcast settler—to a space unmarked by yeomanly improvement, and hence to stigmatize them with the disrepute of unproductivity.

Figure 7. Dick Slack and his lone companion ponder the fraught question of loyalty. Illustration from Clinton Bowen Fisk, *Plain Counsels for Freedmen*, 1866.

For all of their proscriptive certainty and seeming univocity, how-ever, these exhortations to upright industry must also, necessarily, reg-ister the seductions of idleness. Their protestations about the desirability of industry in fact exhibit a relentless fixation on the idle pleasures they claim to disdain—a fixation that, for the most part, is neither avowed or explained.[41] But the vast majority of texts considering activity at the geo-graphical and imaginary limits of American productivity are considerably more ambivalent about the pleasures of the unproductive, often acknowl-edging idleness and mobility alike as the desirable objects of a healthy longing. Such is the case with one of the most influential and beloved depictions of American frontier life, Washington Irving's *A Tour on the Prairies*.

Washington Irving's Tour and the "Busy Hive of Population"

> I listen long
> To his domestic hum, and think I hear
> The sound of that advancing multitude
> Which soon shall fill these deserts.
> —William Cullen Bryant, "The Prairies," 1855

Irving's preoccupation with rethinking the quality and value of activity is apparent throughout his body of work, not only in his *Sketchbook*—in which Rip Van Winkle famously established the idler's presence at the very emergence of the "national literature"—but also, and crucially, in his writings of western adventure and expansion.[42] *A Tour on the Prairies* documents Irving's 1832 adventures accompanying an exploratory detachment issued from Fort Gibson into the contested Indian territories in the vicinity of the Arkansas, the Grand Canadian, and the Red Rivers, and reads as a parodic account of western expansion by an author who is at once an active participant and a removed critical observer.[43] This dual disposition mirrors Irving's notoriously complicated literary and national loyalties. Upon returning to America from his extended visit to England, Irving apparently endured considerable anxiety about reconciling his genteel European personality with the more rugged American context. His subsequent embrace of western themes thus has been read as an effort to capture something of this American character, and to "[throw] aside the indolence of the scholar," as one commentator observed at the time.[44]

Ultimately, what distinguishes Irving's chronicle is his embrace of these ambivalences. Arriving at the frontier after having been shaped by the experience of being "unemployed, unmarried, and expatriated" (in Bryce Traister's words), he was nonetheless equipped with the conventions of gentility and sensibility that could provide unique literary means through which to chronicle prairie experience. Out of these means, he "constructed a voice of early national bachelordom" that "masculinize[d] sentiment by commemorating frontier violence and elevated sentiment as twin manifestations of manly accomplishment."[45] This "bachelor-author" voice facilitated an uncommon openness to the specificity of frontier activity. On the one hand, Irving's expatriate experience, displacing firm ties to a national culture or to the principle of settlement itself, inclined him to understand the value of itinerancy and mobility. But furthermore, his embrace of the alleged unproductivity of the bachelor appears to have positioned him to regard productivity more skeptically than would those for whom its value may have been more of a given. In reference to *Bracebridge Hall*, Traister notes the unusual romantic investments of this bachelor-author and his narrators, who, aloof from heteronormative strictures, are highly attuned observers of "the marriage plots of others."[46] As with the unprocreative bachelor's narratives that are "insistently about marriage," so, too, does the unproductive, unemployed bachelor prove an uncommonly incisive critic of practices of productivity not his own.[47]

Thus, though Irving's travelogue is certainly complicated by the conventional association between ostensibly barren spaces and unproductivity, his treatment of frontier activity is relatively unprejudiced. His conventional depiction of the West as a sometimes sublimely and uncannily "lonely waste" does not, as it did in the prevailing American ideology of the West, disqualify as irrelevant the activity of the region's inhabitants.[48] Quite the contrary, in fact—such activity, and especially that of the natives, is filtered through Irving's romantic lenses and subjected to prolonged consideration, often by personifying the animal inhabitants of the frontier and drawing conclusions based on their apparent qualities.[49] Some of the text's most overwrought passages are thus dedicated to the microcosm of wild prairie horses being broken by Irving's companions. After his sublime initial encounter with the wild horses, Irving reports on the "pride and freedom" they exhibit in the "native wilderness.... How different from the poor, mutilated, harnessed, checked, reined up victim of luxury, caprice, and avarice, in our cities."[50] He goes on to idolize the freedoms of these horses, situating them within an Arab lineage, stressing their nomadism, invoking the smoothness of desert spaces, and enthusing about the pride of their riders, whom he imagines to be pleased "with the idea that their sires may have been of the pure coursers of the desert."[51] Breathless, he concludes with a glorification of unregulated movement:

> The habits of the Arab seem to have come with the steed. The introduction of the horse on the boundless plains of the far West changed the whole mode of living of their inhabitants. It gave them that facility of rapid motion, and of sudden and distant change of place, so dear to the roving propensities of man. Instead of lurking in the depths of gloomy forests, and patiently threading the mazes of a tangled wilderness on foot, like his brethren of the north, the Indian of the west is a rover of the plain; he leads

a brighter and more sunshiny life, almost always on horseback, on vast flowery prairies and under cloudless skies.[52]

Irving's assessment brushes the eastern critique of unbridled frontier movement against the grain, universalizing the "roving propensities of man" while pitting them positively against enclosure and confinement. With the eventual breaking of the wild horse, he is led to reflect upon the loss of a mode of existence threatened not only by the harness but by the very progress of what he characterizes as a civilization predicated on staunching the freedom of movement. Of this animal, "whose whole course of existence had been so suddenly reversed," he eulogizes: "From being a denizen of these vast pastures, ranging at will from plain to plain and mead to mead, cropping of every herb and flower, and drinking of every stream, he was suddenly reduced to perpetual and painful servitude, to pass his life under the harness and the curb, amid perhaps, the din and dust and drudgery of cities."[53] The passage's symmetries and alliterations mount, culminating in a final thrust that lambastes the city with derogations of its "din," "dust," and industrious "drudgery." Irving, anticipating the shackling of his beloved wild horse by the curbs modernity would place on its activity, goes on to even more explicitly lament the prospect of such "painful servitude," continuing: "The transition in his lot was such as sometimes takes place in human affairs, and in the fortunes of towering individuals: one day, a prince of the prairies; the next day, a pack-horse!"[54]

Irving's palpable skepticism about the advance of industrial progress and the yoking of activity under the harness of modernity is heightened in a contrasting example culled from his *Tour*. Appearing as an extended meditation on the mundane fauna of the region, chapter 9 ("A Bee Hunt") documents and dramatizes the apparently inexorable westward dispersion of the bee population.[55] The bee served two simultaneous symbolic functions: first, it fulfilled its entrenched role as the emblem of industriousness, as in the popular children's poem by Isaac Watts.[56] Those connotations qualified it well for its function in early American texts as a figure for the expansion of American civilization, as in William Cullen Bryant's poem "The Prairies," James Fenimore Cooper's *The Oak Openings*, and John Frémont's *Report of the Exploring Expedition to the Rocky Mountains*.[57] In Irving's report, the arrival of the bees appears as an event of world-historical significance for the denizens of the prairie. Of these "industrious little animals," he relates that they have been "the heralds of civilisation, steadfastly preceding it as it advanced from the Atlantic borders": "It is surprising in what countless swarms the bees have over-spread the far West within but a moderate number of years. The Indians consider them the harbinger of the white man, as the buffalo is of the red man, and say that, in proportion as the bee advances the Indian and the buffalo retire."[58] That Irving here addresses the significance of the bur-geoning bee population from the native perspective suggests something of where his loyalties rest, a conclusion further buttressed by an 1820s frag-ment in which Irving attempts to define the American national character, crediting it to the experience of he "who beholds every thing around him changing as if by enchantment—what was once a wilderness becoming a busy hive of population."[59] What is important in the national character is the *beholding*, and not the changing; it is as if Irving wishes to positively spin the reputedly passive position of Native Americans at the margin of headlong expansion, arguing that their inert receptivity—and not the practice of expansion—is in fact the true "American" trait.

"A Bee Hunt" furthermore inverts the accepted relationship of industry to frontier idleness, for it is the arrival of the bee, and not the preexisting character of the Indians or of the frontier itself, that generates unethical behavior—the lustful desire for a bountiful abundance disproportion-ate to effort expended. "The Indians with surprise found the mouldering trees of their forests suddenly teeming with ambrosial sweets," he reports. "And nothing, I am told, can exceed the greedy relish with which they banquet *for the first time* upon this unbought luxury of the wilderness."[60] The Indians thus confront, "for the first time," rewards that are dispro-portionate to their exertion: the native's desire for "unbought luxury" is not an inherent trait that happens to facilitate progress, but rather the product of that progress, and of the industry that itself serves shiftlessness and greedy laziness. When Irving, too, is seduced into a honey-gathering mission in the woods, his narrative gives further rein to a fantastic trans-fer of human commercial character to the bee population, with dramatic results. Despite the blows of the frontiersmen's axes upon a honey-laden tree, the bees "continued to ply at their usual occupations, some arriv-ing full freighted into port, others sallying forth on new expeditions." He ultimately likens them to "so many merchantmen in a money-making metropolis, little suspicious of impending bankruptcy and downfall."[61] The logical outcome is an episode of commercial competition: "Nor was it the bee-hunters alone that profited by the downfall of this industrious community. As if the bees would carry through the similitude of their habits with those of laborious and gainful man, I beheld members from rival hives, arriving on eager wing, to enrich themselves with the ruins of their neighbors."[62] Whatever familiarity with entomology Irving may lack he supplements by his ready assessment of capitalist social relations. But the contradiction inherent in Irving's (literal) naturalization of industry likewise determines his critique, complicating the conventional dyad opposing industry to the unproductive wild. It thus may be said, as Peter Antelyes argues, that instead of positing industry and wilderness as binarily opposed, Irving's criticism instead focuses on the subversion of industry, internally, by greed.[63] In light of Irving's manipulation of point of view and his sympathies with the frontier modes of activity, this might best be put another way: Irving's critique focuses on the way that *purposeful activity itself*—the activity of both wilderness and industry, of horse and bee alike—is vulnerable to corruption by the pursuit of unmerited gain.[64] And with that revelation about the instability of the value of activity, that idleness imagined to lurk beyond the frontier is shown to be an internal disturbance within the realm of industriousness as well.

Redundant and Reluctant Wage Labor

> Eastward I go only by force; but westward I go free. Thither no business leads me.
>
> —Henry David Thoreau, "Walking," 1862

The growth of the busy American "hive" was manifest not only in the absolute movement of industry westward, but also in the changing conditions of industrial production in the East. The frontier's reputation for providing sanctuary to those indifferent to the imperatives of the wage was intensified by the apparent movement toward the western frontier of disgruntled labor-power. One disapproving account of this tendency was expressed in an "extremely doleful anecdote" concerning the mobility of labor, credited to E. G. Wakefield by Marx: "'Our capital,' says one of the characters in the melodrama, 'was ready for many operations which require a considerable period of time for their completion; but we could not begin such operations with labor which, we know, would soon leave us. If we had been sure of retaining the labor of such emigrants, we should have been glad to have engaged it at once, and for a high price.'"[65] Wakefield's apprehension about a labor force enticed by western freedoms and thus too transitory to harness discloses something of the imaginary power of the frontier as a seeming antidote to the work world.[66] Seizing on this episode, Marx applauds the prospect of flight to the frontier from the increasingly constrictive rigors of the wage; like many others since, he imagines the frontier as an escape valve which, in contrast to the relative confinements of the European economies, promised a route of liberation for the exploited American worker.[67] Whereas considerable efforts to curb unproductive vagrancy in England had been commonplace for centuries, the unpredictable movement of such variable capital in the United States posed a new challenge. Though the stakes to be won by meeting this challenge were largely the same— forming and shaping a reliable working class of "free laborers" available for the production of surplus value—the tactics in America would have to take a form adequate to the specific and unprecedented obstacles presented by the open frontier.

England had historically deployed state power, often of an overtly repressive type, to curtail the idle vagrancy of early modern subjects who found themselves cast adrift by the suspension of feudal structures and the concomitant severing of their relationship with land.[68] According to Marx, "the dissolution of the old mode of production" generated a class of "free" men whose living labor was now purchasable.[69] This "setting free," he wryly notes, released a newly unproductive population, a swarm of idlers, internally differentiated only by its constituents' respective inclinations toward vagabondage, begging, or robbery—all attractive alternatives to the prospect of the wage. The task for capital, then, was to capture and refine those lawless and resistant forces, thereby turning them into working subjects and realizing the potential values of their labor. The state intervened to this end, helping to coerce by threat and application of force potentially productive subjects into standardized productive roles. Sir Frederick Morton Eden's exhaustive work *The State of the Poor* (1797) traces precedents for these measures in initial episodic strictures enacted under the reign of Henry VIII. One such measure from the early sixteenth century sought to deter the begging wanderer by the threat of being "whipped till his body was bloody by reason of such whipping. . . . If, however, he offend again he is to be whipped once more, and have the upper part of the gristle of his right ear cut clean off."[70] A third transgression warranted death.

These measures directly targeted the free mobility of the reluctant wage-laborer. An excerpt from the decrees of Henry VIII demonstrates how capital, having sundered the traditional ties of the population to the soil, subsequently resutured the newly created free laborers into a new relationship to the land—a relationship now mediated by capital. According to these dictates, an unproductive vagrant not only risks the aforementioned bloody whippings, but furthermore could be "sworn to return to the place where he was born, or last dwelt for three years, and there put himself to labor."[71] Consistent, then, with the subjection of free men to labor is their attachment to a space. But already in the sixteenth century we note that that space no longer necessarily implies an organic attachment to the soil conferred by one's birthplace; these rules additionally describe an implicitly capitalized space unattached to the property models of the previous mode of production and instead determined by capital— three years' inhabitance and the conduct of "labor."

The American escape valve seemed to provide a virtually limitless trajectory of withdrawal from the emergent capitalist relations of production, a line of flight occasioning an experimental engagement with new conditions in a differently coded kind of space. The challenge to American capitalism, then, consisted less in policing a domestic interior than in securing the frontier against a potentially destabilizing exteriority. This outside, beyond the line of productiveness, promised not necessarily a return to the precapitalist past, however, but rather the cultivation and proliferation of different forms of activity. Marx suggests that this movement was driven by the dream of transforming not only capitalist social relations but also the exploitative affect proper to them:

> The wage-worker of to-day is to-morrow an independent peasant, or artisan, working for himself. He vanishes from the labour-market—but not into the workhouse. This constant transformation of the wage-labourers into independent producers, who work for themselves instead of for capital, and enrich themselves instead of the capitalist gentry, reacts in its turn very perversely on the conditions of the labour-market. Not only does the degree of exploitation of the wage-labourer remain indecently low. The wage-labourer loses into the bargain, along with the relation of dependence, the sentiment of dependence on the abstemious capitalist. Hence all the inconveniences that our E. G. Wakefield pictures so doughtily, so eloquently, so pathetically.[72]

With the "relation of dependence," so, too, is discarded the "sentiment of dependence," in an affective or psychosocial transformation that was regarded by numerous commentators as the driving machinery behind various types of American flight. Horace Greeley argued that such "vagrant instincts and habits" as those exhibited in the West distilled the sentiments of the American majority.[73] And Harriet Martineau, observing the American scene in the 1830s, similarly seized upon the apparent readiness of these Americans to respond to real or perceived oppressions through recourse to geographical mobility: "If a man is disappointed in politics or love, he goes and buys land. If he disgraces himself, he betakes himself to a lot in the west. If the demand for any article of manufacturing slakens [*sic*], the operatives drop into the unsettled lands. If a citizen's neighbors rise above him in towns, he betakes himself where he can be a monarch of all he surveys."[74] The same sentiment may be found metaphorized in Thoreau's claim to embody "the prevailing tendency of [his] countrymen"; in his "Walking" essay, he espouses "a sort of border life, on the confines of a world into which I make occasional and transient forays only," positioning himself as another hoverer about the line of productiveness.[75]

The symbolic significance of flight had, of course, mythologically grounded American endeavor from the Puritan settlements to the Revolutionary-period sermons of Samuel Langdon, George Duffield, Nicholas Street, and others; increasingly, however, the messianic and millenarian presuppositions of these early versions gave way to more immanent and historical models.[76] The teleological outcome presented by the earlier "exodus" mythologists is supplanted—in keeping with the spatial and geographical possibilities of the continent—with a conception of exodus as an ongoing process typified by experimentation, negotiation, and self-constitution. This updated version of the exodus myth implies, in short, a kind of perpetual activity. Whereas a beckoning Utopia once signified the closure of history in the establishment of an eternal paradise, the new promised land was one of process, the historical commencement of the free activity through which Utopia would be *made and remade*. This "march," as Michael Walzer points out, "does not lie beyond history [and its] leader is only a man."[77] Walzer notes that in the biblical account of exodus, the Egyptian tyrant "erects idle and needless trophies to continually employ his tributaries, that they might want leisure to think on other things, as pharaoh did the Jews."[78] It is in response to this combination of, on one hand, alienated labor, and, on the other, the promise of freedom, that conditions are created whereby the former may be eradicated and the latter secured.

The covenant central to the exodus narrative depends upon a degree of political and moral agency among the people, who are required to give their consent; as a consequence, "political leadership in the new society is in principle temporary, charismatic, consensual," and highly consistent with the Jeffersonian vision.[79] The prevalence of exodus narratives in early America provides a critical ideological foundation for the flight of American labor power westward; their overlap ensures that such migration is not merely economic and social, but also, simultaneously, political in character. The exodus from financial dependence on the wage fuses with the attempt to constitute a political subject that is neither transcendent nor fixed; relations among free appropriators of the American territory are negotiated horizontally and continually, rather than through dialectical maneuvering against a perceived oppressor.[80]

The appeal of such an innovative and nondialectical political constitution is what eventually provokes Turner's much-debated nostalgizing of the frontier: "The history of our political institutions, our democracy, is not a history of imitation, of simple borrowing; it is a history of the evolution and adaptation of organs in response to changed environment, a history of the origin of new political species.[81] From the standpoint of Turner and Marx, as well as those who, like Paolo Virno, have adapted the nineteenth-century politics of flight for contemporary applications, this creative movement suggests a nascent strategy targeted at the production of new political institutions befitting expanding political horizons.[82] It, was, however, regarded quite differently by Wakefield, who, in labeling it a "barbarising tendency of dispersion," not only denigrated frontier movement itself, but also invoked the discourse that constructed the unsavory character of those "hoverers" along the line of unproductiveness.[83] The paradox that of course recurs here is that complaints like those of Wakefield, Dwight, and their ilk chastise the pioneer tendency for its unproductivity according to the measure of eastern civilization, while misrecognizing a whole range of activities that, from the standpoint of political constitution, are the most productive of all: the ceaseless work of political self-creation beyond transcendent structures and on the basis of free activity.

Suburbia: *"To Withdraw Like a Monk and Live Like a Prince"*

The divergent notions of frontier activity maintained by the likes of Irving, Marx, Greeley, and Wakefield were, clearly, rather deeply polarized, and these extremes threaten to overshadow the much more moderate position toward space, movement, and idleness that prevailed for much of the century. It is helpful to keep in mind that the more proscriptive discourses concerning unproductivity tended to be targeted at specific practices and social groups regarded as threatening to the consolidation of an ethic of industriousness. It was apparently the case that the fiercest condemnations of idleness were reserved for those operating, by choice or by fate, on the margins of the nation and of the industrial mode of production; for those in the center, a more nuanced definition of the unproductive obtained, which situated idle practices comfortably in a neutralizing dialectic with production. Unlike the attempts of Marx or Irving to exalt supposedly unproductive frontier activity as a radical negation of prevailing political economic trends, the most common response was for idleness to merely play its dialectical role as an assimilable antithesis to production. In this way, by providing an alternative to production, unproductivity ultimately helped to preserve its determinate power.

In this way, regulated "unproductive" spaces offered substitutive satisfactions for dangerous impulses to flight and unadministered movement, without enabling the potentially destabilizing empowerments to which such flight was wont to lead. A valuable example may be found in the new urban and suburban planning models of the period, which sought to fuse the desirable aspects of both country and city, both the wild and the refined. In the process, they contributed to reconfiguring the binary between industry and idleness, substituting for its terms those of work and leisure, and couching the desirability of the latter in representations of the imaginary freedoms afforded by both the West and rural life more generally. The distaste voiced by Irving for the "din and dust" of the city was widely shared, and his recoil from the city's "drudgery" further conveys how the urban organization of space—especially the ascendant grid system—generated dissatisfaction with not only the increasing claustrophobia, pollution, and ethnic diversity of the urban context, but also its atmosphere of imposed industriousness.

Proponents of the urban grid admired its capacity for speeding the measurement, sale, and purchase of real estate, that is, its ability to transform and exploit space as economically productive.[84] Sensing this during his celebrated 1836 visit, Charles Dickens was provoked to comment on the relentless grid that defined Philadelphia, "a handsome city, but distractingly regular. After walking about it for an hour or two, I felt that I would have given the world for a crooked street. The collar of my coat appeared to stiffen, and the brim of my hat to expand, beneath its quakerly influence. My hair shrunk into a sleek short crop, my hands folded themselves upon my breast of their own calm accord, and thoughts of taking lodgings in Mark Lane over against the Market Place, and of making a large fortune by speculations in corn came over me involuntarily."[85] Such a response was not uncommon among European observers, who, often initially intrigued by the striking order and effect of cleanliness that the street grid system conveyed, nevertheless quickly soured on its businesslike indifference to nature.[86] American architecture and landscape architecture reflect this burgeoning contempt for the cramped rectilinearity of the urban environment, as new suburban designs sought to create a sense of leisured ease on the outskirts of corrupted urbanity. As Kenneth Jackson has demonstrated, the increasing availability of detached housing, winding thoroughfares for traffic, and grassy lawns inspired by English and Oriental designs and popularized by Alexander Jackson Davis's 1833 *Rural Residences*, were praised precisely for their disavowal of productivity.[87]

Numerous examples reflect the effort to use suburban design to soothe the harried worker by concealing the businesslike realities of workaday life. The Llewellyn Park development outside of New York City featured walkways along ridges and through the woods of a central open stretch of some fifty acres of rural "wild" known as the "Ramble"—a common name at the time for the meandering of all sorts of different idlers.[88] Similarly, Frederick Law Olmsted's Riverside, Illinois, comprising 1,600 acres accessible to Chicago by means of the expanding commuter rail system, offered curved roadways explicitly intended to "imply leisure, contemplativeness, and happy tranquility."[89] Riverside was to be connected to the business center by a limited-access thoroughfare, providing the commuting businessman a means of "taking air and exercise" while pleasantly traversing the territory separating work from leisure (in another signal of the complex negotiations attendant to productive space, the highway remained unbuilt due to public land use restrictions). That the departure from work into the developing countryside symbolically satisfied the desire for flight from civilization was suggested quite explicitly by Greeley, who advocated the development of affordable cottage housing in Westchester County in the 1850s as a more moderate expedient "for those who were unwilling to

'Go West.'"[90] Such suburban developments provided an aestheticized version of the free westward movement by which they were in part inspired, at times by explicitly borrowing the typical conventions used for representing western "unproductivity," as in an advertisement for a project at Hempstead, Long Island: "Hempstead Plains, hitherto a desert, will be made to blossom as the rose."[91]

Clearly, however, the "natural" suburban setting that made it possible "to withdraw like a monk and live like a prince," as Lewis Mumford put it, depended on the very encroachments of industrial civilization it claimed to elude: the railway, the road, the impermeability of the property line, and the privacy of the detached dwelling.[92] Among those who did register this contradiction was Nathaniel Parker Willis, whose lifelong devotion to the cause of idleness merits specific attention.[93] The notorious dandy-editor was known for tireless advocacy of the restorative powers of rural retreat and for his frequent reference to his own country cottages: Glenmary, where he reposed between 1837 and 1846, and Idlewild, to which he repaired in 1853 and lived out the last of his years.[94] The success of Willis's repackaging of pastoral mythology may be estimated in the claim that "the weather always smiles upon Idlewild," as one contemporary chronicler sighed before going on to note that "the unlovely mask which is worn in cities in defense or defiance of the envy and uncharitableness around, is here laid ingenuously aside, and the better inner spirit is left to manifest itself in freedom."[95] Willis was wont to reinforce these oppositions between rural activity and its more cosmopolitan other, as, for example, in the effusive pomp with which he describes an encounter with a Kentucky backwoodsman, in his collection *Health Trip to the Tropics*:

> We learned, among other things, that a man required no property, beyond a shirt, to "make a gal have him," in that country; that the neighbors would "make a bee" to build his house, and he could get trusted for tools—so that it seems a happy climate where the native can begin life without capital. . . . Looking at the magnanimous, un-careworn, genial and unsuspicious countenance of the man as he talked, I let a small wonder creep through my mind, whether, after all, the mere enjoyment of life were not better attained in this way. Count D'Orsay and this backwoodsman—naturally men very much alike—might weigh happiness at the close of life, with a strong probability that the latter of the two had found the more.[96]

However, in contrast to many who penned similar accounts, Willis tempered his rural mythologies with an acknowledgment of the inherent shortcomings of strategic flight into rurality. Perhaps because his status as a social scene-maker required that he be within visiting distance of friends and acquaintances, he was well aware that the rural retreat could hardly elude the extending tentacles of society, urbanity, and business. His insistence that Idlewild provided a space for "life out of sight, of which the world knows nothing" was patently disproven by his making the claim in print, which thereby would naturally generate a wider thirst for knowledge of the mysteries of life at Idlewild.[97] Disappointment with such compromise likewise colors his conclusion that "wherever there is a butcher shop and a post office, an apothecary and a blacksmith, an 'arcade' and a milliner—wherever the conveniences of life are, in short—there has already arrived the Procrustes of opinion. Man's eyes will look on you and bring judgment, and unless you live on wildmeat and cornbread in the wilderness, with neither friend nor helper, you must give in to compromise—yield at least half your independence, and take it back in commonplace comfort."[98] Nevertheless, at least one contemporary observer regarded Willis's version of the hovering life as having reached "the proper mediating ground for the reconciliation and the harmonizing of the two opposing natures, the moral and the mundane, which especially characterize poets, and Mr. Willis, perhaps, more than most men."[99]

One suspects, however, that such a harmonizing of the moral and the mundane was perhaps ultimately best achieved by the subordination of the countryside to economic ends, and the Procrustean surrender of land and activity to the logic of equivalence. For the suburban developments were compromised from the start by economic reality; as the subdivision became, after 1843, the basic unit of suburban design, the principles of free appropriation and of organic growth were effectively squashed. Private interests, recognizing the intensity of the desire for flight into leisurely settings, wasted little time capitalizing on that want. "The theory that early suburbs just grew, with owners 'turning cowpaths and natural avenues of traffic into streets,' is erroneous," according to Jackson, who stresses how "subdividers lobbied with municipal governments to extend city services, they pressured street car companies to send tracks into developing sections, and they set the property lines for the individual homes."[100] Suburbia's promise of escape from industrial and commercial exigency thus comes at the price of fattening the pockets of the industrial and commercial interests. Flight toward an oasis of unproductive space is achieved in the same gesture by which that space is made productive, transformed by industry and capital.[101] The free activity of movement westward, over real and imagined lines of productiveness, thus becomes the *model* of the movement toward freedom, instead of the *means* of realizing that freedom.

Concerning Hurry, Leisure, and "Inglorious Ease"

> Little does he know of the calm, unexciting, unwearying, lasting satisfaction of life, who has never known what it is to place the leisurely hand in the idle pocket, and to saunter to and fro.
> —A.K.H.B., "Concerning Hurry and Leisure," 1860

The dialectical recuperation that rendered suburban flight essentially innocuous and unthreatening to the productive order was mirrored in conversations about the nature of activity itself. Consider, for example, the comments of the anonymous observer who published an 1857 "Plea for Idleness" in *Putnam's Monthly Magazine*, describing at one point an idler who "was observing the speed and customs of his fellow-men, admiring the architecture of that noble city, or getting a sniff of country air in the suburbs; while improving his mind by grave and suitable reflections. Then, for relief and indulgence, behold him not unamused at some well-managed show, or in a circle of select friends conversing upon matters of art and philosophy, or the affairs of state. Such a life would Plato have approved."[102] And yet this plea advocates an idleness that, in all its amused, contemplative, and leisurely splendor, turns out to be very carefully circumscribed. Our commentator goes on to raise the prospect of "ignoble" idlers, who "having the charge of keeping themselves and friends alive, will yet be hardly prevailed upon to work"; the ensuing salvo against such "horribly immoral, wretched creatures," living in a selfish and "shameless and inglorious ease," characterizes such idleness as a gateway to other immoralities.[103] The distinction is invoked further in its imperative conclusion: "Be, therefore, idle sometimes; but affect not a *vacant idleness*, an incurious dullness, or lethargic quiet."[104]

Such idle "vacancy"—complete with its connotations of empty space—demands to be distinguished from the more commendable leisure advocated above, and by the English author identified only as A.K.H.B., who, in "Concerning Hurry and Leisure," claims to "utterly despise the idler—the loafer, as Yankees term him, who never does any thing—whose idle hands are always in his idle pockets, and who is always sauntering to and fro. Leisure, be it remembered, is the intermission of labor; it is the blink of idleness in the life of a hard-working man. It is only in the case of such a man that leisure is dignified, commendable, or enjoyable."[105] In contrast to the purposeless vacancy of the pathological idler, the dignified leisure advocated by A.K.H.B. and the author of the "Plea" is safely contained, hemmed into an "intermission," a fleeting interval between appropriately productive moments.[106] The same conclusion is reached by "an American" dispatched to Europe—incognito, apparently—to secure "A Glance at the Streets of Paris during the Winter of 1849–50" for the *Southern Literary Messenger*.[107] Describing his rambling through the wonders of Paris, he praises the properly bourgeois leisure of the French, who, "from their earliest infance . . . learn to amuse themselves," a talent lamentably absent from the American mentality, which has yet to reconcile such a dignified idleness with the requisite "talent for affairs, or with the pursuits of an honorable ambition."[108]

Carefully restricted to the intermissions between the more practical matters, such amusement may be balanced with the "affairs" and "ambition" that dignify it. But the intoxication of our Parisian correspondent with the amusing and properly amused denizens of his robust holiday streetscape is dampened as he ponders the contrasting forms of activity that occupy those who lurk along the Seine. There, the contemptibly empty expenditure of idle time appears as a threat of political insurrection and moral decline: "Groups of idlers are constantly gathered along these quais gazing listlessly at the rapid current of the discoloured Seine, or watching the washerwomen as they ply their useful calling in their immense stationary arks with bare coarse arms and with picturesque costume; others are moving slowly along with eyes intent upon the worm-eaten and mouldy volumes and the thumbed and dirty brochures of patriotic or socialist songs and immoral novels which form the collections of the venders of second-hand books."[109] The contrast between the disagreeable idlers and the slightly more noble (or at least more picturesque) laborers is clear, but it remains negligible when compared to the distinction drawn between these "listless" exploits and those of the chubbily amused classes invoked prior. The depiction of this "listless" diversion and the undignified pastimes that abound here impresses the seal of class distinction upon the report of this roving "American."

The need to account at once for the allure of unproductive endeavor and the empty idleness of "listless gazes" and "vacancy" necessitates an adjustment of the long-standing industry-idleness binary. For the supposedly productive classes, it is not idleness that opposes industry, but rather the bourgeois concept of "leisure." While these commentators appear to wrestle somewhat with this reconfiguration of the dominant binary, the following point is quite clear: idleness may be an acceptable pastime, but only if it is an idleness that pays productive dividends (and which therefore can no longer truly be called idleness at all). Such is the strategy employed by A.K.H.B, who ultimately strays so far from the original industry-idleness equation that "industry," too, is discarded, in favor of "hurry." Here one's position in the relations of production determines whether idleness is merely an irresponsible refuge from mind-numbing industrial labors, or the invaluable respite of the upstanding citizen from the twittings of his hectic, bourgeois, lifestyle: "Every earnest man, with work to do, will find that occasionally there comes a pressure of it; there comes a crowd of things which must be done quickly if they are done at all; and the condition thus induced is hurry. I am aware, of course, that there is a distinction between haste and hurry—hurry adding to rapidity the element of painful confusion; but in the case of ordinary people, haste generally implies hurry."[110] The stresses of such "ordinary" people are clearly not those of the millworker or the riverside washerwoman. Few of them would recognize themselves in A.K.H.B.'s winking reminder of "what we should have known from the beginning, that a far larger amount of tangible work will be accomplished by regular exertion of moderate degree and continuance, than by going ahead in the feverish and unrestful fashion in which earnest men are so ready to begin their task." Even less comprehensible would be his exhortation to the kind of self-determination that could only be enjoyed by the comfortable elite: "Consider for how many hours of the day you can labor, without injury to body or mind: labor faithfully for those hours, and for no more. Never mind about what may be said by Miss Limejuice and Mr. Snarling."[111] Furthermore, leisure's proclaimed benefits of developing cultural capital and promoting fitness of body and mind were likely of concern only to the privileged few, the "quiet, gentlemanly, rational" types, concerned with "keeping the humors in due equilibrium and thus conferring an inestimable benefit on the body,"[112] and extending the cultivating effects of higher education by using leisure for mental improvement. Repose in this connection might constitute a form of "instruction . . . supplementary to a good education, college and professional, obtained in the usual way; and it must be sought in intervals of leisure, intercalated in a busy and energetic life."[113]

However much this discourse establishes a bourgeois norm, it reveals one thing held in common by both the man of refinement who partakes of improving and cultivating endeavors and the worker whose hours are not his own: the imperative that time must be productive. The leisurely shall not delude themselves into thinking that their idle pursuits enable them to escape production altogether. Their amusements, too, are re-creation, re-production, the restoration of the energy reserves that make the working day possible once the idle interval has elapsed. Such leisure produces pleasure only for those who know what it is to work. Both idleness and leisure, therefore, are conceptually yoked in a permanent relation to their opposites: "O ye men who have never been overworked and overdriven, never kept for weeks in a constant strain and in a feverish hurry, you don't know what you miss! Sweet and delicious as cool water is to the man parched with thirst, is leisure to the man just extricated from breathless hurry! And nauseous as is that same water to the man whose thirst has been completely quenched, is leisure to the man whose life is nothing but leisure."[114] In an 1850 letter, Washington Irving would come to similar conclusions, locating his own compromise with the reigning notion of productive leisure grounded on rural self-determination. Complete surrender to leisure, he argues, "is one of the most soul wearying, self teasing, temper souring lives in the world." Admitting to having "tried it once … in my younger days," he recounts that "in a little while having nothing to care for I cared for nothing, became a prey to ennui, tired of everything and particularly tired of myself. Fortunately, I was ruined before I was spoiled." To avoid that fate, Irving advises his interlocutor to strive for a productive mixture of leisure with commercial interests: "Cultivate rural habits and tastes and occupations, with which to diversify your commercial pursuits," he counsels. "You will then have rural employments to retire upon instead of a life of leisure."[115] These attempts to salvage an industrious idleness, carefully consigned to the predictability of an "intermission," echo the broader effort to transcend the "vacant" and to stabilize "hovering," "loitering," and "loafing" lives of inglorious ease. In short, they insist upon the application of productive workaday rationality to the question of idle time's delimitation and disposition. In pleading for a productive leisure characterized by stable production, a predictable return of invested time, and the fixation of activity upon the goals of industrious identity or bourgeois morality, they find common cause with the sage Irving, who concludes that, "a rural retreat is a man's own, and at his formation produces a new set of pleasures and interests and ambitions, and every tree he plants awakens a new hope and attaches him to the spot which he has improved."[116] Such "attachments" would, however, seem anathema to the Irving of 1835, to whom we shall return in the next section.

Frontier Activity, Frontier Space, Frontier Freedom

> Space is the constitutive horizon of American freedom, of the proprietor's freedom.
>
> —Antonio Negri, *Insurgencies*, 1999

When we reconsider the activity of the "unproductive" frontier, we note that it is precisely the stable, predictable, and fixed activity described by bourgeois ideologists of leisure that is absent there. Despite an abundance of those who admitted that the "vigor," "rush," and "enterprise" of the frontier constituted a form of activity, fewer are they who credited such activity with contributing to the realization of economic value. One explanation for the seeming contradiction—that of the frontier's avowable rigors being regarded as somehow idle—is to be found in the way that the material experience of the frontier necessitated models of activity that appeared to lack the seriousness, the dedication, and the reliability of eastern production. Indeed, the very premise of the frontier project—that of virtually infinite settlement—seemed to resist conventional ideas of productivity, in that it was a task that would supposedly never be complete.[117]

Irving's early narrative of his tour, enamored as it is with the whimsy and free-spiritedness made possible by the frontier, emphasizes the appeal of such intransitive activity; consider his description of a youthful Osage, who, exemplifying "the glorious independence of man in a savage state," is spontaneously convinced to join Irving's party: "This youth, with his rifle, his blanket, and his horse, was ready, at a moment's warning, to rove the world: he carried all his worldly effects with him; and in the absence of artificial wants possessed the great secret of personal freedom. We of society are slaves, not so much to others as to ourselves; our superfluities are the chains that bind us, impeding every movement of our bodies, and thwarting every impulse of our souls."[118] To Irving, the Osage's magnificent liberty follows from the fickleness of his activity, the freedom of his movement, and his apparent temporariness of duty (which subsequently manifests in the narrative as he abruptly abandons Irving's party). The Osage thus signals the frontier possibilities of manifold interests, transient obligations, free choice, and, ultimately, unemployment. The objects of his endeavor are not fixed; his activity is fluid, shifting, and varied.

Ultimately, it is this activity that shifts, strays, deviates, and digresses from a singular task that so confounded proponents of industry. More than anything else, they expected productive activity to form itself to a fixed task with a product as its proof; activity not lending itself to those expropriative regimes would therefore be misrecognized as idle. Further, where one's objects of exertion proliferate, the "intermissions" intercalated into the work cycle take the form of a shift of task, instead of a momentary suspension of activity with a guaranteed return to the same. For Irving, this propensity is embodied in Antonio, another of his "half-breeds," who "was to be a kind of jack-of-all-work; to cook, to hunt, and to take care of the horses; but he had a vehement propensity to do nothing."[119] Even the generally sympathetic Irving here demonstrates a certain contempt for Antonio's (in-) activity, presumably reserving his validation of free-spirited lifestyles to those who aren't working in his employ.

This transient and unpredictable character of western production is similarly well-captured in an address delivered by Mark Twain to alumni of the California gold rush. His narrative of unprofitable claims and bogus mines "salted" with melted half-dollars is delivered from the perspective of the jack-of-all-trades: "I have been through the California mill, with all its dips, spurs and angles, variations and sinuousities. I have worked there at all the different trades and professions known to the catalogues. I have been everything, from a newspaper editor down to a cowcatcher on a locomotive, and I am encouraged to believe that if there had been a few more occupations to experiment on, I might have made a dazzling success at last, and found out what mysterious designs Providence had in creating me."[120] Twain's playful account suggests the way that the activity of western subjects was informed by the opportunities presented by their material surroundings, and it also illuminates the misrecognition that flummoxed those who found in western exertions proof only of idleness: To "have been everything" is in this case to have somehow *done nothing*. Without a fixed object of exertion, a uniform goal, or an expected outcome, Twain's endeavors come to appear (even to himself) as quixotic and unproductive; his very being—subject to the mysteriousness of Providence's designs and the ambiguities that cloud his true calling—remains nondescript.

Yet Twain's experience of activity fitted to the "spurs and angles, variations and sinuousities" of the western terrain was apparently typical of the frontier life, for simple economic and logistical reasons. James Davis's study of nineteenth-century census data notes that "explicit references to the occupational composition of the frontier are relatively rare," in part because most frontier work aimed at mere subsistence, and was therefore necessarily dominated by various small-scale endeavors around a single homestead.[121] Specialization in certain tasks required a pool of clients that was difficult to cultivate in areas of low population density. But the lack of institutional representation of occupational identity also occurs because eastern schemas for census-taking could not accommodate the qualitative variability and intangibility of frontier labors.[122] The account of one exasperated census taker illustrates these limits: "Sluman Wattles ... was not only a farmer, but a road builder, tailor, shoemaker, lumberman, butcher, hatter, bricklayer, teacher, lawyer and county judge. Another example was Joseph Sleeper, farmer, Quaker preacher, surveyor, millwright, carpenter, stone-mason and blacksmith; and still another Jedediah Peck, who was farmer, lawyer, millwright, preacher, politician and county judge."[123] Despite resisting numerical and imaginary representation back east, this mode of activity was, however, capable of producing not only valuable goods and services, but also subjectivities equipped for a fundamentally experimental relationship with their environment and its transient objects; in other words, a people responsive to the relatively organic needs and material conditions of their frontier surroundings, rather than to the transcendent measures of the wage or the census. In fact, it was precisely the freedom signaled by this quality of American work that William Cobbett lauded in his 1818 *A Year's Residence in the United States of America*. Hailing American laborers as "the best I ever saw," he notes that "an American labourer is not regulated, as to time, by *clocks* and *watches*. . . . Here is no dispute about *hours*. 'Hours were made for *slaves*,' is an old saying; and, really, they seem here to act upon it as a practical maxim."[124]

This type of economic production, indifferent to transcendent measures, demanded a unique diagram of social power, at once abstract and concrete. As Antonio Negri argues in *Insurgencies*: "[Power] becomes completely abstract because it adapts itself to a mass distributed over an enormous space; but at the same time it becomes completely concrete because it leans on the individualized interests of this mass, on their singular insertion into the territory, in terms of appropriation by fact that it must become property by law."[125] Agrarian self-determination depends on this relationship to space. The "individualized interests" of singularities inserted into and coterminous with the American territory were the agents of political and ontological power, instead of merely the passive objects on which such a power would be exercised by government from without. Popular sovereignty, in Negri's words, constructs "a space redefined by the political, conquered through an operation of founding political emancipation—in universal terms."[126] Negri's characterization of the political status of the pioneers as "operational" might be further illuminated by Deleuze and Guattari's conception of "smooth" and "striated" space in *A Thousand Plateaus*, which likewise pivots on the exercise of free activity. The space of America, as Jefferson regarded it, was smooth— not necessarily empty, or featureless, but rather lacking in transcendent structures defining it from above. Activity suited to such space emerges from its specific material character, and is not the product of an arbitrarily imposed template. Instead of subjecting territory to a transcendent governing structure, frontier activity forged governing principles calibrated to its territory. Out of this territory, in which "one 'distributes' oneself in an open space," emerges a practice that Negri, Deleuze, and Guattari would characterize as ontologically productive.[127]

According to the former, the refusal of power structures imposed from without enabled the prospect of a radically democratic subjectivity governed by a virtue that can "pose an inexhaustible frontier to itself, a frontier of freedom, as potentiality of a new man."[128] No longer would binding political relations need to mediate between appropriators and the appropriated—as would be the case in the feudal and nascent industrial capitalist models—but rather such relations were produced between appropriators within their own ranks. The product and the ground of this *horizontal* negotiation between singularities was a new political subject equipped with the capacity for free, immanent activity.[129] Turner more romantically diagnosed something quite similar, asserting that the "physiography of the frontier" ensured that "this new frontier should be social rather than individual."[130] To him, it was "free and competitive movement" that offered the "chance to break the bondage of social rank, and to rise to a higher plane of existence," to cast off aristocratic and traditional sensibilities, and to embrace the "free play" of an activity that organically constituted interdependent and autonomous communities.[131]

This context presented major obstacles to rationalizing templates such as the wage, the census, or parliamentary models of political representation—as is suggested in Wakefield's "doleful anecdote" about redundant labor or in Twain's failure to achieve occupational identity—and thus much of the economic, political, and cultural activity conducted in and through American space was rendered epistemologically unrecognizable as productive. Like the productivities of Native Americans and slaves, the diversity of frontier activity was expelled from rational history itself, and this despite the obvious contradiction that it was precisely the activity of the settler that was called upon to guarantee the specificity of America's spatial identity. This exclusion is evident in Charles Eliot Norton's discussion of the settlers' inability to fulfill the "responsibilities" that would accompany a vertical conception of power. The pioneer is thus disqualified from political agency, except in the form of an idle threat to the established order: "Materialized in their temper; with few ideals of an ennobling sort; little instructed in the lessons of history; safe from exposure to the direct calamities and physical horrors of war; with underdeveloped imaginations and sympathies—they form a community unfortunate and dangerous from the possession of power without a due sense of its corresponding responsibilities."[132] Norton's caustic account, congruent with the other misunderstandings of the political, social, and economic ramifications of western activity considered above, seeks to neutralize the idle threat of the frontier by displacing its population from productive "history" to the realm of mere caprice.[133] Just as the specific economic activity of the frontier would be disparaged as idle, frontier political activity, typified by the horizontality of power, was misrecognized as mere recklessness and irresponsibility. And just as the dialectic of industry and idleness fails to account for the infinite wealth of possible forms of frontier activity, Norton's denigration of western praxis disregards the productive potentials of horizontal political organization.[134] Unregulated movement appears as inactivity, and thus these nondescript beings of the frontier must be *settled* anew.

As the various rationalizations of western space—the "rails, boundaries, and surveys"[135]—transformed "idle" space and the "unproductive" activity proper to it, the process of settlement was transformed into an activity with an end that lies outside it. The republic's expansion increasingly unfolded not according to the logics of individual free appropriation, but rather through the mediation of state and economic power. An armory of abstract techniques of measurement and quantification reinforced the march toward a horizon traced by the ideal of Manifest Destiny. As Emerson somewhat militantly noted at the time: "The railroad is but one arrow in our quiver, though it has great value as a sort of yard-stick and surveyor's line. The bountiful continent is ours, state on state, and territory on territory, to the waves of the Pacific sea."[136]

It is necessary to note that the instrumentalization of idle space occurred not by overcoming its smoothness, but by retaining that smoothness as the *model*, rather than the *means*, for expansion.[137] The righteous rhetoric of Manifest Destiny, for example, borrowed from the logic of smooth space in appealing to a natural mandate for the expand-ing matrix of state power. Such "geographical rationalism" was crucial, for example, in establishing that Texas was meant to be sundered from Mex-ico, a detachment occurring seemingly "in the natural course of events, by a process perfectly legitimate on its own part, blameless on our [own]."[138] That this version of nature's right required the crutch of transcendence was clear from Lewis C. Levin's argument that it was "the eternal laws of God" that provided man with space in which to live, "and told him that the natural boundaries to a country only terminate where oceans inter-vene, and contiguity is obstructed by some formidable obstacle which separates nations and marks out the native home as distinctly as if drawn by the lines of military art. National boundaries and the genius of a people always harmonize."[139] The example of Manifest Destiny is crucial not only because it demonstrates the way that a transcendent ideology of expan-sion comes to supplant the material practice of free appropriation. It also reveals the way in which the threats and potentials of idle terrain beyond the line of productiveness—Irving's "desert world," Wakefield's "waste" territories, Hazen's "barren lands," and beyond—were recuperated in the rendering productive of American space, squeezing from it not only the profitable advantages of the westward expansion, but also the construc-tion of a national mythology that pretended toward the model of horizon-tal power while in fact circumscribing the possibilities of such power. That power, along with the spaces to which it was tailored, would function no longer as the means, but only as the model, of the American democratic project. And thus, as the "vast trackless spaces" celebrated by Whitman gave way to rails, roads, and borders, it was not only the land that would be transformed, but also the value of free activity itself.

Lines of Productiveness

Wrapping western spaces in an increasingly dense meshwork, the railroad—of "great value as a sort of yard-stick and surveyor's line"—was crucial both in effectuating the demographic saturation of the West and in accomplishing the symbolic and real calibration of activity to the standards of productivity. Its power to translate "idle" space into a theater of production made it a persistent icon in nineteenth-century discourse regarding idleness and industry, in which it serves as both the harbinger of a budding, industrious modernity and as the ruination of those benefits associated with free activity and appropriation. Charles Lummis captured much of this in his *A Tramp Across the Continent*, in which he documents a walking tour of 3,507 miles from Ohio to California; there, he justifies his exploit in terms that echo typical period concerns about hurry, gain, and activity: "railroads and Pullmans were invented to help us hurry through life and miss most of the pleasure of it—and most of the profit, too, except of that jingling, only half-satisfying sort which can be footed up in the ledger."[140]

In contrast to Lummis's complaint about the subjection of movement to hurry and profit, Emerson's more positive evaluation of the railroad turns precisely on its ability to make idle spaces pictorially productive by improving upon their inherent character. "In an uneven country the railroad is a fine object in the making," he argues. "It has introduced a multitude of picturesque traits into our pastoral scenery. The tunneling of mountains, the bridging of streams, the bold mole carried out into a broad silent meadow, silent and unvisited by any but its own neighbors since the planting of the region."[141] But this is far more than an aesthetic matter, as Emerson's imagery of industrious exertion—all this tunneling, bridging, and burrowing like a mole—is subsequently amplified. He goes on to invoke the moil of "gangs of laborers" and "the energy with which they strain at their tasks; the cries of the overseer or *boss*." Under that urging is transformed "the character of the work itself, which so violates and revolutionizes the primal and immemorial forms of nature."[142] Like Irving's bees, bringing with them the prospect of ruthless commercial enterprise, the arrival of the iron horse is thus accompanied by an industrious model of work and exertion. For Emerson, the work of railroad expansion is fitted not only with the halter of alienated submission to "the overseer or *boss*," but also according to the revolutionary "violation" of nature's order. As the railroad translates idle western space into an abstractly rationalized

Figure 8. William A. Garnett, "Train Crossing the Desert, Kelso, California," 1974. Gelatin silver print. 13 5/16 x 19 3/4 in (33.81 x 50.17 cm). San Francisco Museum of Modern Art. Gift, by exchange, of Theo Jung. © William A. Garnett Estate.

terrain, it proceeds hand in hand with the translation of free activity into alienated "work." It thereby both metaphorically and literally represents the triumph of capitalized labor over idleness, of the wage regime over free activity.

The scene described by Emerson fuses the industrial and the corporeal, the mechanical and the human; it coincides with the threading together of physical and social energies under the rubric of "work," as diagnosed by Deleuze and Guattari: "The wage regime had as its correlate a mechanics of force. Physics had never been more social, for in both cases it was a question of defining the constant mean value of a force of lift and pull exerted in the most uniform way possible by a standard man. Impose the Work-model on every activity, translate every act into possible or virtual work, discipline free action, or else (which amounts to the same thing) relegate it to 'leisure,' which exists only by reference to work."[143] The free physical deployment of energies in space becomes thereby the *model*, but no longer the *means* of productivity. Its quantifiable counterpart, the measure of social averages known as productive "work," intervenes to mediate and regulate all activity, whether leisurely or productive.

As the railroad emblematizes the coincidence of instrumental expansion and the application of work models upon the free activity of the West, it has come to represent the seeming triumph of the ideology of industry over both idle space and unproductive activity. A photograph from the 1970s offers a visual analogue: in William Garnett's "Train Crossing Desert, Kelso, California" (figure 8), two models of movement across the "idle" space of the desert are counterposed, the businesslike instrumentality of the rail line racing alongside the apparent meanderings of a dried stream beneath it. What appears to be an opposition of the rail's direct purposiveness and the undirected caprice of the stream bed suggests rather two possibilities for progress through this landscape. Indifferent to the stream bed's infinity of configurations, the railroad speeds across this misleadingly "unproductive" landscape of sand, scrub, and wind, overcoding these "barren lands" according to the progressive trajectory of the "road to improvement." Yet these overcodings of the natural by the industrious order would, by the end of the nineteenth century, provoke new ambivalences about the translation of the physical world into the economic and of the body's activity into social and economic meaning. Chapter 4 will turn to an array of geographical, economic, and corporeal reconsiderations of the exhaustiveness of those translations.

4

Vital Reserves Revisited

The Energies of the Social Body

I am only 45 . . . should have—shall have twenty five years of good
work yet.
　　　　—Charlotte Perkins Gilman, "Thoughts and Figgerings," 1905

Of course there are limits: the trees don't grow into the sky.
　　　　—William James, "The Energies of Men," 1907

By the close of the nineteenth century, a signal shift transformed discussions of the limits of productivity—a response to, and a condition of, increasingly rationalized disciplinary systems revolutionizing
notions of work, the home, and the nation, as well as the lived experience
of working bodies. On the one hand, there occurred a rearticulation of
the once explicit moral proscription that leisure time must be used in an
instrumental fashion. In this respect, the emergence of a leisure economy
and a highly orchestrated realm of diverting amusements increasingly
ensured that even time spent away from work proper would nevertheless
produce economic value through consumer practices and the forging of
compliant subjectivities for whom the exhaustive use of time is second
nature. The culmination of this trajectory in a totalizing culture industry
would ultimately prompt Adorno and Horkheimer to plausibly claim that
"amusement under late capitalism is the prolongation of work. . . . What
happens at work, in the factory, or in the office can only be escaped from
by approximation to it in one's leisure time."[1]

Leisure time's warp is complemented by the woof of a new corporeal-
ization of unproductivity, a shift, as Anson Rabinbach put it, "from idleness to fatigue."[2] This tendency occasions a new focus, away from idleness
conceived as a moral boon or danger, and toward unproductivity as a

physiological and directly economic malady. Social attitudes toward the body—including the pathologization of neurasthenia and other inhibitors of the will, the embrace of healthful recreation and play, and intensified technical and managerial attention to the body's physical force as a factor of economic production—gradually make it the privileged site for articulating visions of what productivity is and what it can be expected to achieve.

The end of the century thus witnessed both an intensified subsumption of time by economically productive activity, and a more pronounced emphasis on the practical materiality, rather than the essential morality, of activity. The critical literature on these developments is broad, and as thought-provoking as the primary texts that are typically its focus.[3] But largely unremarked to date is the way that, put into dialogue with each other and viewed through the optic of nineteenth-century discourses on unproductivity, there is revealed in the thinking of key figures such as William James, Theodore Dreiser, and Charlotte Perkins Gilman—despite the diversity of their thematic investments in work—a certain remarkable uniformity. For each is fascinated with imagining precisely what lies *beyond productivity's limits*: energies that are dormant, potentials that are latent, productivities that are unproductive. In short, while they joust for common ground on the question of idleness and work, they nevertheless demonstrate uncanny accord in the grounding faith that there always remains *work yet to be done*.

Each posits the existence of some hitherto untapped repositories gravid with potential productive force yet to be adequately exploited. Exploring the era's common obsession with the various forms of what might be called "reserve" energies, this chapter will consider in particular how this faith is manifest in literal and metaphorical treatments of bodies—physical, political, and corporate. Significantly, the rise to prominence of this notion of the ever-present "reserve" occurs simultaneously with the emergence of widespread alarm about the prospects of exhaustion—for example, the fatigue of bodies pushed to their limits by intensified capitalist production, or the claustrophobia attendant to the closing of the frontier—and hence registers the felt need to discover, preserve, and harness vital energy resources that might ensure that individual and national bodies continue to function under the exigencies of capitalist modernity. Discourses about the fatigue of the body and the exhaustion of land are an index to the emergent national concern with redrawing the "line of productiveness" that was described in chapter 3. But it is especially the work of Charlotte Perkins Gilman—whose obsessive private calculations about her own remaining productive force provide more than merely an epigrammatic thread throughout this chapter, and whose attempt at a total theory of human activity sought to radically redefine work[4]—that helps us to better understand the urgency of redefining the limits of productivity at the turn of the century, and to glimpse the implications of this potential redefinition for the modern and monetarized American metropolis.

William James: Energy "Budgets" and the Second Wind

> 58. Two years to 60. . . . Call it a day.
> —Charlotte Perkins Gilman, "Thoughts and Figgerings," 1918

> Everyone knows what it is to start a piece of work, either intellectual or muscular, feeling stale—or *cold*, as an Adirondack guide once put it to me. And everybody knows what it is to "warm up" to his job.
> —William James, "The Energies of Men," 1907

The term "vital reserves" is derived from the title of a collection of two exoteric lectures about bodily energy delivered by William James, which will, like the wisdom of his Adirondack guide, help us to warm to a consideration of the discourse of exhaustion at the turn of the century.[5] James's 1906 address entitled "The Energies of Men" (first published in 1907) aptly illustrates the notion of the "reserve" in an immediately familiar form, that of the phenomenon of the "second wind," doing so in a way that illuminates many of the key features of such thinking. James's work, like that of others to be considered here, begins by assuming the existence of hitherto untapped reserves of unexploited energy, drawing analogies between the individual body and bodies social and national, all the while delicately balancing often paradoxical concepts of activity, work, and idleness in a way that illuminates their interconnectivity and arbitrariness.

After years of musing, James declares in this lecture that he is developing a physiological theory of the "second wind," describing it as an actualization of "sources of strength habitually not taxed at all" that overcomes the limits on productivity imposed by fatigue.[6] When the body's standard allotment of energy has been exhausted, he argues, fatigue sets in, establishing "an efficacious obstruction on this side of which our usual life is cast" (EM 3–4). But when a body succeeds in having "tapped a level of new energy" beyond this limit, it may access "amounts of ease and power that we never dreamed ourselves to own" (EM 4). His physiological explanation of this recasts the body in terms that are at once corporeal and, perhaps oddly, geological: "Our organism has stored-up reserves of energy that are not ordinarily called upon, but that may be called upon: deeper and deeper strata of combustible or explosible material, discontinuously arranged, but ready for use by anyone who probes so deep. . . . Most of us continue living unnecessarily near our surface" (EM 5). Adding an additional, and suggestively economic, dimension to this description of how one might mine new veins of potential fuel, James counsels the maximization of individual "energy-budgets" such that such magazines of latent force may be most efficiently exploited.

This intriguing if speculative account of such stored energy is complicated by a number of key provisos driven by the conventional difficulty in precisely defining what properly productive activity looks like. The first of these complexities leads James to explain an apparent contradiction between different modes—mental versus physical—of productivity. Drawing a distinction between what he calls "inner" and "outer" work, he argues that the former sometimes is most effective at those moments when it counterintuitively seems to place a curb on the latter: "Let no one think, then, that our problem of individual and national economy is solely that of the maximum of pounds raisable against gravity, the maximum of locomotion, or of agitation of any sort, that human beings can accomplish. That might signify little more than hurrying and jumping about in inco-ordinated ways; whereas inner work, though it so often reinforces outer work, quite as often means its arrest" (EM 9–10). Concluding that "to relax . . . is sometimes a great achievement of inner work," James here introduces a suggestive tableau of ideas that indicates just how complicated the theory of productive energy may be. On the one hand, he introduces the prospect of a productive relaxation, echoing earlier discourses that castigated "hurry" while celebrating downtime as a necessary and generative force; he furthermore contributes to the shift of that discussion about productivity to the corporeal or physiological milieu. Attempting to identify certain "dynamogenic" stimuli that catalyze the energies of men, he bridges the gap between the discourses on idleness and fatigue, noting that these stimuli may function both "morally" and "muscularly" (EM 15).

Just as significant, however, is his assertion that these problems of "economy" are at once both "individual and national." Having elsewhere posited the superiority of a nation whose men maximize their energy-budgets and "run at a higher pressure," at "their most useful pitch" (EM 8), he goes on rather innocently to discuss the dynamogenic qualities of certain moral or intellectual concepts that "naturally awaken" energies, "unlocking innumerable powers which, but for the idea, would never have come into play" (EM 31). Along with idealist evergreens like "Truth" and "Science," most of the ideas included in James's conceptual inventory reiterate the national, and even militaristic, applications of the reserve theory, to wit: "'Fatherland,' 'the Flag,' 'the Union' . . . 'the Monroe Doctrine' . . . are so many examples of energy-releasing ideas" (EM 31).[7]

An attentive look at the second of the two essays collected in *On Vital Reserves*, 1899's "The Gospel of Relaxation," further discloses the specifically national imperative to properly navigate the limits of productivity, as James explicitly notes that as a people, Americans weaken themselves by mismanaging their reserves, and especially by failing to use the inner energies of restraint to curtail the excesses of endless and unceasing outer work. He thus quotes anecdotally from a certain Dr. Clouston: "'You Americans,' he said, 'are living like an army with all its reserves engaged in action. The duller countenances of the British population betoken a better scheme of life. They suggest stores of reserved nervous force to fall back upon, if any occasion should arise that requires it'" (GR 54). Echoing his counterpart's salute to calm and ease, James then inveighs against "those absurd feelings of hurry . . . that breathlessness and tension, that anxiety of feature and that solicitude for results, [and] that lack of inner harmony and ease" that tend to define work under American conditions of total mobilization (GR 61–62).

It must be noted, however, that despite his conclusion that "we must change ourselves from a race that admires jerk and snap for their own sakes . . . to one that on the contrary, has calm for its ideal, and for their own sakes loves harmony, dignity, and ease" (GR 65), this celebration of calm and ease is definitively not an advocacy of keeping such reserve energies forever in abeyance—it is in no way a celebration of ease for its own sake. For throughout the galvanizing final passages of James's address, the point is transparently made that productivity can be amplified by such ease: "It is your relaxed and easy worker, who is in no hurry, and quite thoughtless most of the while of consequences, who is your efficient worker; and tension and anxiety, and present and future, all mixed up together in our mind at once, are the surest drags upon steady progress and hindrances to our success" (GR 63). In 90 percent of cases, the superiority of the European worker, he claims, can in fact be attributed to this (GR 62). The problematic of individual body energy is thereby effectively translated to the national scale. The limits of productivity are imagined to coincide with national political boundaries, and hence to require economically sound management, like any other productive resources. It is therefore perhaps as logical that James would call for a "topography of the limits of human power" (EM 38) as it is unsurprising that just such a mapping of the national budget of productive force was simultaneously under way in discussions of the exhaustion of western lands and their function as energizers of men.

National Exhaustion and the Frontier of Comfort

> *65 years old*—can work probably ten more years . . .
> —Charlotte Perkins Gilman, 1925

William James's theory of vital reserves offers the basic template for a range of discourses that construct an analogy between the individual and the social body, recording a profound anxiety about the exhaustion of those bodies and the idle threat of their unproductivity. As the discussion in chapter 3 of the western "line of productiveness" has suggested, American debates about idleness and fatigue reflected a historically specific sense of how the limit of productivity marks a boundary with exteriority. It was not uncommon for such thinking to indulge a fantasy construction of an exterior repository from which new productivities may be generated. Probably the most prominent exemplar of this is Frederick Jackson Turner, whose yearning for a reassuring outside to civilization, surplus value, and the structuring binds of the social keenly illustrates the turn-of-the-century anxiety consequent to the closing of the frontier and the exhaustion of its power to animate American ideals. In his 1903 essay "Contributions of the West to American Democracy," he remarks on what he calls the demographic *"exhaustion* . . . of the supply of free land," before concluding that America would henceforth need to turn its attention to lands beyond, in search of a supplementary energizing principle for American life.[8] In this essay, he credits the rigorous experience of frontier life with generating a kind of "vital force," an energy that "work[s] *beneath the surface* and dominate[s] the external form" of the nation; elsewhere he notes that these energies "[bring institutional] *organs into life* and shape them to meet changing conditions."⁹ The metaphor of a national body driven by submerged life-giving energies is extended and further made explicit when Turner borrows, from the Italian economist Achille Loria, the notion of a *social physiology*: "The institutional framework of the nation may be likened to the anatomy of the body politic; its physiology is the social and economic life molding this framework to new uses."¹⁰

For Turner and Loria both, it is the value of *land* that is the proper object of an inquiry into social physiology, and it is in this context that the corporeal metaphors are inscribed even more deeply, building on long-standing aesthetic and naturalist ideologies. Consider, for example, John Ruskin's account of how mountains are "to the rest of the body of the earth, what violent muscular action is to the body of man. The muscles and tendons of its anatomy are, in the mountain, brought out with fierce and convulsive energy, full of expression, passion, and strength."¹¹ The naturalist John Muir echoes this invocation of the corporeal energy of the earth; its expression is like that of the forces proper to *work*: "We see Nature working with enthusiasm like a man, blowing her volcanic forges like a blacksmith blowing his smithy fires, shoving glaciers over the landscape like a carpenter shoving his planes."¹² Seemingly split on whether to regard nature as an aesthetic entity or as an organic wilderness, Ruskin and Muir are nevertheless united in their reliance on these figures of bodily force and work, and are thus but a step removed from Turner's own assessment of the meaning of land as a repository of stored energy. These are just a few points along the contour of a broader tradition that might be said to comprise various metaphorical physiologies—aesthetic, economic, and social. And each of these ostensible physiologies betrays a motivating fascination with energy, which is often conceived—as in Turner—as a *reserve* of latent powers.

Very literally realizing the ubiquitous notion of the reserve, in this case as a founding principle of national policy, was the development of America's national park system. The considerable critical effort that has been devoted to chronicling the emergence of the parks affords us the opportunity to note with ease a couple of fundamental patterns in parks discourse—especially the recourse to a notion of energy as reserve, and the appeal to exteriority as its location. Inaugurated with Yellowstone in 1871, and gaining cultural purchase throughout the 1880s and into the early part of the twentieth century, the park system provides a complex example of the intensifying reliance on the idea that the social exterior could house a wellspring of energy (incidentally disproving Horace Greeley's earlier, somewhat sarcastic assertion that "it is likely to be some time yet before our fashionable American spas and summer resorts for idlers will be located among the Rocky Mountains").[13] The commentary on "vital reserves" that accompanied the national park system from its nascency was redeployed in an arena that is simultaneously natural, geographical, corporeal, and political—and, as with all nineteenth-century discourses about productivity, it, too, is riven with contradiction.

Consider how conventions for representing nature tended to describe it in imagery of excess or surplus, beyond the usual sphere of human activity. Thomas Starr King, for example, sermonized in the 1860s that the mountains at Yosemite were "created in an *overflow* of God's goodness."[14] This vision of nature as a primordial excess was complemented by traditional oppositions between nature and culture, and especially of the former as a site promising escape from the latter. Yet this same notion of natural excess also was bent toward teleological ends. As the self-culture advocate James Freeman Clarke argued, God "nowhere leaves the bare skeleton of utility uncovered by the rounded forms of grace." Instead, He "has left a large place in the world for recreation and amusement. Let us see that this is not abused, but used."[15]

Clarke is explicit in his stress on the proper utilization of recreation and pleasure taken in the natural world: "When people live for pleasure, then they are dead while they live. But we should breathe pleasure as we do the air, to strengthen us for work, duty, progress, usefulness."[16] He was echoed by many who esteemed the escape from culture into recreation as a means of restoring and exercising the individual body's energies— and, at the same time, of tactically organizing those bodies into a larger social entity with implications for the national whole. To cite one example, Mary Roberts Rinehart reports in her Glacier Park travelogue that proper roughing it was a pastime that "could take forty-two entirely different, blasé, feeble-muscled, uncertain, and effete Easterners and mould them in a few days into a homogeneous whole: that took excursionists and made them philosophers and sportsmen."[17] And the forging of such robust wholes would not only cultivate militaristic energies (Rinehart: "If we ever have a war, we shall draw hard on the West for cavalry. Our national parks should be able to send out trained skirmishers"),[18] but would also symbolically salve discomfort about the trammeling of the national body by the closed frontier. Frank Norris, for one, makes this explicit in his discussion of the imperialist consequences of the western frontier's exhaustion, when, deprived of a frontier upon which to exercise "our overplus of energy," two possible consequences arise: "Either the outposts fall back upon the main body or the main body moves up to the support of its outposts. One does not think that the outposts will fall back."[19] Such appeals to the national implications of energetic exertion thus dovetailed with Theodore Roosevelt's claim—hegemonic in all senses of the word—that such endeavor promised to conquer unproductivity and lassitude. He exhorted American men to embrace "adventure [and] daring and hardihood and iron endurance"—all traits understood by him as the physical but also the spatial antitheses to the "over-civilized man" who is content to "rot by inches in ignoble ease within our borders."[20]

At the same time that these discourses indicated that the purportedly national line of productiveness had been redrawn globally, however, the parks also provided a symbolic national reserve on the homefront. "We may . . . rejoice," as one *Scribner's* contributor wrote in a nationalistically sanguine comment on the parks, "at any measure tending to encourage the practice of doing our own pleasuring within our own borders."[21] The parks, host to innumerable varieties of such productive self-pleasure, thus also accommodated a range of paradoxes: they are required to be simultaneously both excess and essence; they are both an exterior to the main currents of modern American life and yet interior to the nation-state; they are constructed as a paradoxical site at which one might be abroad at home—there, moreover, to discover the pleasures of strain. This latter contradiction is exacerbated by the inevitable tenuousness of the opposition between productivity and unproductivity. Expressing this tension is a 1914 promotional brochure, drawn from many of a similar stamp in the archives of the Great Northern Railway, which makes a familiar case for the recuperative potentials of western exercise. Here, as elsewhere, the flight from mandatory productivity into tourism serves simultaneously to reinforce that same productivity by reproducing the body and its energies. "The crisp mountain air, combined with the physical exercise of traveling by auto, stage, afoot or on horseback, assures a hearty appetite three times a day and restful sleep at night," the reader is told. "A week or month in Glacier National Park will ginger you up, and enable you to recuperate your energies."[22]

Particularly curious is the way that these awkward ideological juxtapositions were inscribed in the parks from the outset. Early advocates for setting aside park lands argued not only that terrain like Yosemite, being an aesthetic object, by definition could not be productive, but furthermore that it was the *essential unproductivity* of the land itself that justified reserving it. John F. Sears quotes California senator John Conness as contending that terrain like Yosemite's was "'for all practical purposes, worthless.' It was not, in other words, fit for mining, agriculture, or similar pursuits. It could therefore be set aside without interfering with the economic development of the country."[23] The 1871 bill establishing Yellowstone and reflecting the interests of the Northern Pacific Railway and Jay Cooke & Co. would make the same case, classifying the area as a wasteland with no value for any directly economically productive ends.[24] The unusual value of the parks is thus rhetorically grounded in precisely their valuelessness.

Pro-parks ideologue Rinehart went so far as to claim of Glacier that "if the government had not preserved it, it would have preserved itself. No homestead would ever have invaded its rugged magnificence or dared its winter snows." She concludes: "But you and I would not have seen it."[25] Rinehart's glib boosterism, of course, obscures the real difference between Glacier "preserving itself" as a kind of inviolable exterior to modern life and of Glacier being reserved by national park policy to be managed for the purposes of tourism. It is this latter impulse to manage and order that which seems exterior to the limits of productivity that is not only at the heart of the discourse on park reserves, but is also definitive of modernity itself, as Martin Heidegger argues in his "The Question Concerning Technology." A mania for productive order, he suggests, requires that modern man redefine that which is alien as a "standing-reserve"; its mode of being consists in waiting to be put to some use. Such reserving, Heidegger posits, fundamentally alters that which is so reserved, as "whatever stands by in the sense of standing-reserve" is enclosed by the retraced line of productiveness, and henceforth "no longer stands over against us as object." The standing-reserve, Heidegger concludes, is an "*inclusive* rubric."[26] The notion of the reserve thus allows an exterior unproductivity to be folded into the interior of American modernity, and there be ordered and made productive. This logic of inclusion is transparently reiterated in the rhetoric of the proliferating park advertising of the early twentieth century, as the notion that the parks are a wild exterior recedes. The classic slogan "See America First"—a motto adopted for park promotions in 1905 and borrowed by Rinehart for the title of her 1916 volume, patently understands the parks as part of a confined national interior.[27]

As the celebration of exteriority is muted, so, too, does the value of living strenuously—of exertion and adventure of the sort once credited with amplifying vital reserves of corporeal energy—recede from the forefront of this discourse. Rinehart's text ambivalently registers this leisurely new dominant, at one point describing a rendezvous with her touring party as "disappointingly easy," and relating a revealing story, in which she asks her guide to help her find a bear that she might photograph in its natural habitat, as a souvenir of the true wild. Her seeming courage is played for comedy when the guide obligingly leads her to the refuse pile behind the lodge.[28] It is certainly the case that "roughing it" always involved a certain degree of bourgeois playacting, though many concur that a fundamental shift, both symbolic and practical, may be located around the turn of the century. "The Frontier has become conscious of itself," Frank Norris scoffed, noting that it "acts the part for the Eastern visitor."[29] Even acknowledging the roots of this tradition, it is nevertheless hard not to be struck by the degree to which ease displaces exertion as the salient principle of this discourse by the second decade of the twentieth century. Relaxation replaces revitalization; mere sport supplants strain.

One aspect of this general transition is signaled in the description of the parks as "scenic resources" by the Department of the Interior, which somewhat euphemistically represents the value of the parks as one demanding no labor, or at least supplants corporeal labors with those of a visual or spectacular character. This is echoed in the Great Northern's prolific advertising campaigns after 1914, which refer to the parks unthreateningly as "visual panorama[s]" or "floral garden[s]"—a veritable harvest of leisure awaiting cultivation by the cultivated. Simon Evans and Martin Spaul use a concept borrowed from Adorno—the *museal*—to describe the culturally mediated enjoyment so produced. Significantly, Adorno himself says of the term that it "describes objects to which the observer no longer has a *vital* relationship."[30] And thus, as is indicated in the utopian Great Northern pamphlet *Vacations for All*, a parks outing will offer not just golf, tennis, fishing, and photography, but also a good share of "just plain loafing."[31] A brochure promoting walking tours similarly constructs its audience as idle, promising that in the evenings "the main camp fire is lighted and we have two hours of [the] loafing, smoking, and story-telling so dear to the hiker's heart." Of course, the carefully measured "two hours" appears to demystify any promise of leisure without measure, or of ease for its own sake (though elsewhere the address appeals to "visitors who measure time in weeks of pleasure rather than the eons of science").[32]

The neutralization of the once-intimidating frontier and its repackaging as idle spectacle can only be understood within a larger ideological context, in which it is made to demonstrate the inevitability of a universal human progress predicated on the elimination not only of strain but also of those stubborn "other" populations—namely, Native Americans—that needed to be overcome. Shari Huhndorf's analysis of the "symbolic universes" constructed by the expositions of 1876 and 1893, for example, details the transformation of the representational strategies by which they produced a narrative of progressive, white, "Americanness."[33] Philadelphia's 1876 Centennial Exposition, which embraced "progress" as its dominant theme, imagines the implied futurity of a vital reserve yet to be fully exploited by geographical expansion, and realizable only by "placing racial others in the white nation's past." In contrast, at the Columbian Expo of 1893—at which the geographical exhaustion of the West was announced—"native peoples . . . figured as an integral part of white America's identity."[34] This potentially dangerous integration was managed by the spatial layout of the 1893 fair, which positioned the rationally ordered symmetries of the "White City" against the exotic subjects arrayed in the Midway Plaisance's "playground of the multitude," an integration that nevertheless in the same gesture effected a carefully orchestrated exclusion and quarantine of non-Anglo practices.[35] In so doing, the Chicago fair inscribed cultural difference as a distinction between the instrumental rationality of an assumedly homogeneous white viewing subject and its (reserved) other. Thereby distinguishing between productive epistemological order and the unaccountable play of ethnological chaos, the Chicago fair responded to the challenge of policing the increasingly permeable geographical and temporal frontiers distinguishing Anglo and non-Anglo life by foregrounding the antithesis between industry and idleness.[36]

Thus, while the Philadelphia fair plotted the two cultures as temporally separate (with the civilized white world historically supplanting and overcoming the native order that once threatened it), the Chicago expo mapped difference through a symbolic spatial separation. The deployment of a geographical imaginary dedicated to managing Native American integration is evident in concurrent mappings of the industry-versus-idleness boundary in the other "symbolic universes" available to the leisured white tourist. As Leigh Ann Litwiller Berte has argued, one consequence of the tourist economy's expansion at century's end was a "new form of geographical identity—spatial hybridity" that positions the tourist as "an alternative to the wanderer/drifter figure who pathologized mobility as well as to the period's popular organic inhabitant who remains rooted in a native place."[37] The tension, prevalent throughout the nineteenth century, between the attractions of idle nomadism and the cultural imperative of settled productivity, is defused by an emergent "destination geography"—a mapping of tourist space that reinforces a sense of regional authenticity and constructs tourist travel as above all teleological. The various points on the map were understood in this cartographic syntax as fixed localities marking an arrival—not as arbitrary stops along a leisurely ramble—thus satisfying the yearning for mobility while belying the idea that getting there is half the fun.

The implied industriousness of this tourism thus both vanquishes the potential productivities of "open" space and produces yet another relationship to a carefully contained idleness associated with the Native American and the western wild. As the promotion of the national parks as rail destinations exemplifies, idleness coexists with industry no longer as merely a recalcitrant otherness to be overcome, but as a set of practices enclosed within and conducive to productivity itself. Indian play—like playing at being Indians or "going native"—is thus located inside the healthy productivity of white recreations, and in fact, serves the work that they prioritize.[38]

Exemplarily, the Great Northern's later promotional campaigns feature a flyer, the *Great Northern Recreational Map of Glacier National Park*, that recodes Glacier's topography as a constellation of leisurely pastimes, cartoonishly illustrated with an eye toward the careful effacement of signs of strain or conflict. Bears are depicted outfitted for hiking and sightseeing, while mountain goats skate upon the ice of the Sperry Glacier; fish emerge halfway from the water waiting to be speared or netted. Helpful Indians pose for photographers when they are not busy caddying golf clubs or setting bowling pins. Note, in figure 10, how the parallel postures of the white golfer and native caddy, each troubling their foreheads at the lining up of a putt, suggest that, far from embodying an unaccountable unproductivity, the naïve native here instead has something to learn about the practice of productive leisure from the white sportsman.[39] As well-dressed visitors cut capers throughout the park, a profusion of cameras facilitates the preservation of these "scenic resources." And if even these modest rigors should demand too much activity from the potential tourist, the Great Northern finally seeks to remind the public (in its *Hotels and Tours* flyer) that "passengers who do not have time to stop off at Glacier National Park, by taking any of the three trains named above . . . will get a view of practically sixty miles of this great park."[40]

A complementary anecdote from the 1880s, related by J. Valerie Fifer, tells of a young man on his way out of Yellowstone who is asked by an

Figure 9. Great Northern Recreational Map of Glacier National Park (detail). Illustration: J. Scheuerle. Courtesy of Minnesota Historical Society, St. Paul, Minnesota. Mountain goats skate while a benevolent bear dispenses refreshments. No "liquid courage" will likely be needed in these tamed environs, however.

arriving visitor how he liked it. His response was pretty lukewarm. "It is very fatiguing," he replied, averring, after some hemming and hawing, that it was "worth going to see, and particularly as you have [already] come so far."[41] His fatigue was produced, it seems, by the long hikes between major sites in the park; it is surely of a different species than the bereft exhaustion attendant to such tourism today—or even in the leisurely days of 1914. Twentieth-century weariness was one born of the experience of the same, as increasingly the vital dangers of straddling the line of productiveness

Figure 10. Great Northern Recreational Map of Glacier National Park (detail). Illustration: J. Scheuerle. Courtesy of Minnesota Historical Society, St. Paul, Minnesota. Friendly natives help to line up a putt.

were recuperated into the idle pleasures of occupying what Fifer calls the "frontier of comfort."[42] Once domesticated, the lauded exteriority of the parks becomes contradictory, to the extent that it is folded into the regular rhythms of production and reproduction typical of the capitalist economy, and especially, the emergent leisure economy and its soothing rituals of consumption. The force of an unproductive wild that stood over and against mankind, in Heidegger's language, was neutralized with the transformation of that wild into merely a "standing reserve." And if even that—for one might wonder whether it can even be said to any longer have the strength to "stand," so accustomed does this vital reserve become to the consumerist repose made available by what eventually would be known as "America's playground."

Charlotte Perkins Gilman's Work Book

While the parks discourse ultimately addresses the industry/idleness tension through a complicated transformation into mere leisure of what was once strenuous, Charlotte Perkins Gilman's work on vital energies takes the opposite tack, that of reconceptualizing *all human activity as work*. Her project, explicitly driven as it is by the economic situation of women in the nineteenth century, begins with entirely different premises, but shares with these other discourses a certain notion of vital reserves. To her mind, as to any number of feminist economists then and now, it is hardly necessary to seek for energy reserves either deep in the moral and muscular recesses of the active subject or in the remote vales of Yosemite and Glacier—an even more profound reserve was always already at work, albeit much "closer to home." Indeed, the unproductivity of women— whether genuine, mannered, or merely mendaciously represented—occupies a privileged place in the lore of nineteenth-century productivity; it manifests both as the object of politicized cultural representations and as the topic of emergent analytic inquiries in the fields of society and political economy. Whether in the domestic sphere, in the mills, or on the social scene, women played a wide repertoire of culturally and economically indispensable roles that subjected their activity to negotiations of considerable complexity and variability.

The supposed unproductivity of women was constructed and policed in innumerable ways, a fact established by a number of nineteenth-century commentators who objected to the way that they were exchanged as valuable objects according to what would later be called social kinship structures, served as sites for the signifying of a husband's wealth (or as unproductive parasites upon it), or embodied an ideal purity untainted by industrialization—all of which cultural conventions took for granted women's passivity. At century's end, as it became more common for women—including middle-class and married women—to seize opportunities to work outside of the home by choice instead of necessity, it is unsurprising that the culture responded by insisting on an idealized feminine objectivity characterized by passivity, secondariness, and abstractedness from sites of true toil.[43] In economic terms profoundly relevant to the questions raised here, contemporary feminist criticism has built on nineteenth-century antecedents in arguing that the ideology of domesticity enshrined in the works of Catharine Beecher and others effectively defines "women's work"—in its various guises—as a clandestine source of value for capital, immeasurable and unremunerated, a reserve without which modern capitalism would be unthinkable. However, it is equally the case that the study of economics has systematically neglected women's work (on the grounds that economically significant activity must "result in transferable objects for an explicit exchange price"), and that the lived experience of cultural production reflects an assumption of women's unproductivity.[44]

As Marx reported, similarly noting the virtually limitless productive potentials of women's work, "the factory workers in France call the prostitution of their wives and daughters the nth working hour, which is literally correct."[45] In so defining the women's work of prostitution, Marx points up not only a continuity between all forms of value-creating activity, but also a difference. On the one hand, this "prostitution," he says, "is only a specific expression of the general prostitution of the labourer";[46] unlike labor more generally, however, in its potential infinitude the nth working hour transcends measurability. It is a pure surplus, a seemingly inexhaustible reserve. Christine Delphy, assessing the productivity of the care economy, or what she calls the "family mode of production," similarly points out the continuity between compensated work and the invisible, unremunerated work performed by women, suggesting that "there is no essential difference between activities which are said to be 'productive' (like growing wheat and milling it) and domestic activities which are called 'non-productive' (like cooking the self-same flour)."[47] However arbitrary, this sexual division of labor distinguishing "productive" from "non-" or "re-productive" activity, continues to this day to be one of the more fundamental structuring principles of Western "civilization."[48]

At the end of the nineteenth century, Charlotte Perkins Gilman was among those who most pointedly noted the existence of this economic reserve produced by women's work, as the frugal explanation supplied by Mary Ann Dimand indicates: "[Gilman] described the contemporary status of woman as characterized by male appropriation of her produced surplus. Not only did men coopt women's work, but women could not be said to be paid for it at all. Since payments to women by their husbands (or fathers) did not depend on the quantity or quality of their work, and could be withheld at will, these payments were pure transfers. All of the products of the labor of women in the traditional home were surplus and extracted."[49] The remedy Gilman proposed to this unpaid "extraction" was unsentimental: professionalize domestic service and subject it to market forces—a solution that she claimed would render the care economy more efficient and better executed. The fact that the idea of such an explicit surrender of the hearth to the logic of capital still elicits a kind of moral discomfort today testifies to the radicality of Gilman's thinking over a century ago.

Dimand rightly laments that though Gilman was among those who most vigorously inveighed against the arbitrary cheapening of the value of women's productivity by economic prejudices and cultural assumptions, her efforts "are now recognized as feminist documents, yet not considered as economics."[50] Nowhere has this been more persistent than in the case of what is probably Gilman's most experimental economic effort—1904's *Human Work*—which has hardly been deemed worthy of consideration at all. If Gilman, her credentials built on the ubiquity of her gothic tale "The Yellow Wallpaper" and her provocative *Women and Economics*, remains a feminist but not an economic thinker to us today, it is at least in some part due to the neglect of *Human Work*. But in this text it is precisely by reframing the whole question of work to deprioritize explicitly "feminist" concerns—leveraging her analysis into new economic and ontological territory upon the blunt declaration that "work, modern work, has no sex-connotation whatever"—that Gilman makes her most ambitious effort at a total theory of the meaning of human activity.[51]

Human Work is in some ways conventionally exemplary of the turn-of-the-century obsession, in various discourses, with themes of energy, exhaustion, and fatigue. But Gilman's account is philosophically quite distinct from other accounts of "vital reserves," in that she steadfastly avoids defining such vital energy as a hidden magazine of force, awaiting determination by discovery and conquest. Instead, bodily energy is here understood as something that is always already abundant in human life; human beings ignorantly misuse and fritter it away, however, due to a misrecognition of the extent to which it is already at our disposal. Gilman understands this energy as an immanent cause, always there, but visible only in its effects when it manifests in the material world as *work*. Hers is thus an economy of abundance, not, like the others, an economy of lack. Because she begins from the premise that this energy is inexhaustible, she can make claims about the infinite productive potentials of human work that are among the most utopian of her time.

For Gilman, exhaustion is a secondary concern; she rather emphasizes the positive potentialities of the body as a "thermodynamic machine" that converts "energy into use." As Anson Rabinbach has pointed out, this popular nineteenth-century notion of the universe as a field of energy had the consequence that all activity—whether biological or physical, bodily or mechanical, organic or inorganic—could be "reduced to its physical properties, devoid of [a moral or spiritual] context and inherent purpose. Work was universalized."[52] He goes on to explain that given these premises it is no longer possible to distinguish, as John Locke did, between the alienated and degraded "labor of the body" and the supposedly creative and autonomous "work of the hands." In the same way, the distinctions are blurred between mental and physical, or productive and "reproductive," activity. All activity may thus be defined as work.

Gilman develops this idea of the productive immanence of work into an elaborate metaphor in which the thermodynamic machine of the individual human body is both a component in, and a microcosm of, a larger social organism, itself a highly complex pulsing thermodynamic machine. The natural functioning of the human being—its mind, body, and hands— she suggests, is to contribute to the collective manifestation of productive energy; all human work is thus fundamentally social and shared, in contrast to our traditional, egoistic understanding of the binding relationship between individualized modern work and economic reward. According to Gilman, such selfish understandings of energy, in violation of work's primordially collective nature, are to the social body what disease is to the individual body.

Perhaps energized by this argument herself, Gilman declared in a letter just before her death in 1934 that this was her greatest book, and advised her interlocutor "to never mind about reading my books except *Human Work*."[53] Indeed, the ideas collected in *Human Work* represent the culmination of much of Gilman's mature thought. Journal entries dating to 1890 indicate her desire to write on its themes of waste, pain, and pleasure, and an 1891 note outlines what would become a formative contrast between "living and *earning* a living."[54] Yet for all this sustained effort, the book barely found a publisher, and then reached almost no audience. When Gilman pitched the manuscript to McClure, Phillips and Co. in 1903, she initially met with rejection, the publisher expressing disappointment that the book was not "more in the line of [her] others."[55] Because McClure did see some sales potential in another Gilman volume, *The Home*, she was able in April 1903 to leverage a publication deal for both books, on terms rather unfavorable to *Human Work*. Unlike *The Home*, which would pay immediate royalties on any copies sold, no royalties were to be paid on *Human Work* until at least 1,500 initial copies had been unloaded. Gilman's apparent faith that the work would sell itself was misplaced: according to a royalty report found in her papers, by July 1906 sales amounted to only about 600 copies. In the margin of the report, a jotting in Gilman's own hand records the sad calculation that 868 copies remained to be sold before the book would begin to be remunerative.[56]

The author's own acknowledgment of the myriad imperfections of this repetitive, confusing, and occasionally rebarbative book is palpable, when, after 182 pages, she finally announces what she calls her "central thesis concerning work." This thesis declares that "work is an expenditure of energy by Society in the fulfillment of its organic functions. It is performed by highly specialized individuals under press of social energy, and is to them an end in itself, a condition of their existence and their highest joy and duty" (*HW* 182). She likens the individual to a cell in an organism, one nodal point in the web of constant relationships through which social energy moves. Wherever human activity occurs, it draws on a shared "fund" of social energy, transmitting that energy between individuals through their constitutive, productive acts; energy, like the "business of the universe" that transmits it, is *conducted* (*HW* 104). The failure to work she condemns as an impediment to energy's natural course, resulting in displeasure for the individual, and waste, parasitism, or disease for the social organism.

Human work, then, engenders inexhaustible possibilities for social relationships to be formed and reformed by individual creative agents. These relations include the various practical interdependencies that at any given time make any one human life possible, but they also extend historically—since objects, institutions, and knowledge all represent accumulations of social energy expended prior. A created object is therefore not merely dead labor or a practico-inert entity; it is rather an expression of its producer's energy, and furthermore a persisting fund of renewed energy for its consumer, who in turn reproduces its energy for consumption by others. "The universe is an everlasting *production*," Gilman writes, describing how all human work unfolds along a plane of immanence that is both synchronic and diachronic, extending through space and time to unite the human community in collaborative productive relationships that are potentially limitless and infinitely renewable (*HW* 249).

The productive power of human work is intensified when individual bodies enter into such operational linkages with others, thus constituting ever more refined and efficient assemblages. As Gilman describes it, a body is powerful—that is, capable of *making exertions* or *receiving sensations*—only to the extent that it is articulated with other bodies. In one memorable instance, her anatomical metaphor for society almost seems to hearken back to Locke's aforementioned celebration of the "work of the hands": "A hand, taken separately, would have a certain contractile power," she writes, "but as connected with the arm it has far more, as connected with the general nervous system more yet" (*HW* 104). In the same way, a human being increases its powers through its connections with the agents and objects that populate the world that it inhabits.

When we follow this metaphor to its logical conclusion, we find that what Gilman describes is not at all the individuated body of the Enlightenment subject, the self-interested agent of classical economics, or the pleasure-seeking monad of hedonistic theory, but rather a fragmentary, heterogeneous assemblage that is simultaneously and invariably one component in a multitude of larger composites.[57] Gilman conceives of this corporate body not as a unitary agent, but rather as a functional concept distributed in relationships across space and time. In stressing the diversity and dynamism of these relationships, which extend along an inexhaustible continuum of potential linkages and practices, she effectively eluded the "productionist bias" of many invocations of the Marxist labor theory of value, which tend to privilege the *laboring* body over its other applications (though it should be noted that Marx, ever alert to the specificity of the realms of production, consumption, circulation, etc., himself often seems to describe a body that is "overdetermined" and lacking "a center or essential unity" other than that contingently engendered by a specific set of historical relationships).[58]

Understanding the productive body via this model not only challenges the economic orthodoxies of the nineteenth century, but also provides a valuable means to reconsider other turn-of-the-century discourses about the body and its productive energy, as Gilman demonstrates when she alludes, both directly and indirectly, to literary naturalism. One can hear the allusion faintly in her claim that "the Social Organism is as *natural* a life-form as fish, flesh, or fowl. It has been *naturally* evolved, its processes and appearances are as *natural* as those of any other part of creation" (*HW* 99, emphasis added). Moreover, at times she directly condemns the prejudices of literary contemporaries, and especially the lionization, by writers like Jack London, of a heroic, individuated subject—an ideological fetishization that she disparages as "social reversion." Observing that "current literature is full of this," she urges a rejection of the so-called "'call of the wild,' this tempting invitation to give it all up and go back to the beginning," in favor of acknowledging the subject's interdependent position within a complicated and advanced division of social labors (*HW* 103).

It makes sense that Gilman should invoke her literary contemporaries in this connection, given that naturalism, like realism before it, made all but explicit its own preoccupation with vital reserves, in its stated intention to more deeply mine the stuff of the everyday, to excavate deeper strata of human activity always present but misjudged as inconsequential, and to find there potential literary material. The experimental project of naturalism, as Frank Norris was fond of noting, is built out of those quotidian and unheroic pockets of the day's activity that fill the intervals between lunch and dinner.[59] But even more critical here is the fact that naturalism can also be read as advancing a theory of bodily energy. Nowhere is this more pronounced than in the convention of the "plot of decline," as it has been theorized by Philip Fisher. Isolating the collapse of George Hurstwood in Theodore Dreiser's *Sister Carrie* as a typical, though highly self-conscious, instance of this convention, Fisher argues that the naturalist novel's narrative of decline is based "on the history of the body, and not that of social position."[60] A reading of the novel informed by Gilman's arguments suggests, however, that these two bodies—the natural and the social—are necessarily inseparable.

Budgetary Expenditures: Dreiser's Hand-Wringing

> Seventy-two in fall. What I must face is lessening power. . . . Think I could still rise if fed—stimulated in contact with thinkers and doers.
> —Charlotte Perkins Gilman, "Thoughts and Figgerings," 1932

> Our energy-budget is like our nutritive budget.
> William James, "The Energies of Men," 1906

Dreiser's apparent theory of the energies of the human organism describes, with characteristic ponderousness, how the increasing powers of youth tip into inevitable exhaustion and decline with the passage of time. He explains it most overtly like this: "A man's fortune or material progress is very much the same as his bodily growth. Either he is growing stronger, healthier, wiser, as the youth approaching manhood, or he is growing weaker, older, less incisive mentally, as the man approaching old age. There are no other states" (SC, 230). Building on this remarkable passage, Philip Fisher represents Dreiser's argument as implying the "inevitable fall of vitality over time," aging as an ineluctable downslope indifferent to other agents or objects ("neither the theft nor the affair")—and thus he reproduces the tendency to understand human nature as essentially atomized instead of collectively fused with the total social organism.[61]

But Dreiser's novel is somewhat more ambivalent on this question. He in fact repeatedly implies that Hurstwood's decay in the latter half of the novel is contingent, not necessary; it unfolds not according to a logic of inevitable individual decay, but rather as a consequence of Hurstwood's toxic articulation with the rest of the social body. For example, directly after the aforementioned passages that introduce the theory of natural decline, Dreiser qualifies his argument with a discussion of the interdependencies within the social organism: "If each individual were left absolutely to the care of his own interests . . . his fortune would pass as his strength and will." He suggests that a fortune, like a man, is a fund of stored social energy, each being "an organism which draws to itself other minds and other strength than that inherent in the founder . . . it becomes allied with young forces, which make for its existence even when the strength and wisdom of the founder are fading" (*SC* 230). For Dreiser, then, a man is a node in a network of relationships that links him to others, to objects, and to history; he is a relay point for money, energy and the other business of the universe.

Furthermore, it is possible to trace in Dreiser's novel a treatment of such operational linkages as simultaneously both anatomical and social. In a peculiar echo of Gilman and Locke both, Hurstwood's decline is embodied, so to speak, in the particular figure of *hands*—the feature via which the body most regularly interacts with what is alien to it, whether to seal a business deal or to convey a loving caress. Consider how, in the novel's opening movements, hands mediate relations between people, and in so doing form assemblages that—for better or worse—amplify total productive power. At times, the economic quality of these linkages is explicit, as when the hand of a foreman is depicted resting with panoptic gravity on the shoulder of a working girl in the shoe factory (*SC* 26), or when Carrie fumbles at her machine, and "a great hand appear[s] before her" to set a clamp (*SC* 27).

At the end of the working day, "a young machine hand" offers to accompany her into the streets (*SC* 30), the appearance of this "hand" effectively pointing to the prospect of social and erotic pleasure. The business of the workplace later is symbolically coupled with such pleasure, in Dreiser's detailed descriptions of hands involved in romantic transactions. Remember how Carrie's first serious suitor, Drouet, presses money into her palm and subsequently wins her "affection" (*SC* 45):

> She had her hand out on the table before her. They were quite alone in their corner, and he put his larger, warmer hand over it.
>
> "Aw, come, Carrie," he said, "what can you do alone? Let me help you."

He pressed her hand gently and she tried to withdraw it. At this he held it fast, and she no longer protested. Then he slipped the greenbacks he had into her palm and when she began to protest . . . [h]e made her take it. She felt bound to him by a strange tie of affection now. (*SC* 45)[62]

Later, the relentless creepiness of Hurstwood's busy hands produces a similar effect as Carrie gradually aligns herself with his power in chapter 12. At first, when he touches her hand, she "merely smiled." But soon Hurstwood is described as finding in her "so much . . . to applaud," conjuring, in an anticipation of Carrie's later success on the stage, an image of his two hands clapping together (note, however, that in his attraction "there was not the slightest *touch* of patronage"). When she feels the "invisible" hand of his desire touching her, "she relaxed . . . *giving him strength*." Hurstwood, having then "felt" that he is the master of the situation, "reached over and touched her hand"; then, after "extending his hand" to her, he "retained a hold on her hand," and, finally, "*she was touched*" (*SC* 84–86, emphasis added). And so on: as their romantic bond tightens, their corporeal assemblage is consolidated, and Hurstwood's powers increase, synched up as they are to Carrie's own capacity to be herself affected, bound by affection, and energized, by his touch.[63]

If this symbolism seems somewhat, um, heavy-handed, in the novel's first half, consider how differently it functions in the second half, where hands serve the narrative of Hurstwood's decline by betokening poisonous assemblages and diminutions of power that symptomatize the pathologies of the social organism. This is clear in the scenes of Hurstwood's hapless poker playing in chapter 37—in which he "tries his hand" and loses—and the critical scene where Hurstwood, scabbing for work during a transit strike, joins the other "green hands" (*SC* 288) driven by want. There, he awkwardly "laid hand to the [throttle] lever," and clumsily struggles to "handle a brake" (*SC* 290)—instances of a perverse articulation of the body to the labor objectified in tools. His unsmiling companion trains him in by showing him all the "handles" and how to manipulate them, advising in summary that Hurstwood has "got to get the knack of working both arms at once" (*SC* 291). After his bungling of this assemblage (an experience that earns him a bodily injury, it might be noted), complacency sets in, and Hurstwood submits and acclimates to his idleness. His enervation and his aversion to effort are signaled by his complacently "folding his hands behind his back" while on an "idle" urban stroll (*SC* 307), echoing two other scenes where "folding the hands" signifies his impotence—that is, when he folds them to helplessly "wait" for a job (*SC* 283), and when he folds them "weakly" in the shame of being caught in his dishabille by Mrs. Vance (*SC* 255).

Such folding, echoing the gesture made in a game of cards when a gambler has lost, enables Hurstwood to produce no assemblages—only a closed system of egoistic feedback sundered from the real energies of the social world. Of course it is in this utter and complete isolation that Hurstwood's decline culminates; alone and impotent, he captions the scene of his own suicide, muttering "what's the use?" (*SC* 353). When we are gripped by the existential drama of the novel's close, it is easy to overlook the fact that in it, Hurstwood finally poses the ultimate economic question; he puts the very productive value of his isolated existence into doubt, before taking his life, as it were, by his own hand.

The exhaustion of Hurstwood's individual "energy-budget," and his inability to replenish it via linkages to the "fund" of social energies around him, runs parallel to his economic fortunes. Reinforcing this parallel is the fact that throughout the novel, Dreiser's exploration of energy also invokes another kind of social fund endowed with potential power—that of money.[64] Money, in Carrie's classic description, is "stored energy," serving both as a repository of indeterminate imagined possibilities and as the motive force Dreiser's characters ceaselessly seek to realize (money is "something everybody else has and I must get," as Carrie understands it [*SC* 45]). She understands money as a store of absent potential, as a vital reserve with a power analogous to that of shared social energy. But Dreiser's treatment of money elsewhere in the novel insists—like Gilman's exploration of work and energy—that the powers of money are not merely an absent and latent potential, but rather a force that is in fact *always active and present*, and thus ceaselessly and almost magically determinant of human activity.

This ubiquitous monetary power is perhaps best understood via the theory of money advanced by George Simmel in 1889 and 1890. Money, to him, is what mediates social relationships, an infinitely pliable connective tissue of the modern social body. Arguing that money's character is that of an "actus purus," its restless movement is nothing less than that "in which everything else that is not in motion is completely extinguished." While it is said of money that it can be saved, hoarded, stashed, or stored, even in a "state of repose" it exerts an effect that "arises out of anticipation of its further motion."[65] Money never sleeps, Simmel suggests—even in repose it appears to always have one eye open to the possibilities it might realize.

As Simmel goes on to argue, the force exercised by money undermines conventional assumptions about *all* property; property is never merely idle. Typically, men's confrontations with things involve acts of acquisition, or of enjoyment; we are used to imagining these as active engagements with the object world. But the *possession* of things is a mystification of these active relationships—for possession misleadingly appears to us not "as movement but as a stationary, and, as it were, substantial condition."[66] In contrast to this assumption, it must however be noted that economic value is never "substantial," essential, or innate. The value of money is like that of linguistic signs; as Marx and Saussure have demonstrated, it is always differentially produced via dynamic and merely formal relationships with other signs or other money values, determining the meaning of even the most apparently transcendental signified or the most seemingly practico-inert entity.[67] To imagine possession as a *substantial* condition—that is, a state of affairs immune to this dynamic differential movement—is to falsely abstract it from the relationships that define symbolic or economic value.

Simmel's summary on this point proceeds by revealing the erroneous opposition between passivity and activity that lies at the core of such a misapprehension: "The habit of considering possession as something passively accepted, as the unconditionally complying object which, to the extent that it is really possession, does not require any activity on our part, is false."[68] Far from being merely dormant and passive, then, objects of property necessarily imply different types of activity, as any type of ownership is always conjoined with movements that anticipate and movements that go beyond it (in a fashion analogous to the way in which a commodity invites us to mystify and ignore the human relationships that enable its production and consumption). Static possession is only an imagined abstraction naming the aggregate of individual acts by which it may be brought about.

This no doubt coincides with Carrie's definition of money as "something . . . I must get," wherein the possible futures implied in money inform her activity in the present. It furthermore suggests another way of reading Dreiser's predilection toward images of ceaseless movement throughout the book: the incessant rocking of Carrie's chair, the comings and goings of trains, the agency of commodities that speak, beckon, and resist their human interlocutors, and especially the "superfluous action" (*SC* 183) taken by Hurstwood when he fatefully looks into the hotel safe—where a stash of stored energy awaits him, "his eye always seeing the money in a lump, his mind always seeing what it would do" (*SC* 183). Hurstwood encounters this money as a reserve that is at once inert and simultaneously, omnipotently and fatefully, active. For all of its seeming dormancy, it nevertheless affects him. Wavering in his ethical stance, he is startled to find that despite the narrator's claim that "he was quite alone" (*SC* 184), he is actually in the presence of something that determines his action.

Hesitant, hounded by the ungovernable noise of his conscience, "he was tense, as if *a stern hand* had been laid on his shoulder" (*SC* 184, emphasis added). Oscillating back to his desire to make off with the loot, he finds that that inert lump of money, despite being "so smooth, so compact, so portable" (*SC* 185), will nevertheless not fit in his pocket; it will not readily submit to an assemblage with his body. Another option occurs to him: "His *hand satchel! * To be sure, his *hand satchel*" (*SC* 185, emphasis added). One of the features of his theft that has interested critics has been that it is basically passive—"while the money was in his hand the lock clicked. It had sprung! Did he do it?" (*SC* 185)—but with Simmel in mind we must acknowledge how Hurstwood's possession of the money can never be said to be separate from the acts leading up to it (the wavering and various vacillations), nor from those which follow as the money determines his subsequent course—when, "at once, he became a man of action" (*SC* 186). His paralysis overcome, Hurstwood finds in the stored energy of money a galvanizing second wind.

Hurstwood's misadventures with money make literal what elsewhere in the novel is implied. The modern metropolis is depicted as an enveloping repository of social energies that are embodied in things and money, and are transmitted in and through the ceaseless activity of human beings. Even at their most seemingly idle and passive, humans and objects are dynamic conduits for this energy, whether metabolic or catabolic. Isolating the notion of the reserve, then, helps us to better understand the investments—literal and philosophical—not only of Dreiser's characters but also of those many who struggled with the question of energy at the turn of the century. Perplexed by the internal contradictions of the conventional opposition between productivity and unproductivity, and baffled especially by its embodiments on not just the individual, but also the social and national level, these works wrestle with an interconnected and independent modern world mediated by invisible forces, unknown powers, and a productive activity increasingly regarded as ceaseless.

The effort to explain these forces ultimately echoes Carrie Meeber's confusion upon her first arrival in Chicago, where the city's enigmatic "power and force" renders her both fascinated and helpless: "Those vast buildings, what were they? These strange energies and huge interests, for what purposes were they there? She could have understood the meaning of a little stone-cutter's yard at Columbia city, carving little pieces of marble for individual use, but when the yards of some huge stone corporation came into view . . . it lost all significance in her little world" (*SC* 12). Though the naïve Carrie is capable of making sense of production undertaken as an *individual* exertion—in the (very) concrete work of the Columbia City stonecutter—she strains to comprehend the more abstract significance of the "huge stone corporation" she encounters in Chicago. It is the city's *corporateness*—its assembling of the myriad productivities of diverse and disparate individuals into an interconnected social body— that ensures that its "strange energies and huge interests" remain for her at first only the haziest reality. Into this "vast" and yet "far removed" repository of social energies, she must find a productive way to insert herself and her activity: "She sank in spirit inwardly and fluttered feebly at the heart as she thought of entering any one of those mighty concerns and asking for something to do—something that she could do—anything" (*SC* 12). With her successful incorporation into the social body of the modern metropolis, Carrie would join those others who pondered over the magical forces of modernity, crossing the line of productiveness only to confront new conceptions of energy and money that revealed work yet to be done.

5

Conclusion

Idle Thoughts and Useless Knowledge in the American Renaissance, and Beyond

> Free time then does not merely stand in opposition to labor. In a
> system where full employment itself has become the ideal, free time
> is nothing more than a shadowy continuation of labor.
>
> —Theodor W. Adorno, "Free Time," 1969

This study is grounded by the premise that an enriched understanding of the cultural function of unproductivity depends on resisting
the simple binaries that oppose industry to idleness, unproductivity to
productive labor, and "free time" to work time. Adorno's blunt reminder
of this principle is appropriate here, not only for its forceful condemnation
of this traditional opposition between work and its other, but also because
a serious consideration of his work forces us to rethink how this binary
has grounded much of the intellectual agenda of Western modernity, and
no less the critical projects of American studies. A criticism obedient of
the limits of productivity reproduces this central problem of nineteenth-
century America, but also reproduces "nineteenth-century America" as a
limiting object of thought. This final chapter will reevaluate the productivity of thought itself—and its capacity to generate presumably useful
knowledge—and in the process open some of the hoariest of American
"Renaissance" texts to both an improved conception of activity and an
emergent conception of the field's extended horizons.

A contextualization of Adorno alongside Thoreau, Melville, and Hawthorne is not as improbable as it might initially seem. His critical theory
has consistently attracted charges of passivity, stunted political commitment, and—even in his own words—"resignation" in the face of the

visceral modern imperative to act. However, as is demonstrated by Ross Posnock's compelling call to recuperate Adorno—alongside other modern figures whose work lacked a commitment to connecting thought to instrumental action—it is possible to avoid "interpreting this absence negatively, as political paralysis or negativism" and to instead regard such recalcitrant thought as itself an experiment with the possibilities of "new forms of human agency and political action that acquire power and value by deliberately eluding identification and direct affiliation."[1] According to Posnock, Adorno's rejection of merely instrumental thought aligns him with the epistemological skepticism of American Renaissance thinkers, sharing their pursuit of an "energy in impotence" and a "power in refusal."[2] This kind of thinking regards theory as itself practical activity. It thereby renews the challenge to reconsider the ever-tenuous boundary traditionally drawn between theory and practice, a reconsideration aided by an understanding of the productivity and the unproductive in nineteenth-century America.

Posnock, tracing the kinship between Frankfurt-style Critical Theory and American Pragmatism, models an Americanist criticism that militates against both hermetic national boundaries and a rigid synchronic periodization. In the process, he is able to describe a network of delitescent resonances that draws "nineteenth-century America" into an extended set of cultural and critical problematics, thereby liberalizing the "span" of American studies.[3] The choice of Adorno in particular—whose thought is relentless in its refusal of identity and in its insistence upon a continual regeneration of thinking from beyond its own limits—aptly challenges the principle of assimilation common both to systemic thought and to American national mythology. His appearance here, perhaps unexpected, is nevertheless a necessary experiment, despite (or in fact because of) the conventional classification that dismisses him as a culturally chauvinistic exponent of anti-Americanism.[4] In putting him into dialogue with the thinkers of the American Renaissance—those so long regarded as the most American of all—these last sections will explore the improbable kinship born of their shared effort to define new relationships to space, to time, and to the "outside" of thought. In so doing, it promises to bare the epistemological and even ontological limits which, enforced by the productivist ethos, define not only the objects of modern knowledge, but also the very practice of thought.

Adorno and the Play of Shadows

In Adorno, the productivity of the unproductive operates under the cover of work's shadow.[5] The highly rationalized conditions of modern work, he argues, become the model for a new kind of leisure that merely reflects the disciplinary and administered imperatives of late capitalism. In filling so-called "free time" with mere opportunities for commodity consumption or rationalized recreation, industrial leisure represents the logical culmination of nineteenth-century impulses to render free time productive. Such free time increasingly becomes a realm of illusory and orchestrated liberty; it is "enjoyed" only as an abstraction, indifferent to the contents of activity. Such professedly "free" activity, as he notes in one of his *Minima Moralia*, can be little more than *re*-activity; it constitutes merely a "reflex-action" that is "compulsively maintained even in the weary pauses [of] a production rhythm imposed heteronomously on the subject."[6] Quarantined into such intervals and rationalized by the culture industrial apparatus, "unproductive" activity is neutralized; its autonomy, and hence its critical potential, are sacrificed as it is rendered secondary to an economic production now naturalized as the fundamental human trait.

Almost like an eclipse of the sun makes the uncannily lit world seem at once familiar and strange, so too does the making-productive of free time leave oddly indistinct that which seems closest to the modern subject—the very value of his own activity. When the boundary between work and leisure is thereby blurred, one may easily be taken for the other. Adorno senses a logic of mass deception lying behind this: "in secret," he suggests, "the contraband of modes of behavior proper to the domain of work, which will not let people out of its power, is being smuggled into the realm of free time."[7] The ubiquitous euphemism—"free time"—conceals how the invisible, intangible, and immeasurable productivities of leisure lend themselves to exploitation by the economic machinery of modernity. Though this particular shadow has grown longer and more encompassing with the sun now low on the horizons of late capitalism, the discussions in the preceding chapters are intended to suggest how it has loomed over the history of capitalist production, including the idle high noons of early industrialism. Now, like then, the fact that such clandestine production is neither necessarily intentional nor immediately visible hardly means that it is not real and truly productive.

Time and again, it is *shadows* that Adorno invokes when discussing the relationship between work time and free time and between necessity and liberty. The figure appears in numerous passages in his *Minima Moralia*, coloring their lament about the damage already done to free dispensation of time and activity, and intensifying their gloomy foreboding about a modern future envisioned as the eternal return of Monday morning. In the bourgeois world Adorno describes, the dichotomy of work and freedom is hypostatized as the natural order of a universe that is both economic and moral. The embrace of leisure as work's reward (and of work as penance for leisure) seems to so firmly calibrate the rhythms of modern activity that their endless alternation appears immutable.

In another context, Adorno diagnoses this mentality as part of a psychological and social condition called the "bi-phasic paradigm."[8] This syndrome names the enduring belief—maintained by subjects whose business and personal lives alike are determined only by the form of work—in an illusory sense of the depth and diversity of their activity. This illusion, Adorno argues, is created by the simple expedient of splitting the day's activity into two spheres—one for the self at leisure, the other for the self at work. Constructions of this temporality insist upon the purported power of free time to, say, magically transform the ruthless businessman into a sensitive lover after dark (and usually with the benevolent aid of some reasonably priced and readily available consumer good); in the process, not only is an alibi provided for the inhuman mentality required of business, but the basic opposition between the two spheres is hegemonically enshrined as fundamental.

An even more profound consequence of the bi-phasic paradigm, however, is its tendency to denigrate activity that unfolds outside of the templates of ostensibly productive work. "Free time" is given over to activities that are, by definition, insignificant—"hobbies" that kill time instead of realizing its radical potentials, or "interests" that, producing no direct values, are judged inconsequential. Even as such hobbies and interests strive toward some kind of dignity by adopting the pretense of being meaningful at a personal level, they purchase their social acceptability at the high cost of achieving nothing, and thus must be content with being mere "pseudo-activity." The tinkering of the hobbyist is thus little more than a harmless diversion; such activities function as mere "fictions and parodies of the same productivity which society on the one hand incessantly calls for, but on the other holds in check and, as far as the individual is concerned, does not really desire at all."[9] Of course, pseudo-activity *is* paradoxically productive, to the extent that it constructs subjects submissive to the fleeting pleasures of industrial "fun"—willing to exchange consumer dollars for escapist diversion—and hence to the existing order.

Elsewhere in Adorno, we find that even the simplest idle pleasures— swimming, enjoying a stroll—are overshadowed by the pace and punctiliousness of an administered everyday life. Thus does Adorno's nemesis return in the *Minima Moralia* meditation entitled "More haste, less speed"; there, the promise of the archetypal leisurely ramble is ruined by the fascistic felt need to get somewhere: describing the everyday "terror" of "someone running after a bus," Adorno suggests that "the victim's fall is already mimed in his attempt to escape it. . . . He has to look ahead, can hardly glance back without stumbling, *as if treading the shadow of a foe* whose features freeze the limbs."[10] Similar in spirit is Adorno's treatment of an appealing passage in Maupassant, where the true liberation of activity from necessity is described as a state of harmony that is as enchanting as it is impossible to attain. Such a condition, he suggests, would require an entirely new concept of pleasure: "Enjoyment itself would be affected, just as its present framework is inseparable from operating, planning, having one's way, subjugating. *Rien faire comme une bête*, lying on water and looking peacefully at the sky, 'being, nothing else, without any further definition and fulfillment,' might take the place of process, act, satisfaction, and so truly keep the promise of dialectical logic that it would culminate in its origin."[11] Lying on water, looking peacefully at the sky— only in such a state might the dialectic resolve itself. But the shadow of industriousness intervenes, rendering such harmony inaccessible.

Moreover, in invoking here the "promise of dialectical logic," Adorno's rumination on pleasure also highlights the homologous relationship between the broken promise of leisure and that of a freely exercised intellectual method. For industrious rationality likewise jeopardizes the integrity of intellectual practice, itself vulnerable to work's shadow. "Everybody must have projects all the time. The maximum must be extracted from leisure," he complains, going on to add that "*the shadow of all this falls on intellectual work. It is done with a bad conscience, as if it had been poached from some urgent, even if only imaginary occupation. To justify itself in its own eyes it puts on a show of hectic activity performed under great pressure and shortage of time, which excludes all reflection, and therefore itself.*"[12] It is not enough, moreover, to suggest that intellectual activity has fallen under the shadow of production, in the sense that such activity must adjust itself to the imposition of the bottom line from without (a condition that can readily prove inimical to the pleasures of thought, as anyone working in the academy today can attest). Even more critically, the very practice of thought is invested and structured *from within* by the productivist ethos, such that the "labor of the concept" reproduces the formal structures proper to other work. Adorno thus detects a correlation between the way that modern work provides the abstract template for all activity, and the structuring of systemic thought by the formal architecture of the Hegelian dialectic, the latter emphasizing the synthetic product of thought in a simplified dialectical resolution, rather than insisting on the indissolubly negative moment of its process.

Because the science of dialectics cannot be sundered from instrumentality, it is "due for an accounting," as Adorno combatively declares in the opening pages of his *Negative Dialectics*. "One who submits to the dialectical discipline has to pay dearly in the qualitative variety of experience," he argues, noting that pleasure is suffocated by both dialectics and cultural administration, the two appearing as distinct facets of the same historical event. "In the administered world the impoverishment of experience by dialectics, which outrages healthy opinion, proves appropriate to the abstract monotony of that world."[13] Whether a thinking freed of the burden of instrumental "usefulness" might preserve its force in the face of an administered culture is a question similarly posed by the writers of the American Renaissance, in their experiments, at the dawn of the modern age, with the limits of thought.

On the Diffuseness of Useless Knowledge: Thoreau's Skeptical Dream-Work

> They had no idle thoughts, and no one without could see their work, for their industry was not as in knots and excrescences embayed.
> —Henry David Thoreau, "Walking," 1862

Thoreau's 1862 essay "Walking" echoes many of the themes discussed in earlier chapters, famously describing his strolls amid "the desert, the sea, the wilderness" as uncharted "sauntering"—pointed detours from the industrious road to improvement. The term, Thoreau points out, is replete with connotations of both holy pilgrimage and homelessness. The saunter facilitates thought, and frees one from the constraints of civilization through contact with the organic logics of another, natural, order. Such is Thoreau's claim in a provocative scene near the essay's close, when he happens upon an imaginary family lodged in the Concord woods, a family who seemed "to recline on the sunbeams" in such blissful calm that "nothing can equal the serenity of their lives." These exemplars of Thoreau's ideal nevertheless "had no idle thoughts": "They are of no politics. There was no noise of labor. I did not perceive that they were weaving or spinning. Yet I did detect, when the wind lulled and hearing was done away, the finest imaginable sweet musical hum—as of a distant hive in May—which perchance was the sound of their thinking."[14] Despite the vividness of the depiction—which effectively resignifies the industrious "hive of activity" as a noninstrumental site—Thoreau's access to this pastoral panorama is nevertheless blocked, as this noble, idle production recedes into the dim recesses of memory. "It is only after a long and serious effort to recollect my best thoughts that I became again aware of their cohabitancy," he explains.[15]

Seeking respite from the world in the sweet musical hum of this Concord hive, Thoreau describes his geographical withdrawal from society also as a sojourn on the intellectual frontier: it is "the sound of . . . thinking" that envelops him at the line of productiveness. Having staked the essay's rhetorical success on such nonalienated thinking, the fuzziness of his recollection is suggestive; the essay's promised withdrawal from society's ills ambiguously terminates in this unrealized dream space, where "there was no noise of labor," and the certainty of "perceiving" is supplanted by the possibility of "imagining." That it is precisely labor—alienated labor—which Thoreau seeks to flee is established when one considers "Walking" in connection with "Life Without Principle," an exoteric piece published posthumously in the *Atlantic* in 1863. There Thoreau proposes that we "consider the way in which we spend our lives" in a world reduced to "a place of business" (and of busy-ness): "What an infinite bustle! . . . There is no Sabbath," he exclaims. "It would be glorious to see mankind at leisure for once. It is nothing but work, work, work. I cannot easily buy a blank-book to write thoughts in; they are commonly ruled for dollars and cents.[16] Where the ellipsis intervenes there runs this passage: "I am awakened almost every night by the panting of the locomotive. It interrupts my dreams." Again, Thoreau's ruminative repose is aborted; this time the furtive dream of idleness is frustrated by the locomotive, unmistakably emblematic of industry and "incessant business."

There follows a series of dialectical reversals that playfully demonstrate not only the malleability of the concept of "idleness" but also the superficiality of "industry." Thoreau avers that accepting surveying work, along with compensation, will qualify him as "an industrious and hard-working man," yet to seek out what he calls "real profit" provokes only disparaging accusations of idling.[17] Later, Thoreau assails "the ways in which most men get their living, that is, live," condemning their efforts as "mere makeshifts, and a shirking of the real business of life."[18] The economically productive life of the industrious man appears as a living death: "the *real* business of life" and "*real* profit" are the province of the man who seeks no gain.

Having destabilized these seemingly self-evident economic categories, Thoreau goes on to demonstrate their myriad implications, rather practically asserting that "we tax ourselves unjustly. There is a part of us which is not represented. It is taxation without representation." This claim raises not only the obvious political question, but, in this context, also conjures an economic meaning, for in both cases society runs up against imposed productivist limits to truly representing the meaning of men's activity. That activity which is *taxing*—laborious, the product of an external imposition—is unjustly degraded by its translation into an inadequate economic representation. In both aspects, the unrepresentable—whether a structure of political feeling that precedes and exceeds representation in civil society, or an activity that cannot be reduced to instrumental measure—perseveres as a remainder that haunts Thoreau's unrecollectable, unharnessable imagination. Thus may Thoreau reverse the stigma associated with idleness: "To have done anything by which you earned money *merely* is to have been truly idle or worse. . . . Those services which the community will most readily pay for, it is most disagreeable to render. You are paid for being something less than a man."[19] With the wage comes "something less": a "true" idleness, which stifles real, creative, and productive potentials.

In spite of (or perhaps in keeping with) his attempt to point toward that fuzzy remainder, Thoreau's resistance to the industrious spirit at times literally goes nowhere. His disavowals of instrumentalized "facts," the abstract meaninglessness of "news," and the hurry and bustle of frantic activity resembling that of "flies about a molasses-hogshead," lead him to extremes of indifferent idleness. "If I could command the wealth of all the worlds by lifting my finger, I would not pay such a price for it," he boasts, adding that "I would not run round a corner to see the world blow up."[20] Nagged by the trifling distractions of current events or the allure of wealth, Thoreau's only dignified rejoinder is that of complete inactivity—represented in these hyperbolic devices that puncture the seeming gravity of worldly interests—and a stopping short of even lifting a finger. In the obscenity of that (non-) gesture, Thoreau signals his dissatisfaction with compromise, but complete inactivity seems irreconcilable with his previous exhortations to active withdrawal. A tension thus pervades these pieces, as the horizon toward which Thoreau aspires to flee is distant and always compromised, whether by the locomotive's nightly clamor across the wilderness's dreamscape or by the wage that cripples the freedom of activity.

Thoreau's mischievous tone combats, with literary play, the limits imposed by work. It also designates his invocations of free activity as not necessarily—or at least not entirely—a grieving for some type of wild thinking that has been vanquished by instrumentality. Instead, his paradoxical reversals and ironic spirit animate unrealized possibilities of thought that, though nebulous, are nonetheless quite present to him; they mark out the coexistence of multiple orders of perception in one space and time. Such a co-presence of incommensurable ideas manifests when he uses analogies of space and mobility to describe his flight into thought: "Our very intellect shall be macadamized, as it were,—its foundation broken into fragments for the wheels of travel to roll over; and if you would know what will make the most durable pavement, surpassing rolled stones, spruce blocks, and asphaltum, you have only to look into some of our minds which have been subjected to this treatment so long."[21] Rejecting roads, which "are made for horses and men of business," he opts instead for undirected rambles, an itinerary that plunges him into what Robert E. Abrams has termed a uniquely "Thoreauvian space" that is both geographical and conceptual. There, his poetics—embracing dynamic metamorphosis, misty imagery, and the power of the grotesque—reflect a faith that "the present moment itself, no matter how confidently visualized and persuasively conceived, potentially slips away from known images and interpretive profiles to give rise to wholly unsuspected possibilities of visualization and orientation."[22] A proper walk does not merely trace well-known roads of business, bustle, and "macadamized" intellect, but rather always risks dis-"orientation"—the possibility that the walker and his thought will not return from an encounter with the "irremediably negative dimension" inhering in "all positively conceived presence," as Abrams puts it.[23]

Thoreau mocks the conventional walks of the leisured bourgeoisie, in which we "come round again at evening to the old hearth-side from which we set out. Half the walk is but retracing our steps. We should go forth on the shortest walk, perchance, in the spirit of undying adventure, never to return—prepared to send back our embalmed hearts only as relics to our desolate kingdoms."[24] The problem with the "old hearth-side"—which, as Vincent Bertolini has argued, is a privileged location of bachelor meditation[25]—is that it is a space all too well-known. It is that domesticated terra cognita "from which we set out," and only the man who is ready to disavow its familiar confines and to "leave father and mother and brother and sister, and wife and child and friends, and never see them again" can escape a thought that is merely the habitual reproduction of the domestic ever-same.[26] In contrast to the pretense of the known that is embodied in the repose, stability, and certitude of the familiar antebellum hearth, Thoreau depicts an always not-yet-known world, the coordinates of which would be, in Abrams's words, "trans-imagistic, chronically in motion, and categorically unsettled at closer observational range."[27] There, the dynamic overlapping of infinite orders of possible perception produces something like a series of perceptual folds, the traversal of which only momentarily reveals certain transient vistas to the observer, only to have them flit away at the next turn. Such thought is always prepared to take new directions, to fix itself on new objects, and to apprehend many different registers of experience quilted upon them. Such Thoreauvian thinking, embodied in the unpredictable momentum of his literary play, constantly reveals the world to be not only always unsettled, but also always subject to the ongoing intellectual exercise of unsettling received categories and thereby unworking cherished concepts.

As Wai-Chee Dimock affirms in her provocative reading of Thoreau as a postnational thinker, "the map of the world that Thoreau lives in is probably not one that we recognize." For in this world, where not only is the Ganges River "in direct contact with Walden Pond," but where the exhaustive mapping of any space is necessarily impeded by the restless movement of thought, it is precisely re-cognition—that is, a knowing again of the same thing—that is rendered impossible.[28] Such a disavowal of recognition produces, in contrast to a useful knowledge, a different knowledge declared by Thoreau to be "useful in a higher sense": an opening of the limits of the known that embodies a "negative knowledge."[29]

For Thoreau, to walk without destination upon an unrecognizable topography is "perfectly symbolical" of the act of thinking differently, and "sometimes, no doubt we find it difficult to choose our direction, because it does not yet exist distinctly in our idea."[30] Ultimately, his description of such negative thinking, invoking the indirection of thought but also the multiplicity of its simultaneous possibilities, ultimately is what makes legible the dream—of repose, of serenity, of the imagined music of the family in the woods—with which this section began. For what is a "dream-work" other than a text constituted by unpredictable displacements (in which meaning shifts from object to object through reversals and negations) and by superimposed condensations (whereby overlapping registers of signification coexist in a single image)?[31] Thoreau's pretension to embody the universal tendency of the race continually announces a hope that in pursuing this dream, by teasing the established limits of geographical and intellectual mobility, such a utopian state can be approached, through the very tools and materials which lie at hand but remain unfamiliar. With that hopeful sentiment about the potentials, if not the actuality, of thought, he concludes "Life Without Principle" with a call to seize upon and bring to light the contents of those idle dreams: "Thus our life is not altogether a forgetting, but also, alas! to a great extent, a remembering, of that which we should never have been conscious of, certainly not in our waking hours."[32] Remembering and validating the unconscious content of those dreams of idleness means letting them destabilize the "waking hours" of our active lives, unworking the formal categories of thought that police the intellectual and practical limits of productivity.

Moby-Dick: From Thought to Naught

> The Whale can never be 'known' (i.e., caught) . . . as a symbol of the universe he shares the puzzlelike nature of the universe and is shadowy, elusive, paradoxical, inscrutable.
>
> —John Seelye, *Melville: The Ironic Diagram*, 1970

Resonating with Thoreau's barely expressible dreams of "negative knowledge" is Melville's similar inquiry into the shadowy nether realms of thought, in *Moby-Dick*. We saw in chapter 1 how "Bartleby, the Scrivener" attempted to document the spectral pressure of the unproductive on the measurable domain of productivity; *Moby-Dick* likewise defies any easily resolvable binary between these terms. While much has been made of the way that *Moby-Dick* addresses itself to the conditions of modern labor, it should be noted that this novel devotes special attention to modern

idleness as well—respecting its diversity and variety, and especially placing it in relation to the problem of knowledge. Two classic sections of Melville's masterpiece convey this text's skepticism about the utility of modern
knowledge—"The Whiteness of the Whale" and "The Mast-Head"—and
make available another way of understanding Melville's preoccupation
with the productivity of the unproductive.

That *Moby-Dick* is an inquiry into the limits of knowledge is a matter
of common critical concord. The character of Ishmael is depicted uncomfortably straddling two ways of knowing—empiricism and romanticism—
that are often represented as incompatible; he finds himself and the fanati-
cally instrumental Ahab wedded, in Michael Gilmore's words, as "partners
in an epistemological odyssey."[33] Unsurprisingly, the "ways of knowing"
available to the *Pequod*'s crew—like their ways of doing anything else—
have historical limits. These limits, repeatedly sketched by Melville as
grey areas, dimnesses, and shadows, threaten knowledge itself. In the fer-
tile passages bearing on the whiteness of the whale, for example, Ishmael
explains that the horror conjured by Moby-Dick resists "comprehensible
form": "How can I hope to explain myself here," he complains, grudgingly
accepting that, "in some dim, random way, explain myself I must, else
all these chapters might be naught."[34] Ishmael had initiated this account
conversationally, signaling his intention to relate "another thought" about
Moby-Dick, before pausing in midsentence, as if caught out by the realization that "thought" was the wrong term: "There was another thought,
or rather vague, nameless horror concerning him" (*MD* 252). Dim, vague,
nameless, and random—the flaws in Ishmael's understanding introduce a
shadow, occluding his knowledge of the whale's whiteness, and reducing
his initial "thought" to an ineffectual "naught."

Contributing its own resistance to knowledge is an "elusive quality"
that the whale shares with other similarly monstrous beings: the polar
bear, the albatross, the mythic "White Steed of the Prairies," and the white
shark. What they have in common is revealed in a footnote dedicated
to their sublime calm and dignity (*MD* 255). There, Ishmael identifies a
"white gliding ghostliness of repose" as characteristic of the white shark's
typical attitude, and ponders how that character "strangely tallies with
the same quality in the Polar quadruped. This peculiarity is most vividly
hit by the French in the name they bestow upon that fish. The Romish
mass for the dead begins with 'Requiem eternam' (eternal rest), whence
Requiem denominating the mass itself, and any other funereal music.
Now, in allusion to the white, silent stillness of death in this shark, and the

mild deadliness of his habits, the French call him *Requin*" (*MD* 255). The
"silent stillness" and "mild deadliness" that elude knowing are intensified
by an array of other significations of whiteness, a multiplicity so varied
and multiform that Ishmael is provoked to admit that "to analyze it would
seem impossible" (*MD* 259). As a consequence, any effort to apprehend it is
rerouted away from reason and through the realm of "sorcery," "imagination," and, ultimately, a contingent hope "to light upon some chance clue
to conduct us to the hidden cause we seek" (*MD* 259). Confronted with
the meaning of this whiteness, "most men" share in this epistemological
floundering; for all their near-universality, the claims to knowledge made
by such men must remain merely transient and ultimately valueless, for
"few perhaps were entirely conscious of [the meaning of their impressions]
at the time, and therefore may not be able to recall them now" (*MD* 259).
The chapter closes with the suggestion that he is lost who seeks only the
light of knowledge without acknowledging the shadowy unknowns that
render it incomplete. Like the "wilful" Arctic expeditioneers "who refuse
to wear colored and coloring glasses upon their eyes, so the wretched infi-
del gazes himself blind at the monumental white shroud that wraps all the
prospect around him," such violent enlightenment produces not knowledge but only "blank"-ness (*MD* 264). Ultimately, one's desire to "light
upon" the pathmarks to knowledge depends on the recognition of those
dark shadows that, dooming thought to incompletion, resist totality and
produce horror at the monstrous.[35]

Ishmael's skeptical "passivity" about knowledge—to borrow Rogin's
term—contrasts with the depiction of Ahab's ruthlessly instrumental
ways of knowing. Ishmael is content to play with the limits of the know-
able and to test their resistances, but Ahab wants to get things done, using
his knowledge to impose a "forced unity on the world."[36] Bainard Cowan's discussion of how the chapter entitled "The Chart" establishes this
opposition helpfully amplifies the distinction: Ishmael "is more interested
in talking about the feats of navigation than in doing navigation. Ahab,
by contrast, is on the other side of the scientific imagination, doing the
charting with skill but not particularly interested in it."[37] The language of
these passages again discloses how, despite the "unloitering vigilance" of
Ahab's instrumental reason and the "sleeplessness of his vow" to avenge
himself, his thought—like his brow—is darkened by the unknowns that
haunt him (*MD* 270). Poring over the chart, he is confounded by the "various lines and shadings which there met his eye," mirrored in the "shifting gleams and shadows" on his forehead, the seat of thought (*MD* 266,

267). Describing the peculiarity of his searching gaze, Melville reprises the figure that closed the earlier chapter regarding the whiteness of the whale: the "formless" spirit that "glared" out of Ahab's eyes resembled a "ray of living light, to be sure, but without an object to color, and therefore a blankness in itself" (*MD* 272). In its objectless intransitivity, Ahab's knowledge founders.

Such passages, among others to be found throughout the novel, enact *Moby-Dick*'s critique of instrumental reason, as it is embodied in all these various systems, measures, analyses, and charts. The charge of disutility here levied against such knowledges—since they fail to produce the promised totalizing understanding of the nature of things—is continually energized by Ishmael's overt ambivalence toward this instrumental way of knowing. Even his remarkable quest for empirical data about whales and whaling tends to be accompanied by a probing self-reflexivity that calls the bases of such knowledge into question. Ishmael's "imagination," as Cowan notes, "always tends to ascend to a meta-level above the action he is observing"; that is, he muses not only over the object of thought, but on the practice of thought itself, via a process that might be described as dialectical (in the best sense of this critical term).[38] However, the type of reflexive abstraction to which Ishmael is sometimes tempted—in its most narcissistic and indulgent forms—is hardly immune from a similar critique of utility, as the "Mast-Head" chapter indicates. There it becomes clearer that the treatment of knowledge in *Moby-Dick* is not, as the prevailing critical wisdom might seem to suggest, merely a negative critique of the shadows inherent in empiricist epistemology. It is furthermore an inquiry into the positive potentials of a different thinking that would begin from unproductivity.

Our narrator's cautious caveats about the dangers of such romantic flights have been widely read as an attack on transcendentalism of the Emersonian persuasion. Not so broadly acknowledged is that this treatment of thought at its *other* unproductive extreme (Ishmael's excessive speculation playing the counterpart to Ahab's unapologetically empirical instrumentality) unfolds in the midst of a sustained meditation on idleness. Marking another trajectory from *thought* to *naught*, Ishmael's momentarily enthusiastic embrace of sublime meditation seems fundamentally to compromise his ability to do his job, as Rogin notes: "Ishmael's meditative whaleman, like Emerson's transparent eyeball, becomes 'nothing.' But in seeing 'all,' the 'sunken-eyed young Platonist' fails to see the whales he was sent up to find."[39]

Melville does at first seem to emphasize the duties that attend this type of labor: he opens the chapter with a number of images of the efforts necessary to erect ancient mast-heads, and even alludes to the way that Admiral Nelson's modern mast-head in Trafalgar Square is obscured by "that London smoke" from which one might deduce the fires of industrialization. But the most salient of these images contrasts the alleged "incompetence" of a decadent modern lookout like Ishmael with the dedication of Saint Simeon Stylites, a "dauntless stander-of-mast-heads." The latter "was not to be driven from his place by fogs or frosts, rain, hail, or sleet," Melville reports, and "valiantly facing everything out to the last, literally died at his post" (*MD* 207–8). The dedication of Stylites—to a "post" that is clearly intended both to name his literal perch ("Stylites," in Greek, meaning "of the pillar")[40] and to imply the job he was there so committed to doing— suggests something like the absolute horizon of industriousness toward which any pretender to mast-standing must aspire. That this arguably sets an unattainable standard for productivity is a suspicion confirmed by the rest of the chapter, which demonstrates that any simple opposition—such as the one earlier drawn by Rogin positing that the stander-of-mast-heads may simply do his job, or not do his job—is too reductionist. Upon the mast-head, productivity and its supposed other are so complexly intertwined that the binary becomes all but meaningless.

As we are told twice in the chapter's third paragraph (*MD* 207), standing mast-heads is a "business" (e.g., "the business of standing mast-heads, ashore or afloat, is a very ancient and interesting one"); however, according to paragraph 4, the practice is also "exceedingly pleasant" (*MD* 209). The unique intensities unleashed by this fusion of business and pleasure are thereafter rhapsodically detailed, with considerable insistence on the unusual deliciousness of this tropical lassitude: "The tranced ship indolently rolls, the drowsy trade winds blow; everything resolves you into languor. . . . [A] sublime uneventfulness invests you" (*MD* 209). Another series follows, picking up on the rhythm and the punctuation of the first, but instead disclosing how sailing above the tropical seas mutes the usual dissonance of the instrumental, modern world. "You hear no news; read no gazettes; extras with startling accounts of commonplaces never delude you into unnecessary excitements; you hear of no domestic afflictions," Melville notes (*MD* 209). Even the prospect of financial crisis—"bankrupt securities; fall of stocks"—is smoothed, as Melville's line calms from semicolons to a dash that resolves all such cares of the modern world into a simple matter of home economy. You are "never troubled with the thought of what you shall have for dinner—for all your meals for three years and more are snugly stowed in casks, and your bill of fare is immutable" (*MD* 209–10).

However untroubled and carefree, the elevated state of the stander-of-mast-heads may only at considerable risk resolve into pure walleyed vacancy. A constant reminder of this peril is provided by the awkwardness of the mast-head's perch, a clumsy contrivance requiring that a degree of alertness and vigilance be folded into sublime ease.[41] Yet if the purity of the whaleman's reverie is corrupted by the constant strain of vigilance, so too is the purity of his work tainted by the pleasures of idleness. The delights of this post are contingent upon one's harnessing the machinery of production and turning it toward the ends of pleasure. Check out the resonances of autonomy, sovereignty, and erotic possibility that pervade Melville's description: "There you stand, a hundred feet above the silent decks, striding along the deep, as if the masts were gigantic stilts, while beneath you and between your legs, as it were, swim the hugest monsters of the sea, even as ships once sailed between the boots of the famous Colossus at old Rhodes" (*MD* 209). The lookout's shift is thus transformed into an idle ramble over the surface of the globe, as the whaleman strides through "silent" surroundings and communes with the gods.

The intermingling of work and pleasure is bolstered by the narrator's meditation on the narrative of "Captain Sleet" (William Scoresby Sr.), which had offered a thoroughgoing, obsessive, and "very scientific" record of all the trifling details pertaining to the provision of mast-heads. This, Melville notes, in a familiar phrase fraught with seeming contradiction, was "plainly a labor of love" for Captain Sleet, who purported to spend his time atop the mast-head immersed in figuring the deep mysteries of mathematics and navigation. But "for all his learned 'binnacle deviations,' 'azimuth compass observations,' and 'approximate errors,' he knows very well, Captain Sleet, that he was not so much immersed in those profound magnetic meditations, as to fail being attracted occasionally towards that well replenished little case-bottle, so nicely tucked in on one side of his crow's nest, within easy reach of his hand" (*MD* 211–12). Acknowledging that even the dedication of the stalwart Captain Sleet could prove vulnerable to the charms of idleness, Ishmael goes on to narrate his own encounter with the mast-head in terms that unambiguously foreground his own penchant for unproductivity, beginning with a paean to the "*serenity* of those seductive seas in which we South fishers mostly float," and going on to describe his climb: "I used to *lounge* up the rigging very *leisurely, resting* in the top to have a chat with Queequeg, or any one else off duty whom I might find there; then ascending a little way further, and throwing a *lazy* leg over the top-sail yard, take a preliminary view of the watery pastures, and so at last mount to my ultimate destination" (*MD* 212, emphasis added). Ishmael will readily admit that he "kept but sorry guard," but facetiously cites the "thought-engendering altitude" as a mitigating factor (*MD* 212). Yet even if the altitude is "thought-engendering," the minds of the young men who often climb to it apparently remain quite removed from productive ends. Twice in the next paragraph, Melville describes them as "absent-minded," enlisting the convention of "vacancy" that designates an unproductive idleness. With one additional invocation of that absence in the next paragraph, he finally makes the convention explicit, voicing a condemnation of the "vacant, unconscious reveries [imparted to] this absent-minded youth by the blending cadence of the waves with thoughts" (*MD* 214).

Living a "rocking" life, hovering above the undifferentiated formlessness of the liquid world, the young whaleman adopts its indifference as his own, and "at last he loses his identity," finally risking the ultimate sacrifice: "And perhaps, *at midday*, in the fairest weather, with one half-throttle shriek you drop through that transparent air into the summer sea, no more to rise for ever" (*MD* 215, emphasis added).[42] In his permanent and irrevocable abandonment of identity to such thought, and at the risk of himself becoming part of the formlessness of the sea, Melville's whaleman embodies the fleeting thinkability of another kind of living, what Branka Arsić calls "the possibility of *living at midday*," unworking certainty, and embracing the contingency of existence itself.[43] Such a thinker risks being transformed into that which he is not, a risk that calls into doubt "the finite person," revealing the shortcomings of a theory of being in which there is no provision for "loose" or unascertainable existences.[44]

Such an existence as is here described—"this sleep, this dream"—is echoed in the formless ascertainability of Bartleby (whose refusal, as chapter 1 explained, demands to be thought via categories other than those of the atomized, self-interested individual), and that parallel is further reinforced by a number of detailed resonances between the two works. Just as Melville declares his whaleman bereft of the necessary "interest"—as young men of romantic inclinations would apparently "rather not see whales than otherwise" (*MD* 213–14)—"Bartleby," too, muses on what young romantics would "rather" do, or rather, what they would prefer *not* to do. Furthermore, each account turns on the blindness of gazes fixed on "productive" horizons—whether the instrumental blindness of Ahab or the romantic "reveries" of Ishmael and Bartleby—all of whom look but yet do not properly see. Ultimately, the measure for Ishmael's unproductive gaze is the uninterrupted vigilance of the fifth-century Syrian Stylites; in "Bartleby," Melville instead references the fourth-century Egyptian Evagrius Ponticus, who celebrates the quest for wisdom by warning monks to resist the temptations of distracted reverie that threatens to set in around noontime. That the noonday demon is invoked in both scenes (as well as in *Redburn*'s invocation of "noon, when an interval of silence falls upon the docks") indicates how deliberately Melville uses temporality to place questions about unproductivity at the heart of these works.[45] Noon would logically seem that time of the day in which knowing would be most certain—for in the absence of shadows one might then see things "as plain as day"—but in Melville's work it is precisely there that knowledge and the certainty of the thinking subject are demonstrated to be at their most vulnerable.

Consequently, it is not enough to read *Moby-Dick* as merely a negative critique of instrumental knowledge—for it is clearly also an exploration of the positive productivities of unproductive thought, and their potential for reconceiving the value of the unproductive subject, whether the becoming-formless of Ishmael or the unascertainability of Bartleby. In both *Moby-Dick*'s depiction of becoming at sea and in the imagining, in "Bartleby," of an infinite and impersonal horizon of activity, the very constitution of the subject itself is put at stake. In "this sleep, this dream" of an unproductive thinking there emerges a whole other order of existence, a provisional solution to Melville's quest for, in Arsić's words, "a being that is not doing."[46] Those dreams, the stuff of a becoming that is forever unfamiliar to and nonidentical with itself, are the lifeblood of "loose existences," whose ontological possibility exists only in the shadows of midday.

"Between Speech and a Snore": The Custom House and Its Limits

> The life of the Custom House lies like a dream behind me. . . . [The old Inspector] and all those other venerable personages who sat with him at the receipt of custom, are but shadows in my view.
> —Nathaniel Hawthorne, *The Scarlet Letter*, 1850

The custom house described by Hawthorne is a workplace where work of any sort is all but impossible. In fact, a saturating spirit of idleness is depicted as pervading even Salem's topography, with its "long and lazy street lounging wearisomely through the whole extent of the peninsula." The only seeming relief from the "flat" and "unvaried surface" of this apparent desert of unproductivity is provided by a rogue's gallery of idlers, affectionately described in all their appealing variety, who have sought refuge in the tale's titular office. Among them, we are introduced to a Collector, never "characterized by an uneasy activity"; an insatiable Inspector, dedicated above all else to the "delight and profit of his maw"; and others bearing an "almost slumberous countenance," a "lack of efficiency for business," and a "repose" in which they are content to indulge their "half-torpid systems" and to "go lazily about what they termed duty."[47] The description of their ineffectual labors illustrates how even the most apparently dedicated zeal frequently works at cross-purposes to the imperative of getting something done, as in one of the narrator's observations about the counterproductive consequences of their dereliction. Whenever "a wagon-load of valuable merchandise had been smuggled ashore, *at noonday, perhaps*, and directly beneath their unsuspicious noses," they respond with a concentrated display of energy, a flurry of busywork the "vigilance and alacrity" of which was manifest only at "the moment that there was no longer any remedy" (*SL* 15, emphasis added). In an odd obverse to Adorno's observation that the modes of work are smuggled into the realm of leisure, these "workers" secret the contraband of leisure into the domain of work—and again, it is noontime when the binary is scrambled.

Yet the well-intentioned narrator finds himself powerless to reprimand his staff for their midday lapses, instead generously opting for an ironic and "grateful recognition of the promptitude of their zeal" (*SL* 15). This recognition—or better, mis-recognition—of their activity reproduces that by which the value of his own activity has been subject to misunderstanding. His sympathy is understandable, given his complaint that "an idler like [him]self" had received an unfair hearing when tried by the prevailing law of productivity. His own unproductivity manifests in a desire to write, a perverse calling that attracts the imagined scorn of his Puritan ancestors, and reveals the shadowy bad conscience of one laboring under the insistence of the work ethic.

> No aim, that I have ever cherished, would they recognize as laudable; no success of mine—if my life, beyond its domestic scope, had ever been brightened by success—would they deem otherwise than worthless, if not positively disgraceful. "What is he?" murmurs one gray shadow of my

forefathers to the other. "A writer of story-books! What kind of a business in life,—what mode of glorifying God, or being serviceable to mankind in his day and generation,—may that be? Why, the degenerate fellow might as well have been a fiddler!" (*SL* 9)

It is telling that at the outset of this work the narrator feels the need for inoculation against such a failure of "recognition," and his initial preoccupation with the problem of productive activity and its refusal of practical measure permeates the remainder of the sketch. Throughout, he understands the problem of his productivity as both a problem of thought and a problem for thought. For one thing, his job demands that he take a disciplinary posture toward the unproductivities of his staff, and though he "knew it," he nevertheless cannot translate thought into action: "I could never quite find in my heart to act upon the knowledge" (*SL* 14). More significantly and famously, however, the fact of his imprisonment in the custom house curtails the productive powers of his imagination, eliciting the disagreeable "suspicion that one's intellect is dwindling away" and making him vulnerable to a torpor that mutes his vitality not only at work, but also haunts him on his "seashore walks," his "rambles into the country," and "in the chamber which I most absurdly termed my study" (*SL* 43, 39).

His nagging anxiety has been crystallized, of course, by the discovery, on an "idle and rainy day," of the long-forgotten materials that will constitute the romantic history he must write.[48] The custom house, however, is no place to execute this office, and, afflicted by the "miserable dimness" of the images populating his fancy, he laments, like Thoreau and Melville above, a failure to properly *see*. Even at night—when the faculties of the romantic author should be at their most penetrating, in contrast to the empirical certainties promised by a shadowless noon—he is inhibited by the impossibility of the task before him. One would expect, he asserts, that the odd confluence of moonlight with the dim projections of the coal-fire would illuminate his nocturnal setting in such a way as to bring uncannily to light the mysterious hidden value of even the most trivial things. "Moonlight," distinct from the clear productivities of "a morning or noontide visibility," should "[make] every object so minutely visible"; all details thus "completely seen, are so spiritualized by the unusual light, that they seem to lose their actual substance, and become things of intellect. Nothing is too small or too trifling to undergo this change, and acquire dignity thereby" (*SL* 39–40). The fire should bring the value of these unrecognized trifles into the light of the imagination, liberating the mind from mundane actuality and loosing it into romantic fancy. "Glancing at the looking-glass, we behold—deep within its haunted verge—the smouldering glow of the half-extinguished anthracite, the white moonbeams on the floor, and a repetition of all the gleam and shadow of the picture, with one remove further from the actual, and nearer to the imaginative" (*SL* 41).

The charms of this setting are, however, constantly interrupted by the "rude contact of some actual circumstance," preventing him from assuming a "productive" course of action: "The wiser effort would have been to diffuse thought and imagination through the opaque substance of to-day, and thus to make it a bright transparency . . . to seek, resolutely, the true and indestructible value that lay hidden in the petty and wearisome incidents, and ordinary characters" (*SL* 42). So many of our key themes intersect in the narrator's frustrations. In contrast to the labors of the workplace, the night promises a unique kind of visibility, in which the real work of imaginative creation should supposedly flourish, catalyzed by the ability to make sense of the shadowy values of the everyday and to translate that critical knowledge into imaginative labors. In short, just as the value of Hawthorne's activity is culturally stigmatized due to a misrecognition, so too are the incidents he wishes to narrate misunderstood as merely "petty" and "ordinary"; to rescue them from obscurity will require a redoubled intellectual effort capable of navigating the shadows of the imagination. This, however, is impossible as long as the author labors at the custom house. The office makes its usual demand for a productivity understood in terms of "the many intricacies of business," and expected to operate with the "regularity of a perfectly comprehended system" (*SL* 26). But however tempting it is to attribute the romance writer's plight to the confining rationality of the productive world, Hawthorne's sketch suggests something somewhat more subtle. For while the custom house is truly the wrong location from which to conduct an imaginative endeavor, that seems to him to be the case not only due to the demands of regular work, but also due to the idleness and lethargy that pervade the space.

Of the deficiencies of the custom house, we may say that the problem is simultaneously *both* productivity and its opposite. At once, Hawthorne recoils against the work form that requires that he direct his activity toward the hope of remuneration and barter his power for "a pittance of the public gold" (*SL* 39). But in a curious reversal, his surrender to work comes *at the expense of* productivity: it is work that renders one unproductive. The broad roster of sluggards that conduct custom house business is a testament to this paradox, as they compromise themselves and their activity in order "to be made happy, at monthly intervals, with a little pile of glittering coin. . . . It is sadly curious to observe how slight a taste of office suffices to infect a poor fellow with this singular disease" (*SL* 44).

Hawthorne's is thus both an indictment of work and of the peculiar kind of unproductivity that it engenders. It reflects the conceptual and logical inseparability of the two. And it raises the prospect that the real work—of writing this romantic work—cannot be conducted until the artificial productions of waged labor in the poisonous custom house are ended. To Hawthorne's delight—though through no effort of his own, it is acknowledged—this liberation from the workplace is effected, as a change in administration puts him on the wrong side of the political bureaucracy. Thus, after three years in the custom house, living in a "an unnatural state, doing what was really of no advantage nor delight to any human being, and withholding myself from toil that would, at least, have stilled an unquiet impulse in me," our surveyor finds himself out of work, or as he puts it, "decapitated" (*SL* 48). The word conjures a couple of different possibilities, the head standing both as a symbol for the capacity for thought and for the sovereignty attendant to holding official power. Hawthorne clarifies that it was only at the expense of the latter head that the first could be made to flourish. "The real human being, all this time with his head safely on his shoulders," thus takes up the task of writing, kick-starting his "intellectual machinery," "rusty through long idleness," and allowing Mr. Surveyor Pue's historical chronicles to come "into play" (*SL* 48–49).

Despite his protestations, our narrator's cavalier attitude toward these administrative developments constitutes something more than mere passivity; it also models a kind of differently productive thinking. It frees him from the confinements of remunerable work in the custom house while, in the same gesture, opening his thought to a radical relationship with time: history is thereby allowed to come "into play." This occurs not because the narrator launches a quest to overmaster and know the historical details, but instead through his submission to a power that is described not so much as cognitive but as affective: the burning urgency of the prenational past, figured in the scarlet letter that continues to smolder into the narrator's time, is restored to life anew and threaded into the present. Only when putting aside the dusty empiricism of the historian does this romantic author gain access to the vistas of "deep time," where mere historical chronology is eschewed and a "linear model of supersession" is replaced "with a fractal model of looping."[49] In some respects, Dimock's explanation of such a nonsynchronous temporality echoes the description, advanced by Deleuze and Guattari in their late work *What Is Philosophy?* of a properly "philosophical time." In their argument, philosophical time involves a very specific relationship between thought and its nonconceptual other; understanding this relationship should enable us to better confront the dreams, sleeps, and shadows central to Thoreau, Melville, Hawthorne, and even Adorno—each of whom is a philosopher in this fashion.

Deleuze and Guattari claim for philosophy "a grandiose time of coexistence that does not exclude the before and after but superimposes them in a stratigraphic order."[50] To truly think means apprehending a horizon of connections that cannot be contained by any supposedly exhaustive analysis; such thought is always only the provisional construction of a constellation of concepts, at once a local and limited assemblage and simultaneously a subset of the unlimited milieu of the as-yet unthought. This unthought milieu, while exceeding any local thought, is the precondition of that thought. Deleuze and Guattari, describing this ultimate historical horizon, or "plane of immanence," understand it as the nonconceptual realm "presupposed" by the thinkable; the former is the substrate of the latter. But it "is presupposed," Deleuze and Guattari argue, "not in the way that one concept may refer to others but in the way that concepts themselves refer to a nonconceptual understanding."[51] The connections through time and space that are implied by the plane of immanence are therefore not analogous to simple intertextuality; resonating more profoundly through them is the fact that all conceptual thought shares a common and vertiginous relationship to the unthought.

Thus, to approach the plane—to instantiate it—is never a matter of mastery, as one would pretend toward in the architecture of a totalizing philosophical "system" capable of knowing all or of making everything ascertainable. That kind of thinking always pulls up short at the limit demarcating the unthought. Real philosophy instead requires "a sort of groping experimentation," they argue, deploying "measures that are not very respectable, rational, or reasonable. These measures belong to the order of dreams, of pathological processes, esoteric experiences, drunkenness, and excess."[52] It involves a plunging into the chaos of the undifferentiated, a chaos that is not "the absence of determinations" but is rather an infinite field characterized by the ceaseless coalescence and disappearance of determinations. The danger of instrumental thought lies in subordinating the plane of immanence to the concepts that populate it—that is, of taking concepts to be fixed entities that, once thought, are independent of the plane that makes them possible. In attempting to delineate a plane of immanence, one should not pretend to discover a universal or a transcendent category, autonomously capable of embracing all. To think in this way would be to reproduce the productivist ethos, and to reify our concepts as a truth indifferent to practices of unworking.

That is why for Deleuze and Guattari there must be a multiplicity of these planes, their intersection indicating the existence of an endlessly generative milieu of possibilities for thinking differently. Throughout *The Scarlet Letter*, Hawthorne's legendary romantic ambiguity ensures the coexistence of various interpretive standpoints, mirroring the experience of his Salemites, who capably propose alternative readings not only of the scarlet letter, but also of the star shower that follows Dimmesdale's revelations on the scaffold. Mirroring their encounter with the fleeting heavenly constellation that illuminates the sky with the form of the letter *A*, Hawthorne's narrator can only grapple with the past by extracting a particular and unstable configuration of thought out of its ethereal chaos of historical events. Pressing to his chest the cloth letter *A*—the unraveling product, he says, of a "now forgotten art"—he finds that it burns in his time, too, and in so doing it makes possible the text of his thought. The stars momentarily align. He, like the reading public of Salem, is led to the conclusion that this *A* might be made to mean "able."

Such ambiguous reflections as those of Hawthorne's narrator are of a piece with the thought-experiments of our other American Renaissance thinkers. They conduct a common inquiry at the limits of "useful knowledge," finding there various species of formlessness, nondescription, and the "negative thought" of different orders that are co-present but only dimly ascertainable. This kinship reverberates in the conclusion of Hawthorne's introductory sketch, which revisions the village of Salem, no longer as a hamlet enervated by the routine of the workday, but instead as a locale emerging from the "haze of memory." As Hawthorne describes this imaginary "overgrown village in cloud-land," free from quotidian obligation, we cannot help but recall Thoreau's similarly hazy dream of a town in which there circulated "no idle thoughts," or, for that matter, Melville's depiction of the sympathetic boss pondering the loose existences of a supporting staff that lives for the "dinner-hour as the nucleus of the day" (*SL* 45). This tradition of thinking about activity, and specifically of thinking about the activity of thought, is arguably characteristic of the whole of the American Renaissance—as in Emerson's critique of instrumental "penny-wisdom," or Whitman's serenade to a self that might "lean and loafe at my ease"—but is also manifest in the plethora of similarly rich ways in which the unproductive energizes those cultural practices conducted beyond, beneath, and around the Renaissance as well. These American thinkers, asserting with generosity and nuance the importance of idle practice for "a man who [feels] it to be the best definition of happiness to live throughout the whole range of his faculties and sensibilities" (*SL* 45), gesture toward the radical productivities of the unproductive.

Their depiction of a thought indebted to the plane of immanence that subtends it is of interest not only because such thinking assumes the underlying commonness of the thinkable, but also because it functions as a homology for the situation of activity itself. For the unproductive is precisely this: an infinite horizon of common and limitless activity out of which locally valuable practices are arbitrarily brought to significance. The discourses analyzed here, in their stretching and unraveling of the limits of "productivity," all point to this infinite horizon, demonstrating that what has been thought of as unproductivity is in reality the onto-logical ground out of which an arbitrary and normative "productivity" itself may be formed. As is apparent in the experiments of the American Renaissance thinkers with the negativity of space, the outside of thought, and the plane of immanence—experiments linking them with not only the Puritan legacy, but also with twentieth-century German critique and fifth-century Syrian saints—such a rethinking of the productivity of the unproductive also draws the temporal, spatial, and epistemological cer-tainty of "America" and the "nineteenth century" into a zone of indeter-minacy. While "productivity" represents a reductive fixing of limits and a privileging of some types of activity over the rest, so too does "nine-teenth-century America" function to abstract, frame, and fix a space and a period, pinking its edges so as to inhibit unraveling. This last analysis, addressed to these most recognizably "American" works in the canon, sought there something more than merely the familiar and the known. In so doing, perhaps, it mirrored a thinking that, unfolding amid the supposed certainties of midday, might unexpectedly discover there the intriguing shadows cast by other suns.

Lazy Existence

When Hawthorne is finally able to dispense with the rigors of the work-place and take seriously the real concerns of his existence, he does so by allowing Mr. Surveyor Jonathan Pue's own work to "come into play." Hawthorne's surrender of his rusty "intellectual machinery" to this "play" enables him to overcome the atrophy of his own imaginative capacities, and to unleash the novel productivity of that which had hitherto been unproductive. In stepping outside of the well-worn routines of workplace rationality and the state of vacant indolence to which they lead, he pursues the prospect of thinking differently, of escaping the bad faith of a system that produces only expected results and thereby neutralizes man's creative powers. Though his gesture unquestionably articulates a widespread American romantic ideal, it just as crucially challenges the very definition of a modern thought tailored to the hegemonic insistence on the synthetic possibilities of dialectical logic. This instrumental thinking, as we have seen, is identified by Adorno as a perverse outgrowth of Enlightenment rationality, a mutation in which the dialectical model of thought frees man from his "self-incurred tutelage" (in Kant's memorable phrase) only to imprison him anew within the formal fetters of the dialectical model. The shadow of Hegelianism is the template for such thought; its tutelage is not without its own violent misrecognitions of value.

In fact, as Adorno argues, such familiar thought, indifferent to the contents marshaled under its systemic inevitability, has to ignore the very "matters of true philosophical interest at this point in history." These matters, he suggests, are "those in which Hegel, agreeing with tradition, expressed his disinterest. They are non-conceptuality, individuality and particularity—things which ever since Plato used to be dismissed as transitory and insignificant, and which Hegel labeled 'lazy Existence.' Philosophy's theme would consist of the qualities it downgrades as contingent, as a *quantité négligeable*. A matter of urgency to the concept would be what it fails to cover, what its abstractionist mechanism eliminates, what is not already a case of the concept."[53] The transitory, insignificant, and contingent persistently belie the claims of systemic philosophy, the Hegelian variant of which, by "covering" and "placing these things in prefabricated categories" and subjecting them to the measure of its own imperial logic, evades its true responsibilities and loses sight of its own possibilities. Only a thought that is courageous enough to force us "to immerse ourselves in things that are heterogeneous to it" would deserve to be called philosophical.[54]

Calling for a dramatic intervention into the conventions of dialectical thought, Adorno argued for an "unleashed dialectics" that would be shorn of its striving toward systematicity and thereby become capable of embracing a crucial category of experience that has been overshadowed by the dialectical machinery. That category is "play":

> As a corrective to the total rule of method, philosophy contains a playful element [*das Moment des Spiels*] which the traditional view of it as a science would like to exorcise. For Hegel, too, this was a sensitive point; he rejects "types and distinctions determined by external chance and by play, not by reason." The un-naïve thinker knows how far he remains from the object of his thinking, and yet he must always talk as if he had it entirely. This brings him to the point of clowning. He must not deny his clownish traits, least of all since they alone can give him hope for what is denied him. Philosophy is the most serious of things, but then again it is not all that serious.[55]

An unleashed dialectics commences only by acknowledging the element of play upon which it depends, and which the dialectic in its Hegelian variant traditionally has concealed in the formal shadow of its productive work. For it is only by respectfully confronting philosophy's playful aspect that the system may recognize itself as system and come to awareness of its merely posited character. Without that sensitivity toward play, philosophy is not only ridiculous but lacking in self-reflexivity—it is little more than science. And thus Adorno's critique pinpoints, as the ultimate vulnerability of the Hegelian machinery, its instrumental industriousness. Dialectics, like the other machineries of our perverse enlightenment, is a killjoy.

Adorno's championing of philosophical play—that intellectual activity traditionally derided as transient, inconsequential, unproductive, or nugatory because of its consignment to the uncharted shadows free of measure and standardization—mirrors my own insistence on the validity of those cultural practices that challenge the rationalization of activity and ceaselessly trouble the existing categories by which its value may be judged. In terms of thought, the infinite variability of play contests the stability and ossification of philosophical standpoints and ensures, like Ishmael's constant doubt and redoubling of his intellectual activity, the fluid renewal of the known. Knowledge cannot be merely a passive object, but rather is a relentless process and an ongoing exploration of the dynamic horizon of intellectual possibility. Hence Adorno's claim that consciousness itself comprises inner and outer modes, the dialectically hermetic and "productive" logics of the former constantly being challenged and galvanized by the insatiable dynamism of the latter: "Mobility is the essence of consciousness; it is no accidental feature," he says. "It means a dou-bled mode of conduct: an inner one, the immanent process which is the properly dialectical one, and a free, unbound one like a stepping out of dialectics."[56]

To leap clear of the dialectical machinery's shadow is, however, not merely to release one's self and one's thought into an indiscriminate free play. Quite the contrary, in fact—for opening thought to the play of its exterior represents a burden. Embracing the challenge of Adorno's unleashed dialectic entails a sentence of perpetual exertion in the philosophical worksite. Such a "qualitative change in dialectics" as would embrace play actually means that "thought would *be burdened with more toil and trouble* than Hegel defines as such, because the thought he discusses always extracts from its objects only that which is a thought already."[57] In a version of the refrain now familiar from the preceding chapters, work such as Hegel's deliberate exertions in fact does too little—it evades the real work of philosophy, which is to wrestle with the nugatory. Just as the object is said to be primary because it can exist without the subject (whereas the subject depends for its existence on the materiality of objecthood), the nugatory, or the misrecognized and infinite activity that in its multiplicity appears as "unproductive," needs no assimilation in order to be what it is. It thus appears as autonomous and ontologically central. Contingency, singularity, and particularity constitute the primary material of play's infinite economy; the philosophical system is but a dim, shadowy reduction.

Being unproductive is still being. It is only that the shadows cast by industrial modernity—of measure by the wage, of disciplinary time and space, of thought systematized in keeping with the dialectical imperative—misrepresent such being as nothingness. Writing on the philosophical tendency toward ruthless systematization that was inaugurated in the seventeenth century, Adorno diagnoses at its core an anxiety. It is a fear of the monstrous and menacing particularity that hovers in the shadows of thought just as it haunts the social power that seeks to gird itself against imagined idle threats.

> [The bourgeois *ratio*] trembled before the menace that continued underneath its own domain, waxing stronger in proportion to its own power. This fear shaped the beginnings of a mode of conduct constitutive for bourgeois existence as a whole: of the neutralization, by confirming the existent order, of every emancipatory step. *In the shadow of its own incomplete*

emancipation the bourgeois consciousness must fear to be annulled by a
more advanced consciousness; not being the whole freedom, it senses that
it can produce only a caricature of freedom—hence its theoretical expansion of its autonomy into a system similar to its own coercive mechanisms.[58]

Systemic philosophy sought to mitigate the terror unleashed by fearsome
baroque infinity; so too have the regressive structures of bourgeois society
reinforced themselves against the imagined dangers of unproductivity. In
the process, however, a slightly different shadow appears—that which continually indicts "bourgeois existence as a whole" for its stunted enlightenment. In a final reversal, our thinking finally enables us to see that is
the specter of play that overshadows that of work, and not the other way
around. In doing so, those shadows, dreams, and idle thoughts remind
us of the bourgeois project's incompletion—its inability to meaningfully
realize modernity's promise, its belligerent refusal to valorize the unproductivity of the productive, and its contentment to continue toiling in the
shadows that shield bourgeois society from the truly unlimited potentials
of its own activity.

Notes

NOTES TO INTRODUCTION

1. Of course, the "American" identities forged by these various productivities reflected considerable distinctions along the lines of gender, race, class, and region. The responsibility of respecting these profound overdeterminations is one of the primary challenges faced by this book; it is also, in some part, the source of the joy to be taken in the inexhaustibility of its topic.

2. Adriano Tilgher, *Work: What It Has Meant to Men through the Ages*, trans. Dorothy Canfield Fisher (New York: Harcourt, Brace, 1930), 90.

3. For a sketch embracing many of the key figures, see Tom Lutz's engaging *Doing Nothing: A History of Loafers, Loungers, Slackers, and Bums in America* (New York: Farrar, Straus and Giroux, 2006), esp. chaps. 4–6.

4. James Freeman Clarke, *Self-Culture: Physical, Intellectual, Moral, and Spiritual* (Boston: James R. Osgood, 1882), 384. There will be more to say on the subject of bees.

5. Ibid., 388. On the increasing significance of play as part of the discursive "production of unproductivity" between 1880 and 1900—with the ultimate consequence that "play, not work, appeared to be the mode through which a culture expresses itself"—see Bill Brown, *The Material Unconscious: American Amusement, Stephen Crane, and the Economies of Play* (Cambridge and London: Harvard University Press, 1996), 9.

6. Ibid., 269–70.

7. Eugen Fink, "The Oasis of Happiness: Toward an Ontology of Play," in *Game, Play, Literature*, ed. Jacques Ehrmann (Boston: Beacon Press, 1968), 21, provides welcome nuance here, imagining the specific productivity of play in a way that is incompatible with Clarke's conception and the typical nineteenth-century representation more generally: "It is frequently said that play is 'purposeless' or 'undirected' activity. This is not the case. Considered as a whole it is purposive and each individual phase of play action has its own specific purpose, which is an integral part of the whole. But the immanent purpose of play is not subordinate to the ultimate purpose served by all other human activity. Play has only internal purpose, unrelated to anything external to itself."

8. William James, "The Gospel of Relaxation," in *On Vital Reserves: "The Energies of Men" and "The Gospel of Relaxation"* (New York: Henry Holt, 1911), 65. I shall return to James's account in greater detail in chapter 4.

9. Ibid., 63.

10. See Karl Marx, *Capital: A Critique of Political Economy*, vol. 1, ed. Frederick Engels, trans. Samuel Moore and Edward Aveling (New York: International, 1967), 313. Surplus value is *absolutely* determined by the prolongation of the working day; however, within the given parameters of the working day, relative surplus values arise from "the curtailment of the necessary labour-time, and from the corresponding alteration in the respective lengths of the two components [i.e., the necessary and the surplus] of the working-day" (315).

11. Kiarina Kordela, *$urplus: Spinoza, Lacan* (Albany: State University of New York Press, 2007), 43.

12. Ibid.

13. Ferdinand de Saussure, *Course in General Linguistics* (Chicago and La Salle, Ill.: Open Court Press, 1983), 68–69: "The word *arbitrary* also calls for comment. It must not be taken to imply that a signal depends on the free choice of the speaker (. . . the individual has no power to alter a sign in any respect once it has been established in a linguistic community.) The term implies simply that the signal is *unmotivated*: that is to say arbitrary in relation to its signification, with which it has no natural connexion in reality."

14. Henry David Thoreau, "Life Without Principle," in *The Writings of Henry David Thoreau*, vol. 4, *Cape Cod and Miscellanies* (New York: AMS Press, 1968), 456–57. Thoreau's fundamental claim that "the ways in which most men get their living . . . are . . . a shirking of the real business of life" (463) is one that is refashioned in various ways throughout the nineteenth century, as we shall see in the pages that follow, including my expanded discussion of Thoreau himself in chapter 5.

15. Patricia Seed, "Afterword: Further Perspectives on Culture, Limits, and Borders," in *Border Theory: The Limits of Cultural Politics*, ed. Scott Michaelsen and David E. Johnson (Minneapolis and London: University of Minnesota Press, 1997), 254.

16. Russ Castronovo's contribution to *Border Theory* provides an apt reminder that heroic narratives—such as those inclined to read the border "as a site of contested cultural production" that facilitates "articulations of oppositional consciousness"—tend to downplay the fact that the limit, here figured as national, is also "laden with 'traps' . . . that suture homogeneity and confirm hierarchical structures." "Such boundaries," he argues, serve "as occasions to imagine, often aggressively, fixed and unrelenting standards of citizenship and belonging" (see Castronovo, "Compromised Narratives along the Border: The Mason-Dixon Line, Resistance, and Hegemony," in *Border Theory*, ed. Michaelsen and Johnson, 196).

17. Consider, by way of illustration, the complicated situation of the "good student" who is keenly aware of just how many absences are allowable in a given semester. Taking just one more "sick day" than is acceptable—thereby crossing the limit of acceptable activity established by the syllabus—requires a complex evaluation of marginal utility. Is it worth risking a destabilization of the pedagogical assemblage? Does the student wish to transform the once-benevolent professor into something else—an agent of punishment? Perhaps only the "good student" who thereby becomes an "underachiever" truly can know.

18. Gilles Deleuze and Félix Guattari, *A Thousand Plateaus: Capitalism and Schizophrenia*, trans. Brian Massumi (Minneapolis and London: University of Minnesota Press, 1987), 438.

19. Homi Bhabha's formative account, in "Dissemination: Time, Narrative, and the Margins of the Modern Nation," in *The Location of Culture* (London and New York: Routledge, 2004), represents the limits of national thinking in a similar way, positing the uneasy coexistence between the pedagogically fixed nation and the "recursive strategy of the performative" that constantly displaces narrative authority at the former's limits (209). "The performative intervenes in the sovereignty of the nation's *self-generation* by casting a shadow between the people as 'image' and its signification as a differentiating sign of Self, distinct from the Other of the Outside" (212). In this shadow of the national self, the relentlessness of the performative gesture necessitates a constant changing of the rules governing the engagement between the so-called self and its other.

20. Deleuze and Guattari, *A Thousand Plateaus*, 438.

21. John Carlos Rowe, *The New American Studies* (Minneapolis and London: University of Minnesota Press, 2002), xvii.

22. This theoretical interest abroad is illustrated by a healthy tradition encompassing the speculations of the exiled Frankfurt school, the fascination of Gilles Deleuze and Giorgio Agamben with Melville, and recent Italian Marxist interventions, including Antonio Negri's study of the U.S. Constitution and his complex exploration of the privileged role of the United States (in his work with Michael Hardt) (see Deleuze [with Claire Parnet], "On the Superiority of Anglo-American Literature," *Dialogues*, trans. Hugh Tomlinson and Barbara Habberjam [New York: Columbia University Press, 1987]; Negri, *Insurgencies: Constituent Power and the Modern State*, trans. Maurizia Boscagli [Minneapolis and London: University of Minnesota Press, 1999]; and Hardt and Negri, *Empire* [Cambridge and London: Harvard University Press, 2000]).

23. Deleuze and Guattari, *A Thousand Plateaus*, 436.

24. Paul Giles, "The Deterritorialization of American Literature," in *Shades of the Planet*, ed. Wai-Chee Dimock and Lawrence Buell (Princeton and Oxford: Princeton University Press, 2007), 54–55.

25. In this connection, it might be pointed out that the premises of *Idle Threats* challenge the prevailing periodizations not just of practitioners of a traditional American studies, but also of those postmodernists and "post-Marxists" who sometimes describe the transition from the modern into the postmodern, or from industrial into postindustrial production, via a more or less rigid historical schema—usually locating a watershed somewhere just after the middle of the twentieth century at which the "real subsumption" of society under capital can be said to have been realized. To the extent, however, that this subsumption centrally involves a renegotiation of the boundary between work and leisure, in which the productivity of the former is extended to all social practice, an argument can be made that this transition too needs to be reperiodized in light of the cultural dominants of an ever-lengthening long nineteenth century. See the work of Moishe Postone—for example, his *Time, Labor, and Social Domination: A Reinterpretation of Marx's Critical Theory* (Cambridge: Cambridge University Press, 1996), 12–13—for another take on the analytical limits of this linear historical schema.

26. Roland Greene, "Wanted: A New World Studies," *American Literary History* 12, no. 1/2 (Spring-Summer 2000): 344. Dimock's recent efforts in this direction are particularly helpful (see Wai-Chee Dimock, "Planet and America, Set and Subset," in *Shades of the Planet: American Literature as World Literature*, ed. Dimock and Lawrence Buell [Princeton and Oxford: Princeton University Press, 2007]). Rejecting the notion that "America" names an autonomous and self-evident given, she proposes instead to loosen its boundaries both spatially and historically. Accordingly, she seeks to "nest" America within a dynamic system of sets, wrapping it into the folds of larger conceptual fields and showing how the membranes between those sets are penetrated by innumerable and multiform relays that resonate across multiple and heterogeneous planes. "America" might thus be said to function as one set subordinate to a broader conceptual plane understood as "modernity" more generally, with that latter plane itself coming increasingly to echo "America" itself in the age of real subsumption by capital. Other critical interventions have similarly embraced an augmented "span" for a criticism that can no longer be merely period- or nation-based; among them, Gayatri Chakravorty Spivak's framework of "planetarity" offers a horizon that might radically broaden the scope of the field while resisting the dangers of totalization (see Spivak, *Death of a Discipline* [New York: Columbia University Press, 2003]).

27. Dimock, "Planet and America," 5.

28. Cesare Casarino, *Modernity at Sea: Marx, Melville, Conrad in Crisis* (Minneapolis and London: University of Minnesota Press, 2002), xl.

29. Ibid., xxxv.

30. Deleuze and Guattari, *A Thousand Plateaus*, 439, emphasis added.

31. Priscilla Wald, *Constituting Americans: Cultural Anxiety and Narrative Form* (Durham and London: Duke University Press, 1995), 299.

32. James, "The Gospel of Relaxation," 60.

33. See Siegfried Wenzel, *The Sin of Sloth: Acedia in Medieval Thought and Literature* (Durham: University of North Carolina Press, 1960). Though the Bible is replete with references to sloth and idleness—there are twenty-nine verses on the topic in the Book of Proverbs alone—it is not until the fourth century that *acedia* is accorded the status of a deadly sin. Cassian is particularly important for locating the sources of *acedia* inside the slothful person, thereby making it a pathology, and one treatable with manual labor at that (22); Aquinas is primarily responsible for abstracting and universalizing the concept (46). On the biblical origins, see Gary F. Allen, "A Study of Slothfulness and Industriousness in the Book of Proverbs" (Th.M. thesis, Dallas Theological Seminary, 1983).

34. Wenzel, *The Sin of Sloth*, 185, describes this conceptual breakdown as follows: "One is frequently compelled to think that *acedia* has become a mere name, a label stuck on a cage whose inhabitants live rather uneasily together and are ready to break out and defect into different directions."

35. Max Weber, *The Protestant Ethic and the Spirit of Capitalism*, trans. Talcott Parsons (New York: Charles Scribner's Sons, 1958), 62. An enormous body of commentary addresses the viability of the Weber thesis. A frugal exposition of some of the key themes

in the controversy is provided in Herbert Applebaum, *The Concept of Work: Ancient, Medieval, and Modern* (Albany: State University of New York Press, 1992), 332–37. See also Fernand Braudel's persuasive repositioning of Weber's argument in *Civilization and Capitalism, 15th–18th Century*, trans. Sian Reynolds, vol. 2, *The Wheels of Commerce* (New York: Harper and Row, 1982), 568, 578–81.

36. Weber, *The Protestant Ethic*, 157.

37. "Work thus conceived stands at the very opposite pole from 'good works.' . . . They, it was thought, had been a series of single transactions, performed as compensation for particular sins, or out of anxiety to acquire merit. What is required of the Puritan is not individual meritorious acts, but a holy life—a system in which every element is grouped round a central idea, the service of God, from which all disturbing irrelevancies have been pruned, and to which all minor interests are subordinated" (R. H. Tawney, *Religion and the Rise of Capitalism: A Historical Study* [1926, repr., Gloucester, Mass.: Peter Smith, 1962], 242).

38. Weber, *The Protestant Ethic*, 158.

39. On Cassian and the exhortation to manual labor as a prophylactic against idleness, see Wenzel, *The Sin of Sloth*, 18–22.

40. Tilgher, *Work*, 58, sums up this productive paradox of Calvinism as "the command to ceaseless effort, to ceaseless renunciation of the fruits of effort." See also Weber, *The Protestant Ethic*, 172.

41. Weber, *The Protestant Ethic*, 157.

42. Ibid., 159. The extremes to which this ideology may be extended are exemplified in, among others, Hubert V. Mills, *Poverty and the State: Work for the Unemployed* (London: Kegan Paul, Trench, 1886), 8: "I would take care that all healthy men had the opportunity of earning a livelihood easily; but when this was done, I would excuse no man's indolence; I would give to no beggar; I would have the State provide starving idleness with a coffin, but nothing more; and would teach the people to say good riddance to it. There are but two unpardonable sins. Selfish pride is one, idleness is the other."

43. Ibid., 161, emphasis added. Applebaum, *The Concept of Work*, 329–30, concurs, locating this systematic character in the teachings of Calvin: "the moral conduct of the average man was deprived of its planless and unsystematic character, and subjected to a consistent method for conduct as a whole."

44. See Robert Seguin, *Around Quitting Time: Work and Middle-Class Fantasy in American Fiction* (Durham and London: Duke University Press, 2001) for a kindred account of the American ambivalence toward work in the twentieth century.

45. A recent example from a context just slightly removed illustrates quite bluntly this tendency to accept the basic binary as natural and symmetrical. See Sarah Jordan, *The Anxieties of Idleness: Idleness in Eighteenth-Century British Literature and Culture* (Lewisburg, Pa., and London: Bucknell/Associated University Presses, 2003), 22: "In order to have a model of productivity, a culture also must have a model of nonproductivity. In order to enforce productivity, a culture must also disparage and punish nonproductivity."

A considerably more visible work, Sianne Ngai's captivating *Ugly Feelings* (Cambridge and London: Harvard University Press, 2005) deserves special mention in this connection. *Ugly Feelings* persuasively argues for both the materiality and the cultural significance of affect, and in particular attends to a certain breed of "intransitive feelings" characterized by "inaction" (22). As she explains in her introduction, her "exclusive focus" lies in assessing such "Bartlebyan" affects, which manifest an "obstructed agency with respect to other human actors or to the social as such" (3); in her accounting, negative affects are nonstrategic (she argues that they are instead "diagnostic"), inactive, and intransitive. As she explains in a telling passage, they may be "dysphoric or experientially negative, in the sense that they evoke pain or displeasure. They can also be described as 'semantically' negative, in the sense that they are saturated with socially stigmatizing meanings and values . . . and as 'syntactically' negative, in the sense that they are organized by trajectories of repulsion rather than attraction, by phobic strivings 'away from' rather than philic strivings 'toward.' In the case of these explicitly agonistic emotions, informed by what one psychoanalyst calls the global affect of 'against,' the negativity at stake is algorithmic or operational, rather than value- or meaning-based, involving processes of aversion, exclusion, and of course negation" (11–12).

In short, as obstructions or blockages of agency, these affects are read by Ngai as impeding the exercise of subjective power. They are thus cast as resolutely negative—as impediments to "normal" agency, or as hindrances, perhaps, to non-"ugly" feelings. To the extent that this negativity satisfies a certain Frankfurtian bias toward critical reflexivity, I am sympathetic (as my final chapter illustrates); I furthermore find entirely welcome Ngai's identification, in her introduction, of two paradigmatic instances of "narrative inaction" that, like "Bartleby," attribute negative affect to "a worker's increasingly alienated relationship to the corporation that employs him, as well as to the institutions of the state" (13). However, her continual linkage of such "negative" and "nonstrategic" affect with failure, resignation, and pessimism risks occluding the positive productivities of such feelings. In contrast, I will argue that idle practices may afford a strategic political potential, serve as a source of pleasure, and foster sympathy, community, and human attraction. They may be beautiful indeed. It is thus perhaps best at the outset to distinguish these practices from the "ugly feelings" Ngai discusses.

46. I am indebted to John Conley for sharing with me a description of the odd productivity of Bartleby, the scrivener, which illustrates precisely the kind of conceptual shift I am proposing. Bartleby is not idle—he is, rather, *idling*—and the odd force of this practice cannot be measured or otherwise made ascertainable (John Conley, "Bartleby and Communism," in *Failure: Experiments in Aesthetic and Social Practices* [Los Angeles: published in conjunction with the *Journal of Aesthetics and Protest*], 154).

47. This idea might be likened to that put forth in Postone, *Time, Labor, and Social Domination*, that "labor," far from being an ahistorical source of all value, is actually a reductionist category—that is, a constructed template that is historically specific to the capitalist mode of production.

48. The literature on "women's work" in the nineteenth century is expansive. For one constellation of critical and historical accounts of women's so-called unproductivity, see

the discussion of Charlotte Perkins Gilman's political economy in my chapter 4. The concept of a "national manhood" is advanced by Dana Nelson, *National Manhood: Capitalist Citizenship and the Imagined Fraternity of White Men* (Durham and London: Duke University Press, 1998).

49. Ibid., 14.

50. Christopher Castiglia's *Interior States: Institutional Consciousness and the Inner Life of Democracy in the Antebellum United States* (Durham: Duke University Press, 2008) makes a valuable contribution to theorizing the particular stakes of such interiority in nineteenth-century America. Crucially, he reveals the fundamental contradictoriness of such interior states, speaking specifically of the seeming impossibility of managing the unruly self in this context: "Citizens possessed of riven interiorities shuttle perpetually *between* self-control and appetite, desire and deferral, wait and want. That shuttling . . . is the necessary result of the interiorization of social division" (10). In a similar vein, Deleuze, reading Foucault's late work, notes that the agency of the subject in relationship to such social forces depends upon the variable configuration of the body, of power relations, of the state of knowledge, and of relation to the undifferentiated outside of thought—the confluence of these factors is what makes possible the constitution of a subject in a given field of forces. He goes on to argue that a modern subjectivity negotiates "two present forms of subjection, the one consisting of individualizing ourselves on the basis of constraints of power, the other of attracting each individual to a known and recognized identity, fixed once and for all. The struggle for subjectivity presents itself, therefore, as the right to difference, variation, and metamorphosis" (see Gilles Deleuze, *Foucault*, trans. Seán Hand [Minneapolis and London: University of Minnesota Press, 1988], 104, 106).

51. Some recent studies of nineteenth-century masculinity have tended simultaneously to offer important insights into the professionalization of masculine life—in particular, the emergence of the professional author and the white-collar subject more generally—while, in their fixation on the problem of men's relation to their work, subtly undervaluing the emergence of nonwork bases for male identity. See, for an example of this related mode of inquiry, John Evelev, *Tolerable Entertainment: Herman Melville and Professionalism in Antebellum New York* (Amherst and Boston: University of Massachusetts Press, 2006). Thomas Augst's *The Clerk's Tale: Young Men and Moral Life in Nineteenth-Century America* (Chicago: University of Chicago Press, 2003) is exceptionally subtle in navigating the everyday spheres of masculine work and leisure.

52. Vincent J. Bertolini, "Fireside Chastity: The Erotics of Sentimental Bachelorhood in the 1850s," in *Sentimental Men: Masculinity and the Politics of Affect in American Culture*, ed. Mary Chapman and Glenn Hendler (Berkeley and Los Angeles: University of California Press, 1999), 21. For a more historical account of the social practices of bachelordom, see Howard P. Chudacoff, *The Age of the Bachelor: Creating an American Subculture* (Princeton: Princeton University Press, 1999).

53. Bertolini, "Fireside Chastity," 21.

54. Katherine V. Snyder, *Bachelors, Manhood, and the Novel 1850–1925* (Cambridge: Cambridge University Press, 1999), 32. Bryce Traister, in "The Wandering Bachelor: Irving,

Masculinity, and Authorship," *American Literature* 74, no. 1 (March 2002): 117, affirms that the bachelor's neglect of sexual reproduction "served as a metaphor for his economic unproductivity in the marketplace at a time when men's productivity was conceptualized as the male counterpart, or complement to, female domestic consumption."

55. See the argument made by Traister, "The Wandering Bachelor," 122.

56. Lori Merish, *Sentimental Materialism: Gender, Commodity Culture, and Nineteenth-Century American Literature* (Durham and London: Duke University Press, 2000), 4–5.

57. Joseph Fichtelberg, *Critical Fictions: Sentiment and the American Market, 1780–1870* (Athens and London: University of Georgia Press, 2003), 7.

58. Ibid., 236.

59. With the rise of finance capital and the increasing importance of the white-collar facilitator, this type of "passive" economic productivity would become that much more hegemonic. In this connection, see Howard Horwitz's extended discussion, in chapter 7 of *By the Law of Nature: Form and Value in Nineteenth-Century America* (New York and Oxford: Oxford University Press, 1991), of the curious economic power wielded by Frank Cowperwood in Dreiser's *The Financier*.

60. For an account of surplus in the attention economy, see Jonathan Beller, "Cinema/ Capital," in *Deleuze and Guattari: New Mappings in Politics, Philosophy and Culture*, ed. Eleanor Kaufman and Kevin Jon Heller (Minneapolis: University of Minnesota Press, 1998). A very useful account of the diversity and profundity of these contemporary developments is provided in Randy Martin, *Financialization of Daily Life* (Philadelphia: Temple University Press, 2002).

NOTES TO CHAPTER 1

1. Dan McCall, *The Silence of Bartleby* (Ithaca and London: Cornell University Press, 1989). For an engaging summary of some of the achievements and the excesses of the Bartleby Industry, see chap. 1, 1–33. Two exceptionally important recent contributions to the field—Sianne Ngai's *Ugly Feelings* (Cambridge and London: Harvard University Press, 2005) and Branka Arsić's *Passive Constitutions or 7 ½ Times Bartleby* (Stanford: Stanford University Press, 2007)—regard Bartleby as the key figure in their extended treatments of the affective significance of passivity. My account is sympathetic to both works, despite harboring some hesitation to adopt Ngai's classification of myriad manifestations of negative affect as "Bartlebyan," an approach that collapses key distinctions between various types of negativity: as Arsić notes, "there remain differences among passivities" (67).

2. Robert Grant White, *Law and Laziness; or, Students at Law of Leisure* (New York: printed for the author at the Golden Rule Office, 1846). White, himself a lawyer, is best known today for his later contributions to Shakespeare scholarship. As is evident in Laura Rigal's *The American Manufactory: Art, Labor, and the World of Things in the Early Republic* (Princeton: Princeton University Press, 1998), the association of students at law with idleness boasts a robust tradition. Her account of *The Port Folio*, published in Philadelphia

from 1801 to 1824 and notable for its staff's "attempting to make themselves legendary for laziness rather than hard work" (117), relates the "Lounger's Diary" of a law student character by the name of Meander, who records such eventful entries as the following: "I rambled through the woods for two hours. . . . Did *nothing* very busily till four. Seized with a lethargic yawn, which lasted till seven, when a dish of coffee restored animation" (quoted, 127).

3. In the course of its 7 ½ provocative interpretations of Melville's tale, Arsić's *Passive Constitutions* similarly pursues these implications of the story, though without a deliberate emphasis on the specifically *economic* meaning of Bartleby's unproductivity. In the spirit of her claim that "as is the case with all originals (Oedipus, Hamlet, Don Quixote, or Milton's Satan), any interpretation [of Bartleby] will apply" (10), I humbly offer my more economically oriented account—Bartleby 8.0, if I may—as a complement, not an alternative, to her readings.

4. Herman Melville, "Bartleby, the Scrivener: A Story of Wall Street," in *The Piazza Tales, and Other Prose Pieces, 1839–1860*, ed. Harrison Hayford, Alma A. MacDougall, G. Thomas Tanselle et al., vol. 9 of *The Writings of Herman Melville* (Evanston and Chicago: Northwestern University Press and the Newberry Library, 1987), 19. Hereafter cited parenthetically.

5. Thomas Augst, *The Clerk's Tale: Young Men and Moral Life in Nineteenth-Century America* (Chicago and London: University of Chicago Press, 2003), 237. For Augst's interesting expansion on the theme of the narrator's failed "ethics of reading" and its challenge to contemporary criticism, see 244–48.

6. Notably, this claim is sanctioned only through the emulative economics of the lawyer's own employment in the service of John Jacob Astor, "who had no hesitation in pronouncing my first grand point to be prudence; my next, method" (Melville, "Bartleby," 14).

7. It has been fiercely argued in many circles that the sequel to "Bartleby" undermines the text's frugal perfection, anticlimactically appending superfluous and misleading surmise. To such critics, it is precisely this breakdown of evidentiary purity that cannot be permitted; they thus fail to recognize how the narrator's final lapse—his sober method giving way to idle speculation—is an element of the story that is perfectly necessary to convey Bartleby's impact. For some varied perspectives on the sequel paragraph, see McCall, *The Silence of Bartleby*, 128–33.

8. Such certainty would be total and seamless, as is alluded to by René Descartes, *Discourse on Method and Meditations on First Philosophy*, trans. Donald A. Cress (Indianapolis: Hackett, 1998), 10: "the true method" makes possible "arriving at the knowledge of everything." On the ambivalent and tactical function of "prudence" in the seventeenth century, see José Antonio Maravall, *Culture of the Baroque: Analysis of a Historical Structure*, trans. Terry Cochran (Minneapolis: University of Minnesota Press, 1986), 62: "[Prudence] was probably what gave the baroque the appearance that, beneath its sometimes hallucinating excesses and exaggerations, it was a culture whose disorder somehow made sense, was regulated and under control." McCall, *The Silence of Bartleby*, 115–16, suggests a

more proximal reference point for Melville's fixation on prudence: Lemuel Shaw's decision in *Brown v. Kendall*, which lionized "common sense and common usage."

9. McCall, *The Silence of Bartleby*, proffers a number of instances of this ambivalent narrative voice, through which the lawyer "put[s] to himself his own most profound misgivings about himself" (121) and develops a "habitual way of alternately saying yes and no" (122).

10. Marvin Hunt, "'*That's* the Word': Turning Tongues and Heads in 'Bartleby, the Scrivener,'" *ESQ* 40, no. 4 (1994): 279. Hunt's stress is rightly on the failure of these two instrumental idioms.

11. This point is well illustrated in David Kuebrich, "Melville's Doctrine of Assumptions: The Hidden Ideology of Capitalist Production in 'Bartleby,'" *Northeast Quarterly* 69, no. 3 (September 1996): 404. It is easy to sympathize with Kuebrich's interpretation of Bartleby as a class warrior whose protest is targeted at any kind of employment whatsoever, and hence at the wage system itself: "by stressing that he is not 'particular,' Bartleby is also asserting that he is not 'unique' but a member of a class: dependent, wage-earning employees" (400). Yet this is only part of the story, for Bartleby's preferences also exclude leisure activity, rural retreat, travel, the companionship of young men, etc. And, as McCall, *The Silence of Bartleby*, 108, argues, the imposition of a rigid class structure on the story seems to underemphasize the self-reappraisal of the narrator: to see Bartleby "as a representative of a class, an unwitting victim of a social and economic system, is not so much creative interpretation as it is obtuse paraphrase." Squaring this evidence with Kuebrich's reading would take some doing. On Bartleby's downward mobility, see Richard John, "The Lost World of Bartleby, the Ex-Office Holder: Variations on a Venerable Literary Form," *Northeast Quarterly* 70, no. 4 (December 1997): 631–41. John provides an interesting account of political patronage in the 1840s and its impact on those who both benefited and suffered from it.

12. Arsić's chapter "Bartleby or the Impersonal (White Wall and Green Screen)" comes to the same conclusion after juxtaposing "Bartleby" with key sections of *Moby-Dick* and reexamining the relationship between Melville's tale and Emerson's essay "The Transcendentalist." I will revisit these discussions in my chapter 5, in the meantime echoing her definitive correction to the individualizing tendency: "To raise the question of his identity, to ask 'Who is he?' 'Who is that man?' misses the point, insofar as it aims at positioning him, at giving him a determinate being. To try to pose and answer that question is to double the attorney's effort to bring Bartleby under the force of the law" (*Passive Constitutions*, 98).

13. Hunt, "*That's* the Word," 281.

14. Michael Hardt and Antonio Negri, *Empire* (Cambridge: Harvard University Press, 2000), 203. Their account at once overstates the case and also ultimately reinforces the individualizing paradigm, as will be addressed further below.

15. Ronald Wesley Hoag, "The Corpse in the Office: Mortality, Mutability and Salvation in 'Bartleby, the Scrivener,'" *ESQ* 38, no. 2 (1992): 125. Hoag argues that Bartleby's arrival is that of death pretending to be life; confronting this masquerade, the lawyer's

understanding of mortality and the human condition is transformed. My argument below will be almost exactly the opposite of his.

16. James C. Wilson, "'Bartleby': The Walls of Wall Street," *Arizona Quarterly* 37, no. 4 (Winter 1981): 339–40. Consider, by way of example, the narrator's ambivalent musing after Bartleby's second invocation of the formula "I would prefer not to": "I pondered a moment in perplexity.... Nothing so aggravates an earnest person as a passive resistance.... I regarded Bartleby and his ways. Poor fellow! thought I, he means no mischief; it is plain he intends no insolence; his aspect sufficiently evinces that his eccentricities are involuntary." Then confusion and retreat ease into self-interest: "He is useful to me. I can get along with him. If I turn him away, the chances are he will fall in with some less indulgent employer, and then he will be rudely treated, and perhaps driven forth miserably to starve. Yes. Here I can cheaply purchase a delicious self-approval. To befriend Bartleby; to humor him in his strange wilfulness, will cost me little or nothing, while I lay up in my soul what will eventually prove a sweet morsel for my conscience" (49–51).

17. In Descartes, *Meditations*, 63, the toil of reason is cause for reflection on this fragile encounter: "This undertaking is arduous, and a certain laziness brings me back to my customary way of living. I am not unlike a prisoner who enjoyed an imaginary freedom during his sleep, but, when he later begins to suspect that he is dreaming, fears being awakened and nonchalantly conspires with these pleasant illusions. In just the same way, I fall back of my own accord into my old opinions, and dread being awakened, lest the toilsome wakefulness which follows upon a peaceful rest must be spent thenceforward not in the light but among the inextricable shadows of the difficulties now brought forward."

18. Ann Smock, "Quiet," *Qui Parle* 2, no. 2 (Fall 1988), notes, for example, how Turkey is held to a paradoxical standard throughout this investigation, in which he, at his best, would "busily subside, industriously rest" (91).

19. Additional parallels that indicate Melville's debt to the earlier story may be added to those discussed in detail below. Among these are White's assertion that a student at law of leisure "of spirit, will become a Solicitor in Chancery" (*Law and Laziness*, 38), the post held by Melville's narrator. The scene in which Melville's narrator gives Turkey a hand-me-down coat also echoes one in White's story, where a "ragged" bum in a "wretched" hat swaps clothes with an inebriated student, and thereafter "might [be] taken for a gentleman returning from a ball" (24–25).

20. Ibid., 6–8.

21. Ibid., 22.

22. "It is a mournful view of human nature, of which we have had a glimpse,—this sight of the American Aristocracy just when they have, with much pain, become adept in the profession of idleness, and are awakening to the discovery that they have mistaken their vocation" (ibid., 26). White somewhat abruptly concludes his tale with a moralizing salvo against those men binarily made up of "the Lawyer by license, and the idle man by nature" (48).

23. Smock, "Quiet," 85.

24. This situation draws the attention of Gilles Deleuze, "Bartleby; or, The Formula," in *Essays Critical and Clinical*, trans. Daniel W. Smith and Michael A. Greco (Minneapolis: University of Minnesota Press, 1997), 73: "This is what the attorney glimpses with dread: all his hopes of bringing Bartleby back to reason are dashed because they rest on a *logic of presuppositions* according to which an employer 'expects' to be obeyed, or a kind friend listened to, whereas Bartleby has invented a new logic, a *logic of preference*, which is enough to undermine the presuppositions of language as a whole." Smock describes the peculiarity and the implications of the contract even more suggestively: she notes that it "consists in acquitting one of the parties to it of the duties that otherwise would comprise its terms. But such would seem to be the conditions of employment, or usefulness generally; or of busy-ness; *unemployment*. . . . Perhaps to work is to save yourself work" (86). Thus does "work" become the avoidance of real activity—of significant or substantial or meaningful endeavor; busy-ness is the avoidance of the real business of being.

25. Leo Marx, "Melville's Parable of the Walls," in *Melville's Short Novels*, ed. Dan McCall (New York and London: Norton, 2002), 252, writes, "In fact, writers like Nippers and Turkey are incapable of action" because they merely cower before authority and therefore fail to achieve anything significant.

26. Citing the scene in which Bartleby's behavior leaves the attorney paralyzed with doubt, "thunderstruck" like a man killed by lightning, Arsić argues that "by the force of Bartleby's will the attorney is relegated to a spectral existence" (*Passive Constitutions*, 20).

27. See, for example, Paul Lafargue, *The Right to Be Lazy*, trans. Charles H. Kerr (1883; repr., Chicago: Charles H. Kerr, 1989), 42, which predicts that "work will become a mere condiment to the pleasures of idleness." The tendency of most cultural criticism on this point has been merely to recalibrate the relative values of industry and idleness, while the tenability of the binary itself is seldom raised as a concern.

28. Lars Nerdrum, *The Economics of Human Capital: A Theoretical Analysis Illustrated Empirically by Norwegian Data* (Oslo: Scandinavian University Press, 1999), 68.

29. Gary S. Becker, "Investment in Human Capital: A Theoretical Analysis," *Journal of Political Economy* 70, no. 5, pt. 2 (supplement to October 1962): s9. The essays collected in this volume represent the first large-scale statement of human capital theory. A schematic list of such investments in human capital, suggested by Mark Blaug and cited by Nerdrum, *The Economics of Human Capital*, 53, includes such factors as schooling, on-the-job training, health, information retrieval, job searching, and migration. While the tendency has been for the proportion of value predicated on such inputs to rise in the postwar economy, it should be noted that such factors have always made an unheroic contribution to capitalist production. Thorstein Veblen, for example, notes how the printing trade in particular exploited these possibilities during the nineteenth century: see his *Theory of the Leisure Class: An Economic Study of Institutions* (New York: Modern Library, 1931).

30. Nerdrum, *Economics of Human Capital*, 52–53. A pithy account of the centrality of the theory of human capital to the neoliberal "epistemological transformation" of economic analysis may be found in Michel Foucault, *The Birth of Biopolitics: Lectures at the*

College de France, 1978–79, ed. Michel Senellart, trans. Graham Burchell (New York: Palgrave MacMillan, 2008), esp. 222–27.

31. Theodore W. Schultz, "Reflections on Investment in Man," *Journal of Political Economy* 70, no. 5, pt. 2 (supplement to October 1962): s2; Becker, "Investment in Human Capital," s10, emphasis added.

32. The conclusions reached by Schultz, "Reflections," s2, indicate the political stakes of restricting this analysis to individualized economic agents: "These changes in the investment of human capital are the basic factors reducing the inequality in the distribution of personal income," he claims. "One of the implications of this formulation is that modifications in income transfers, in progressive taxation, and in the distribution of privately owned wealth are relatively weak factors in altering the distribution of personal income." (This is bourgeois economics, after all!) Foucault, in *The Birth of Biopolitics*, 226, observes that the object of neoliberal analysis might most accurately be described as something slightly different than a mere individual: man as an "ability-machine," or as "entrepreneur of himself."

33. Becker, "Investment in Human Capital," s9–s10.

34. See Fritz Machlup, *Knowledge: Its Creation, Distribution, and Economic Significance*, 3 vols. (Princeton: Princeton University Press, 1980, 1982, 1984), esp. vol. 3, *The Economics of Information and Human Capital*. Machlup provides an extensive bibliography charting economic interventions in the field of human capital and the knowledge economy (336–400). For a statistical account of the growing significance of workers involved in knowledge-production during the transition into "postindustrialism," see Michael Rogers Rubin, Mary Taylor Huber, and Elizabeth Lloyd Taylor, *The Knowledge Industry in the United States, 1960–1980* (Princeton: Princeton University Press, 1986).

35. Machlup, *Knowledge*, 3: 430.

36. Further clarification would insist that this is hardly a "recently invented concept"—as Machlup asserts—but is rather a notion introduced by Marx in the mid-nineteenth century. A quote from *Capital*, cited in Mario Tronti, "Social Capital," *Telos* 17 (Fall 1973): 114, illustrates his early understanding of economic phenomena as the expression of a pure field of aggregated externalities: "social capital is forced to socialize the very knowledge of social labor. The single capital, with its limited perspective, comes to see that its profit now does not come only from the labor expanded by him or by his branch of production, and that average profit is different from immediate surplus-value. But to what extent this profit is due to the aggregate exploitation of labour on the part of the total social capital, i.e. by all his capitalist colleagues—this interrelation is a complete mystery to the individual capitalist; all the more so, since no bourgeois theorists, the political economists, have so far revealed it."

37. Larry A. Sjaastad, "Costs and Returns of Human Migration," *Journal of Political Economy* 70, no. 5 (October 1962): 87.

38. Antonio Negri, "Twenty Theses on Marx: Interpretations of the Class Situation Today," trans. Michael Hardt, in *Marxism beyond Marxism*, ed. Saree Makdisi, Cesare Casarino, and Rebecca E. Karl (New York: Routledge, 1996), 157. Ultimately, with the

continued intensification of the forces of production, all activity finds itself effectively enclosed by capital in a condition Marx termed "real subsumption." As Negri explains, real subsumption has been achieved when "the capitalist process of production has attained such a high level of development so as to comprehend every even small fraction of social production ... [its] form of value ... is a form in which there is an immediate translatability between the social forces of production and the relations of production themselves" (152). Gilles Deleuze's "Postscript on Control Societies," trans. Martin Joughlin, in *Negotiations* (New York: Columbia University Press, 1995), following on Foucault's analysis of disciplinary society, addresses a similar development by contrasting disciplinary production to contemporary "metaproduction"; "what [metaproduction] seeks to sell is services, and what it seeks to buy, activities" (181). And it is money that perhaps best conveys how contemporary control society differs from its predecessor: "discipline was always related to molded currencies containing gold as a numerical standard, whereas control is based on floating exchange rates, modulations depending on a code setting sample percentages for various currencies" (180).

39. Karl Marx, *Grundrisse*, trans. Martin Nicolaus (London and New York: Penguin, 1973), 694.

40. Ibid., 711–12. As Paolo Virno, "Notes on the General Intellect," trans. Cesare Casarino, *Polygraph* 6 (1993): 35, astutely notes, here "models of social knowledge cannot be compared to different forms of labor; rather, they are themselves an immediate productive force. They are not units of measure, rather, they are the measureless presupposition of heterogeneous operative possibilities."

41. Michel Foucault, *Discipline and Punish*, trans. Alan Sheridan (New York: Vintage, 1979), 138.

42. Leo Marx, in his "Melville's Parable of the Walls," 250, queries: "the office in which he had worked was enclosed by walls. How was this to be distinguished from the place where he died?"

43. Ibid., 241.

44. Lois Severini, *The Architecture of Finance: Early Wall Street* (Ann Arbor: University of Michigan Research Press, 1981), 57–58.

45. J. S. Gibbons, quoted ibid., 83.

46. The green of the grass peeking through the stones of the Tombs, especially in contrast to the blank monotony of the office's views, is read by Leo Marx as a testament to Melville's affirmative tendency: "green seems virtually inherent in time itself, a somehow eternal property of man's universe" (Marx, "Melville's Parable of the Walls," 254).

47. Emphasis added.

48. Marx, "Melville's Parable of the Walls," 255. A pretty apt description of the potentials of such a space is offered by White, *Law and Laziness*, 42: the office is "a *safe screen* for quiet and gentlemanly inebriety, a little eddy beside the swift current of business where all worthless things circulate for ever, a corner where the idle bask in the sun, pout at the passing world, which will not notice them" (emphasis added).

49. Foucault, *Discipline and Punish*, 195.

50. Ibid., 200, emphasis added.

51. Smock, "Quiet," 78. For some complementary riffage on the question of *communication*, and in particular a description of its relationship to the impersonal force of a language that exceeds any containing context, recall the opening passages of Jacques Derrida's "Signature, Event, Context," in *Margins of Philosophy*, trans. Alan Bass (Chicago: University of Chicago Press, 1982), 309–11. In *Law and Laziness*, too, idle office chatter proliferates, always exceeding the disciplinary context, meandering through "a golden haze of poetry and metaphysics" that softens the sharp edges of duty, and featuring "not a word of law, nay, the one who should broach *that* topic, would be a bore, and lose his character for knowledge of life" (White, *Law and Laziness*, 11–12).

52. White, *Law and Laziness*, 19.

53. On this passage and Evagrius more generally, see Siegfried Wenzel, *The Sin of Sloth: Acedia in Medieval Thought and Literature* (Chapel Hill: University of North Carolina Press, 1967), 4–6.

54. Michael Hardt, "Prison Time," *Yale French Studies* 91, ed. Scott Durham (1997): 64–65, notes that the "rationality" of time equally inflects both the economic and the legal: the time of the office works according to the same logics as that of the prison: "Like the equations between labor-time and value, our society sets up an elaborate calculus familiar to all of us between crime and prison-time. . . . The calculations are utterly arbitrary . . . but, while we may often question relative values on the two sides of the equation, we seldom doubt the viability of the calculus itself."

55. E. P. Thompson, "Time, Work-Discipline, and Industrial Capitalism," *Past and Present* 38 (December 1967): 95.

56. Foucault, *Discipline and Punish*, 154. The specific "modernity" of such time has prompted wide discussion. Particularly helpful in linking this discussion to the constitution of activity under capitalist totality is Moishe Postone, *Time, Labor, and Social Domination: A Reinterpretation of Marx's Critical Theory* (Cambridge: Cambridge University Press, 1996), 214–15: "Just as labor is transformed from an action of individuals to the alienated general principle of the totality under which the individuals are subsumed, time expenditure is transformed from a result *of* activity into a normative measure *for* activity" (emphasis added). One might note innumerable other illustrations of time's constitutive role in the American national mythology, such as Benjamin Franklin's exhortations to gain—"He that idly loses five shillings' worth of time . . . might as prudently throw five shillings into the sea" (quoted in Weber, *Protestant Ethic*, 50)—or the historical primacy of clock manufacturing in the United States, as described in Michael O'Malley, *Keeping Watch: A History of American Time* (New York: Viking, 1990), 7, 31.

57. So it appears in Evagrius's account, as well as, for that matter, throughout nineteenth-century discourses on unproductivity, as my chapter 2 argues.

58. Thompson, in "Time, Work-Discipline, and Industrial Capitalism," 95, credits the industrial ethic with according time a "firmer accent," and traces its New World trajectory from Franklin to Henry Ford.

59. Weber, *The Protestant Ethic*, 157–58.

60. Ibid., 48–49.

61. Ibid., 49–50.

62. Ibid., 52.

63. On the emptying of space and time in exchange economies, see Alfred Sohn-Rethel, *Intellectual and Manual Labour: A Critique of Epistemology*, trans. Martin Sohn-Rethel (London: Macmillan, 1978), esp. 48–53.

64. Louis Althusser, "Contradiction and Overdetermination," in *For Marx*, trans. Ben Brewster (1969; repr., London: Verso, 1996), 119, italics in original.

65. Foucault, *Discipline and Punish*, 225. Antonio Negri, *Time for Revolution*, trans. Matteo Mandarini (London: Continuum, 2003), 65, helpfully puts this definition of discipline into economic terms: discipline "is the homologue of hierarchy in the social redistribution of wealth; it represents the hierarchy of functions in the process of social production. . . . Value is surplus-value, is command, is hierarchical and disciplinary absoluteness of command."

66. Negri, *Time for Revolution*, 75.

67. On the individualism of Bartleby's strategy, see Hardt and Negri, *Empire*, 203–4. On the cooperative fundament of refusal, see Negri, *Time for Revolution*, 73: "Behind the category of relative surplus-value hide the movements of productive co-operation that—*originally* (it should be forcefully underlined)—presents itself as the *refusal* of capitalist command over production and as the attempt, always frustrated but not for that less real, of constructing an autonomous time." Even Bartleby's ambiguous final "sleep," which brings him into communion with "kings and counselors," might be regarded as tapping into a fundamentally collective experience. As Jean-Luc Nancy claims in his quirky essay *The Fall of Sleep*, trans. Charlotte Mandell (New York: Fordham University Press, 2009), 17: "Sleep itself knows only equality, the measure common to all, which allows no differences or disparities. All sleepers fall into the same, identical and uniform sleep. This consists precisely in not differentiating."

68. White, *Law and Laziness*, 41.

NOTES TO CHAPTER 2

1. Thomas Cole, "Essay on American Scenery," *American Monthly Magazine*, January 1836, 1–12. Excerpted in John W. McCoubrey, *American Art 1700–1960: Sources and Documents* (Englewood Cliffs, N.J.: Prentice-Hall, 1965), 100–101.

2. While the possibilities of antebellum rail travel have been the chief critical concern in this regard, the opening of the Erie Canal in 1825 also deserves special mention, as it was one of the primary means by which Cole undertook his "tours of the picturesque" (see Patricia Anderson, *The Course of Empire: The Erie Canal and the New York Landscape, 1825–1875* [Rochester: Memorial Art Gallery of the University of Rochester, 1984], 38). Something of the leisurely ease of such pleasure junkets was reported by Dewitt Clinton, who noted at the time that "for 8 dollars you can go, in four days, 200 miles without a jolt or the least fatigue, and employ the whole time in reading, writing, rational conversation,

amusement, or viewing the most interesting region of the globe" (quoted ibid., 19). The rail system would later greatly serve such poachers of the picturesque; a description of such an outing appears in the unpaginated essay by John K. Howat in *John Frederick Kensett: 1816–1872* (New York: American Federation of Arts, 1968): "Proceeding along in five days from Baltimore to Wheeling, the trip was conceived to allow the fifty assembled aestheticians to 'collect' the most picturesque views along the right of way. . . . The trip was distinguished by 'countless incidents which made the time pass so agreeably.'" On Dunlap's persistent propensity to idle behaviors and the vicissitudes of his career as a history painter, see McCoubrey, *American Art*, 45–48.

3. The nineteenth-century equation of repose with aesthetic contemplation is a relatively new development, the concept having previously been largely reserved for the formal quality of masses in proper alignment. The most sustained consideration of this development is found in John Bryant, *Melville and Repose: The Rhetoric of Humor in the American Renaissance* (New York and Oxford: Oxford University Press, 1993), which demonstrates great sensitivity in its deft discussion of the tensions inherent to the term. Though Bryant notes that it "had its vogue in the Romantic era, losing the richness of its meaning in our rather less-than-reposeful century" (4), I will argue that it is only in the context of such "less-than-reposeful" conditions that the term becomes most freighted with significance.

4. Exemplary in this regard is Nathaniel Parker Willis's *American Scenery*, which illustrates the translation of repose, often in league with the prevailing pastoral conventions, into other vocabularies. In this connection, see Sarah Burns, *Pastoral Inventions* (Philadelphia: Temple University Press, 1989), 13–14. As the following chapter notes, another significant site for the export of pastoral ideology was the architecture of suburbia; the first significant edge developments in Boston and New York date to the 1830s and 1840s. For a more extended account, see Kenneth T. Jackson, *Crabgrass Frontier: The Suburbanization of the United States* (New York and Oxford: Oxford University Press, 1985), esp. 20–44. In the literary context, there may be no more compelling adaptation of the term than in the opening paragraph of Melville's *Pierre: or, The Ambiguities*, ed. Harrison Hayford, Hershel Parker, and G. Thomas Tanselle, vol. 7 of *The Writings of Herman Melville* (Evanston and Chicago: Northwestern University Press and Newberry Library, 1971), 3. There, nature seems to become self-conscious of its own truths, an awareness predicated upon the complete cessation of all activity: "Not a flower stirs; the trees forget to wave; the grass itself seems to have ceased to grow; and all Nature, as if suddenly become conscious of her own profound mystery, and feeling no refuge from it but silence, sinks into this wonderful and indescribable repose."

5. Richard Henry Dana, "Preface," *Idle Man* 1 (1821): 8–12.

6. Richard Henry Dana, "Musings," *Idle Man* 4 (1822): 38.

7. Ibid.

8. Ibid., 46. The relationship between nature and spiritual truth in American visual culture has been widely discussed. Barbara Novak, *Nature and Culture: American Landscape and Painting, 1825–1875* (New York and Oxford: Oxford University Press, 1995), esp. chap. 1, provides a useful overview, as does Albert Gelpi, "White Light in the Wilderness:

Landscape and Self in Nature's Nation," in *American Light: The Luminist Movement, 1850—1875*, ed. John Wilmerding (New York: Harper and Row; Washington, D.C.: National Gallery of Art, 1980), 291–312, which analysis considers key American literary figures as well.

9. This widespread sentiment also finds a home in Washington Allston, *Lectures on Art, and Poems* (1850; repr., Gainesville, Fla.: Scholars' Facsimiles and Reprints, 1967), to which I shall return.

10. Theodor W. Adorno, *Aesthetic Theory*, trans. Robert Hullot-Kentor (Minneapolis: University of Minnesota Press, 1997), 62.

11. In *Aesthetic Theory*, Adorno argues that "in every particular aesthetic experience of nature the social whole is lodged" (68), insisting that the appreciation of natural beauty is a product of human endeavor, and not of the seamless transmission of spirit. Such appreciation demands, for example, the historical acculturation of viewers that makes it possible for them to appreciate landscape views, as is pointed out in Kenneth John Myers, "Culture and Landscape Experience," in *American Iconology*, ed. David C. Miller (New Haven: Yale University Press, 1993), 74.

12. Adorno, *Aesthetic Theory*, 65.

13. The transition apparently facilitated by "repose" persists as an unresolved issue in art historical accounts of the period. For while it has been acknowledged that repose, especially in the wake of Cole's essay, is ever more significant as an experiential and aesthetic category, the distinction between these two functions of the concept is seldom observed—its meaning is taken for granted instead of being contextualized.

14. Given its magnitude, the critical literature on the sublime might itself be described as sublime. On the American reworking of the concept, chiefly in visual culture, see the similar treatments of Novak, *Nature and Culture*, 37; and Earl A. Powell, "Luminism and the American Sublime," in *American Light*, 69–72. Powell refers to this new sublime as a "transcendental" or "contemplative" one. In addition to the classic figurings of Longinus and Burke, I have found helpful the general context provided by Samuel H. Monk, *The Sublime: A Study of Critical Theories in XVIII-Century England* (Ann Arbor: University of Michigan Press, 1960), esp. chaps. 9 and 10 on painting, as well as the frameworks offered by Peter de Bolla, *The Discourse of the Sublime* (Oxford and New York: Basil Blackwell, 1989) and *Of the Sublime: Presence in Question* (Albany: State University of New York Press, 1993), which features essays by Jean-Luc Nancy, Philippe Lacoue-Labarthe, J. F. Lyotard, and others.

15. Cole, in McCoubrey, *American Art*, 104.

16. Quoted in Powell, "Luminism and the American Sublime," 75.

17. See the classic work of Leo Marx, *The Machine in the Garden: Technology and the Pastoral Ideal in America* (1964; repr., Oxford and New York: Oxford University Press, 2000), esp. chap. 4. For a further assessment of the political function of "sublimity" as a guarantor of national destiny, see Howard Horwitz's discussion of the "domestic" or "manifest" sublime in *By the Law of Nature: Form and Value in Nineteenth-Century America* (New York and Oxford: Oxford University Press, 1991), 36–38, as well as Rob Wilson's claim in "Techno-euphoria and the Discourse of the American Sublime," in *National*

Identities and Post-Americanist Narratives, ed. Donald E. Pease (Durham and London: Duke University Press, 1994), about the currency of such discourses of "democratic longing," enabling subjects to "identify not so much with the power of the state as with a sublimated spectacle of national empowerment increasingly materialized into a railway train, an electronic dynamo, an airplane, or a bomb" (208).

18. Marx, *Machine in the Garden*, 194.

19. Ibid. Consider the parallel treatments in Charles Caldwell's 1832 assertion that "objects of exalted power and grandeur elevate the mind that seriously dwells on them, and import to it greater compass and strength. Alpine scenery and an embattled ocean deepen contemplation, and give their own sublimity to the conceptions of beholders. The same will be true of our system of Rail-roads" (quoted in Marx, *The Machine in the Garden*, 195), and in Charles Fraser's assertion that steam power was "triumphing over time and space, outstripping the winds in speed, annihilating every obstacle by sea or land, and almost defying the organic influences which regulate the surface of our globe" (199).

20. Quoted in Emily Morse Symonds (pseud. George Paston), *Little Memoirs of the Nineteenth Century*, (1902; repr., Freeport, N.Y.: Books for Libraries Press, 1969), 194.

21. William Ware, *Lectures on the Works and Genius of Washington Allston* (Boston: Phillips, Sampson, 1852). Buoyed, perhaps, by landscape's rise to respectability between the time of this painting and the time of his writing, this Unitarian clergyman provocatively comments that the painting would benefit from the excision of its historical aspect: "It would have been a great gain to the work if the Scripture passage could have been painted out, and the Desert only left" (89). Considered in light of Allston's professed desire to realize a "Grand Historical Style" (and his failure to do so), this suggests just how dramatic was the ascension of landscape painting. For at the time of the painting's execution, its landscape elements would have been those in need of justifying their existence, against the widely held superiority of history painting, which, despite being generally economically unprofitable, enjoyed a certain esteem as a more noble genre. For more on Allston's self-acknowledged failure to dignify history painting, see Kathryn Wat, "Word Over Image: Benjamin West, John Singleton Copley, Washington Allston, and the (Dis) Illusion of Grand Manner History Painting" (Ph.D. diss., University of Delaware, 2000), esp. chaps. 6 and 7.

22. For a further evaluation of *Elijah in the Desert* and Allston's facility with repose, see Ware, *Lectures*, 72, 83–90.

23. Ibid., 69. Ware's "purplish folds" is a formulation borrowed from Allston's *Lectures on Art*. The purplish prose owes a similar debt.

24. Margaret Fuller Ossoli, "A Record of the Impressions Produced by the Exhibition of Mr. Allston's Pictures in the Summer of 1839," in McCoubrey, *American Art*, 60.

25. The response to this effect is documented in David Bjelajac, "The Boston Elite's Resistance to Washington Allston's *Elijah in the Desert*," in *American Iconology*, 41. This diffuse coloring, in which light seems to emanate from beyond the canvas, was key to the idealist aura of immaterial ephemerality that helped to popularize Allston's work among eastern elites, and was also arguably an important forerunner to the mystificatory

enlightenment of the later works now called luminist. Allston's tireless labors to achieve his desired effects are documented throughout his collected letters, and are also suggested by the protracted saga of his unfinished *Belshazzar's Feast* (see Bjelejac, *Millenial Desire and the Apocalyptic Vision of Washington Allston* [Washington, D.C., and London: Smithsonian Institution Press, 1988]; and Wat, "Word Over Image").

26. Margaret Fuller, in McCoubrey, *American Art*, 60.

27. Allston, who while at Harvard produced a student composition entitled "Procrastination Is the Thief of Time," maintained his alertness to the corrupting dangers of his situation throughout his career. Included among the many platitudinous apothegms with which he decorated the walls of his studio was the following: "The love of gain never made a Painter; but it has marred many" (see Allston, *Lectures on Art, and Poems*, 168). The letter to Robert Rogers (28 October 1797), as well as reference to Allston's college theme, are found in *The Correspondence of Washington Allston*, ed. Nathalia Wright (Lexington: University of Kentucky, 1993), 12, 19.

28. Allston's "The Hypochondriac" first appeared in *Idle Man* 2 (1821): 38–60, and is reprinted in *Lectures on Art, and Poems*, from which this quote is drawn (182). It bears a great resemblance, in form, content, and title, obviously, to the *London Magazine* essays written by James Boswell between 1777 and 1783, and collected under the title *The Hypochondriack*, ed. Margery Bailey, 2 vols. (Stanford: Stanford University Press, 1928). Boswell roughly equates hypochondria with melancholy, suggesting that the former is a "fantastically wretched" version of the latter (1: 140), and suggesting that he would "recommend to those who are subject to fits of languor not to the leave themselves to their own minds alone for occupation, but to engage in some profession which calls them to stated duties" (1: 148). The most intense of Boswell's hypochondria essays is found in vol. 2, no. 34, pp. 40–46.

29. Allston, "The Hypochondriac," 182.

30. Ibid., 183.

31. Ibid., 190.

32. Ibid., 191.

33. Ibid., 196.

34. Washington Allston, "Introductory Discourse," in *Lectures on Art, and Poems*, 11.

35. Ibid.

36. Ibid., 17. Compare this description of a harmonious emotional state with that, found elsewhere in the *Lectures*, which similarly describes the experience of the sublime as one in which merely human interests are chased away. The sublime experience is "too vast to be circumscribed by human content" (61); the sublime object "is not in man: for the emotion excited has an outward tendency; the mind cannot contain it" (53).

37. Ibid., 70, emphasis added.

38. Ibid., 70–71.

39. Ibid., 73.

40. Beauty resonates with the universal essence of each individual mind. Allston's discussion of Beauty considers the outer, material world only in light of its "immediate

relation to Man"; he defines "the Human Being as the predetermined centre to which it [the outer world] was designed to converge" (see Allston, *Lectures on Art, and Poems*, 52).

41. Ibid., 53.

42. Ibid., 55.

43. Ibid., 64.

44. Washington Allston, "Art," in *Lectures on Art, and Poems*, 105.

45. Washington Allston, "Composition," in *Lectures on Art, and Poems*, 149–50.

46. Ibid., 152.

47. Allston, "Introductory Discourse," in *Lectures*, 68.

48. Cole quoted in McCoubrey, *American Art*, 105. The unique character of the waterfall increasingly helped to define repose. It captures how, rather than merely being a state of rest characteristic of inert masses, later versions of repose came to imply *completed movement*. Consider the later definition provided by Henry Rankin Poore, *Art Principles in Practice* (New York and London: Putnam's, 1930), 75–76, where rest is a product of incessant activity, and likewise is expressed in endlessly rushing waters: "Repose is not the quality of inaction in art but rather the tranquilizing effect of witnessing motion that is consistent and eventually final. Repose in art is not the inaction of those elements which ought to be actively coordinate; it is rather the sensation of movement in a whirlpool, the logical result of dynamic forces so correlated as to produce equilibrium, such an equation of forces as produce balance—and under this sensation we rest."

49. Allston, "Composition," *Lectures*, 144, 145.

50. Ibid., 192.

51. Ibid., 145.

52. Ibid.

53. Sergio Bologna, quoted in Antonio Negri, *Marx Beyond Marx: Lessons on the "Grundrisse,"* ed. Jim Fleming, trans. Harry Cleaver, Michael Ryan, and Maurizio Viano (New York: Autonomedia, 1991), 25. For the impact of this condition on Marx's intellectual development, see especially the early chapters of *Marx Beyond Marx*. For further discussion of the significance of the 1857 monetary crisis, as the earliest demonstration of the new monetary system's propensity to internal crisis, see Eric Hobsbawm, *The Age of Capital, 1848–1875* (New York: Vintage, 1996), 67–68.

54. Note the repeated recourse to "nature" and "natural value" throughout the money chapter of Karl Marx, *Grundrisse*, trans. Martin Nicolaus (London: Penguin, 1973), 115–238. According to Antonio Negri, "Value and Affect," trans. Michael Hardt, *boundary2* 26, no. 2 (Summer 1999): 81, it is characteristic of the period of formal subsumption of labor under capital that use value and necessary labor are represented as not only "natural" but also as external to the capitalist regime: "The price of 'necessary labor' (to reproduce the proletariat) is thus presented, in this period, as a quantity that is natural (and/or historical), but in any case external—a quantity that mediates between the productive effectivity of the working class and its social and monetary inclusion." It might be added that like the category of "natural beauty" considered above, the notions of "natural labor" or of a "natural product" already presuppose an historical, "unnatural" counterpart: exchange.

55. These instances of romantic-Gothic sublimity are drawn from Marx, *Grundrisse*, 146, 147, 158, emphasis added.

56. Ibid., 188.

57. Ibid., 197. Negri, *Marx Beyond Marx*, 27, argues that this emphasis on the sociality of capitalist production and circulation is the unique strength of the *Grundrisse*'s analysis: "While in *Capital* the categories are generally modeled on private and competitive capital, in the *Grundrisse* they are modeled on a tendential scheme of *social capital*."

58. Ibid.

59. Allston, "Composition," *Lectures*, 152.

60. Marx, *Grundrisse*, 202.

61. Ibid., 222.

62. Ibid., 224. The prospect of wealth is thus, in itself, generative—of a condition in which "money does not have a dissolving effect, but acts productively," by generating the circumstances in which greed and industriousness may flourish.

63. The above complaints of Cole and Allston about the bogey of "gain" are weak tea compared with those of Asher B. Durand, whose screeds in *The Crayon* provide an exemplarily stinging response to this concern. See Durand, "Letters on Landscape Painting," *Crayon* 1, no. 7 (February 1855): 97–98.

64. Marx, *Grundrisse*, 224.

65. Foremost among these appraisals of luminism is that of Barbara Novak. The collection *American Light*, ed. Wilmerding, compiles numerous plates with commentary from the likes of Novak, Powell, Stebbins, Wilmerding, and others, and includes Novak's essay "On Defining Luminism." Additionally, chapter 12 of Wilmerding, *American Art* (Baltimore and Middlesex, England: Penguin, 1976), 93–99, is devoted to an introduction to luminism by way of Ruskin and Jarves; his essay "Luminism and Literature," in *American Views: Essays on American Art* (Princeton: Princeton University Press, 1991) considers certain luminist conventions resonant with the contemporary trends outlined by F. O. Matthiessen in *American Renaissance*. Robert Hughes, *American Visions: The Epic History of Art in America* (New York: Knopf, 1997) provides a short exoteric account that stresses the biographical trajectories of the various artists (see esp. 167–74 on Kensett, Heade, and Lane). Andrew Wilton and Tim Barringer, *American Sublime: Landscape Painting in the United States* (Princeton: Princeton University Press, 2002) provide a more recent overview of the works and the field, while challenging the "luminist" label as too narrow and exceptional (see 25–26).

66. A broader application of the category "luminism," which documents luminist effects internationally and both earlier and later than luminism's accepted time frame, is offered in Theodore E. Stebbins Jr., "Luminism in Context: A New View," *American Light*, 211–36.

67. Barbara Novak, "On Defining Luminism," *American Light*, 27–28, emphasis added.

68. See Cole, "Essay on American Scenery" in McCoubrey, *American Art*, 103, 108. Cole was particularly taken by water, noting its suggestion of repose ("in the unrippled lake, which mirrors all surrounding objects, we have the expression of tranquillity and peace").

In his invocation of shorelessness he not only contrasts these bodies of water with those hemmed into the painting's center by Claudean conventions, but also borrows another figure from Dana, "Musings," 41: "All that his mind falls in with it sweeps along in its deep and swift and continuous flow, and bears them on with the multitude that fills its shoreless and living sea."

69. Such was the verdict, in 1844, of the *Art-Union* (London), quoted in Lisa Fellows Andrus, "Design and Measurement in Luminist Art," in *American Light*, 46.

70. Albert Boime, *The Magisterial Gaze: Manifest Destiny and American Landscape Painting, c. 1830–1865* (Washington, D.C., and London: Smithsonian Institution Press, 1991).

71. Powell, "Luminism and the American Sublime," 78.

72. Baur, in his early study, describes this simplification and abstraction of luminist mass in the purist vocabulary of eighteenth-century repose. What prevails here is "a balanced grouping of masses with some simplification of volumes and structure" (quoted in Wilmerding, *American Light*, 13).

73. A similar effect is achieved in Gifford's *Hook Mountain, Hudson* (1866) and in Kensett's *Newport Coast*, from the 1850s, as well as in numerous of Heade's works.

74. Ralph Waldo Emerson, "Nature," *The Writings of Ralph Waldo Emerson*, ed. Brooks Atkinson (New York: Modern Library, 1950), 6–7, famously articulates the experience of transcendent sublimity as follows: "I became a transparent eyeball, I am nothing; I see all; the currents of the Universal Being circulate through me; I am part or parcel of God. . . . In the tranquil landscape, and especially in the distant line of the horizon, man beholds somewhat as beautiful as his own nature."

75. Novak, "On Defining Luminism," 27–28.

76. Jarves, quoted in Wilmerding, *American Light*, 14.

77. The idea that a luminist composition is capable of "stopping" or "halting" time has provoked considerable discussion, as in Powell, "Luminism and the American Sublime," 72, which invokes "absolute stillness," and Novak, "On Defining Luminism," 44, which declares that luminist paintings "reach to a mystical oneness above time and outside of space. . . . [O]neness with Godhead is complete." Hughes, *American Visions*, 168, describes how, in the painting of Fitz Hugh Lane, "each image offers a small moment in time, but infinitely stretched out."

This mystified temporality is only heightened by luminism's characteristic light effects. Novak notes, in "On Defining Luminism," 25, that "luminist radiance occurs not because of interactions, overlaps, and dissolutions of stroke, but because of minute tonal modulations . . . the coalescence of these tonalities mimics the effect of radiant light and negates the idea of paint," noting, significantly, that luminist light is not really "atmospheric" in frequency—so dense are the particles of matter that represent it that "air cannot circulate" between them. Here she may be wishing to distinguish between properly luminist light and the atmospheric effects of someone like Washington Allston, who first imported certain "atmospheric" glazing techniques he culled during his travels abroad. It has been demonstrated (as in Wilmerding's introduction to *American Light*) that the effects of high luminism—the glowing streaks of color that would have been alien to the comparatively drab palette of the Hudson River painters—were the product of innovation in painting technology. The year 1856, he points out, marked the availability of a new palette, including mauve and magenta, later to be followed by cobalt blue and cobalt yellow. The proliferation of synthetic color, then, is likely as much a reason for the different light effects as is painterly technique (see 15–16).

78. So much did the rigid geometry of luminism rely on such schemas that Heade—probably the most meticulous of the luminists in this regard—has been charged with being formulaic (see Andrus, "Design and Measurement," 46). Such geometrical precision is likewise apparent in Bierstadt's 1862 *Moat Mountain, Intervale, New Hampshire*, where geometrically placed trees shrink toward the horizon as an index of recession; the effect—very similar to that of Heade's haystack paintings—is heightened by alternating strata of shadow and light.

79. Quoted in Powell, "Luminism and the American Sublime," 78. Cole acted on this principle in such works as *Mountain Sunrise, Catskill* (1826), likely a composite of sketches he took while sojourning through the Hudson River valley in 1825–26 (see Powell, "Luminism and the American Sublime," 73–74).

80. Spurred by Eli Whitney's desire to "give every part [of a machine] its just proportion—which, once accomplished, will give expedition, uniformity, and exactness to the whole," the system of interchangeable parts was used in twenty industries by 1860, including the manufacture of farm machinery and watch components (see Robert Heilbroner and Aaron Singer, *The Economic Transformation of America* [New York: Harcourt Brace Jovanovich, 1977], 43–45). An extreme, and extremely nationalist, example of this assimilative tendency in landscape painting is Bierstadt's "Among the Sierra Nevada Mountains, California" (1869), which, painted by Bierstadt while in Rome, brings together a greatest-hits assemblage of natural features, in what Rob Wilson calls "a private composite of the American Sublime, rearranged to serve a vision of national grandeur" (Wilson, "Techno-euphoria," 214).

81. Records of Heade's wanderlust are presented in Theodore Stebbins, *The Life and Work of Martin Johnson Heade* (New Haven: Yale University Press, 1975). His letters, for example, document plans, ever aware of financial imperatives, to travel in Paris, London, Rome, and Scotland, this last location justified by his expectation that "there's some fine scenery there, & I believe the associations would give them a ready sale" (30).

82. See, for example, *The Railroad in American Art: Representations of Technological Change*, ed. Susan Danly and Leo Marx (Cambridge: MIT Press, 1988). *Starrucca Viaduct*, governed by a Claudean compositional strategy, is not regarded as a luminist work; I treat it here due to its exceptional character among American landscape representation generally. *Starrucca Viaduct* engineering data are drawn from Wilton and Barringer, *American Sublime*, 140.

83. Stebbins, *Martin Johnson Heade*, 45–47.

84. Burns, quoted ibid., 126.

85. Ibid., 116.

86. John Durand, in McCoubrey, *American Art*, 9.

87. John Galt, in McCoubrey, *American Art*, 37.

88. James Guild, "From Tunbridge, Vermont, to London, England—The Journal of James Guild, Peddler, Tinker, Schoolmaster, Portrait Painter, From 1818 to 1824," *Proceedings of the Vermont Historical Society*, n.s., 5, no. 3 (1937): 268. Itinerant purveyors of paintings were common prior to the Civil War and the rise of photography, the latter of which devalued the "likenesses" attainable by their "craft."

89. John Trumbull, in *The Autobiography of John Trumbull*, ed. Theodore Sizer (New Haven: Yale University Press, 1953), 160–62.

90. Even relatively notable history painters found that despite the much-trumpeted social utility of their work, making a living at it was not so easy. See William Dunlap, *The Rise and Progress of the Arts of Design in the United States* (1834) 1: 344–50, for example, for a biographical account of how his "experiment in great historical painting yielded little profit" until late in 1822, when some of his paintings generated both acclaim and accounts. After that success, and prior to his "next exertion as an artist," Dunlap, "having some taste for the picturesque and more for rambling," spent some time in the country "in clambering rocks and making sketches." Ultimately, he concludes that "I had none of that facility which attends the adept in drawing, and now felt the penalty—one of the penalties of my idleness and folly when I had the Royal Academy of England at my command."

91. *National Advocate*, April 21, 1818, reprinted in McCoubrey, *American Art*, 44. Vanderlyn's money troubles appear to have been quite dire and protracted: in an 1814 letter (issued from Paris) to Washington Allston, he sought Allston's advice on whether to shift his emphasis to panorama painting, complaining that "I have never received a *sol* for any historical picture, save the small one I painted for Mr. [Joel] Barlow at the time you was here, for which I rec'd 25 Louis. 'Tis true I have not painted many, but enough however to run myself in debt and to discourage me" (see Allston, *Correspondence*, 78). Barbara Novak, *Nature and Culture*, 20, notes the common scale and principle behind the public panoramic spectacles and such large-scale history painting works as Thomas Cole's *Course of Empire* series, effectively deflating the overblown claims to nobility made by painters of the latter. One surmises that it was perhaps precisely the delicacy of the boundary between art for the consuming public and that directed toward the intellectual elite that generated attempts such as those of the *National Advocate* to emphasize the distinction between the formats.

92. In McCoubrey, *American Art*, 44.

93. Durand, in McCoubrey, *American Art*, 113.

94. Ibid.

95. See Kenneth John Meyers, "Culture and Landscape Experience," 74. The connection between such appreciation and class status is made rather transparent by Durand, "Letters on Landscape Painting," *Crayon* 1, no. 7 (February 1855): 98: "To the rich merchant and capitalist, and to those whom even a competency has released from the great world-struggle, so far as to allow a little time to rest and reflect in, Landscape Art especially appeals—nor does it appeal in vain."

96. W. J. T. Mitchell, "Imperial Landscape," in *Landscape and Power*, ed. Mitchell (Chicago and London: University of Chicago Press, 1994), 14.

97. Dana, "Musings," 28.

98. Ibid., 40.

NOTES TO CHAPTER 3

1. William B. Hazen, from his 1875 pamphlet *Our Barren Lands*, reprinted in Edgar I. Stewart, *Penny-an-Acre Empire in the West* (Norman: University of Oklahoma Press, 1968), 176–77. Stewart helpfully compiles key documents in what was a fierce public dispute (involving, among others, General George Custer, the editorialists of the *Minneapolis Tribune*, and advocates for the Northern Pacific Railway) about the merits of expansion west of the Missouri River and east of the Sierra Nevadas. Hazen's rejoinder, that of a military man who had been himself stationed at various frontier outposts throughout the region, was not merely an episodic skirmish targeted at this particular quixotic campaign, nor was it an isolated salvo reflecting only the opinions of one maverick individual. As we shall see, it instead articulated a broader sentiment distrustful of western activity that would be vindicated in 1873, with the abortive effort to extend the Northern Pacific rails past Bismarck.

2. Hazen's contribution to *House Executive Document No. 45* (30th Cong., 2nd sess.) is quoted in Stewart, *Penny-an-Acre Empire in the West*, 8. As an illustration of the persistent draw of these ideas, consider the case of the 1987 "Buffalo Commons" land-use proposal for the shortgrass prairie region between the 98th meridian and the Rocky Mountains. Noting that many counties in the region sustained population densities at or below the demographic levels set as the standard for "frontier" lands (and that density levels faced further decline), the proposal called for a radical land-use vision that would "deprivatize" the region and "recognize its unsuitability for agriculture," removing human barriers and stocking the area with buffalo, with an eye toward ultimately restoring the plains grasslands to their unbounded primal state. The idea is forwarded in Deborah Epstein Popper and Frank J. Popper, "The Great Plains: From Dust to Dust," *Planning* 53, no. 12 (December 1987): 12–18.

3. Hazen, *Our Barren Lands*, in Stewart, *Penny-an-Acre Empire in the West*, 140.

4. For the classic account of the myth of the western desert, see Henry Nash Smith, *Virgin Land*, rev. ed. (Cambridge: Harvard University Press, 1970), esp. 175–83. On the symbolic draw of western vacancy, see also Sacvan Bercovitch, *The Office of the Scarlet Letter* (Baltimore and London: Johns Hopkins University Press, 1991), 92–97.

5. See Howard Lamar, "Image and Counterimage: The Regional Artist and the Great Plains Landscape," in *The Big Empty: Essays on Western Landscapes as Narrative*, ed. Leonard Engel (Albuquerque: University of New Mexico Press, 1994), 75–92. Smith, *Virgin Land*, 175, traces the desert motif to the 1810 publication of Zebulon Pike's journal documenting his plains expedition.

6. Horace Greeley, *An Overland Journey from New York to San Francisco in the Summer of 1859*, ed. Charles T. Duncan (New York: Knopf, 1964), 82.

7. Quoted in Stewart, *Penny-an-Acre Empire*, 257. This western desiccation figures in, among others, two key texts to be considered here: Washington Irving, *A Tour on the Prairies* (London: John Murray, 1835); and E. G. Wakefield, *England and America* (London: Richard Bentley, 1833). The latter outlines a proposal for sale of "waste" lands by colonial powers, so as to promote the interests of any old country through its "applying this system to desert countries at her disposal" (242). The connotation of idleness associated with desert space dates back at least as far as the fourth century (see Siegfried Wenzel, *The Sin of Sloth: Acedia in Medieval Thought and Literature* [Durham: University of North Carolina Press, 1960], 5).

8. On the shared conventions of prairie and sea description, see Robert Thacker, *The Great Prairie Fact and Literary Imagination* (Albuquerque: University of New Mexico Press, 1989), esp. 118–22, on Melville; and Edwin Fussell, *Frontier: American Literature and the American West* (Princeton: Princeton University Press, 1965).

9. In striking this parallel between the western and southern economic frontiers, I follow the example of Paul Giles, who, in his account of the rise of the United States to economic supremacy in the late nineteenth century, argues that "the joining together of the North and the South . . . ran in parallel with the joining together of the East and the West; America was metamorphosed from a series of local economies into an imposing continental edifice" (see "The Deterritorialization of American Literature," in *Shades of the Planet: American Literature as World Literature*, ed. Wai-Chee Dimock and Lawrence Buell [Princeton and Oxford: Princeton University Press, 2007], 44). In keeping with Deleuze and Guattari's theory of the many registers of capitalist global organization, discussed in my introduction, I would, however, wish to maintain that this consolidation of a unified economic culture did not merely homogenize, but also opened up new localisms and heterogeneities in the process.

10. Irving, *A Tour on the Prairies*, 19. Eric J. Sundquist, *Empire and Slavery in American Literature, 1820–1865* (Jackson: University Press of Mississippi, 2006), 25, cites Irving's assertion, in *Astoria*, that "the central plains were uninhabitable—a 'Great American Desert,'" and his corollary anticipation of "the rise there of 'new and mongrel races, like new formations in geology, the amalgamation of the 'debris' and 'abrasions' of former races . . . ejected from the bosom of society into the wilderness.'"

11. Smith, *Virgin Land*, 177–78, 211–49, considers in some detail the perceived threat of frontier barbarity, noting the variations on this theme that emerge along the literary trajectory stretching from James Fenimore Cooper to Edward Eggleston and Hamlin Garland. On the broader question of "anxiety" in Irving's literary production, see Jeffrey Rubin-Dorsky, "Washington Irving: Sketches of Anxiety," *American Literature* 58, no. 4 (December 1986): 499–522; and *Adrift in the Old World: The Psychological Pilgrimage of Washington Irving* (Chicago and London: University of Chicago Press, 1988).

12. In a passage redolent with images of comfortable eastern repose, Stanley T. Williams quotes Philip Hone's diary to suggest that episodes of frontier hardship were "events of ordinary occurrence to the settlers of the great West, but matters of thrilling interest to comfortable citizens who read of them in their green slippers, seated before a shining

grate, the neatly printed page illuminated by a bronze astral lamp; or to the sensitive young lady who, drawing up her delicate little feet on the crimson damask sofa, shudders at the hardships which the adventurous tourist has undergone" (Williams, *The Life of Washington Irving*, vol. 2 [New York: Octagon, 1971], 82–83).

13. Note the considerable literature that has emerged to correct the usually masculine bias of the most recognized nineteenth-century texts in this regard. See, for example, Annette Kolodny, *The Land Before Her: Fantasy and Experience of the American Frontiers, 1630–1860* (Chapel Hill: University of North Carolina Press, 1984); and Lillian Schlissel, *Women's Diaries of the Westward Journey* (New York: Schocken, 1982).

14. Timothy Dwight, quoted in Frederick Jackson Turner, *The Frontier in American History* (1920; repr., New York: Holt, 1985), 251. Elaborating further on the pioneers' motivations, he sarcastically diagnoses their bitterness as well as their penchant for idle talk: "After exposing the injustice of the community in neglecting to invest persons of such superior merit in public offices, in many an eloquent harangue uttered by many a kitchen fire, in every blacksmith shop, in every corner of the streets, and finding all their efforts vain, they become at length discouraged, and under the pressure of poverty, the fear of the gaol, and consciousness of public contempt, leave their native places and betake themselves to the wilderness" (ibid., 251–52).

15. Among these subjective weaknesses was the common linkage made between idleness and drunkenness, with the former usually serving as a gateway to the latter (though the opposite could also undoubtedly be the case). One of many illustrations of the insatiable thirst of the settler may be found in E. V. Smalley, "Features of the New North-West," *Century: A Popular Quarterly* 25, no. 4 (February 1883): 531–32, where the index of settlement's encroachment into the territory is the availability of liquor: "The first harbinger of civilization in all the vast interior between Eastern Dakota and the settled country on the Pacific coast, is the saloon." The author sketches the saloon-keeper as the true settler of the West, the nomad who establishes the trajectories of settlement. The saloon "does not follow population; it takes the lead. . . . If there is any reason to suppose that settlers will go into any distant and isolated section a year hence, you will find the whisky seller already on the ground with this tent or his 'shack,' patiently waiting for customers."

16. Greeley, *Overland Journey*, 153. Other extreme instances of Greeley's rhetoric include his claims that "braves are disinclined to any such steady, monotonous exercise of their muscles" (153) and that Californian Indians are "generally idle and depraved" (354). Consider Hegel's similar claim in *Introduction to the Philosophy of History*, trans. Leo Rauch (Indianapolis: Hackett, 1988), 85, that "America has always shown itself to be physically and spiritually impotent . . . after the Europeans landed, the natives gradually perished at the mere breath of European activity. . . . The main character of the native Americans is a placidity, a lassitude, a humble and cringing submissiveness . . . and it will take a long time for the Europeans to produce any feeling of self-confidence in them."

17. Greeley, *Overland Journey*, 152. Greeley argues that "the Indians are children. Their arts, wars, treaties, alliances, habitations, crafts, properties, commerce, comforts, all belong to the very lowest and rudest ages of human existence . . . they are utterly

incompetent to cope in any way with the European or Caucasian race" (152). For more on this convention, see Mick Gidley's "The Figure of the Indian in Photographic Landscapes," in *Views of American Landscapes*, ed. Mick Gidley and Robert Lawson-Peebles (Cambridge: Cambridge University Press, 1989), 214.

18. Gidley, "The Figure of the Indian," 199.

19. William Cronon, "Telling Tales on Canvas: Landscapes of Frontier Change," in *Discovered Lands, Invented Pasts*, by Jules David Prown et al. (New Haven and London: Yale University Art Gallery, 1992), 70.

20. Susan Hegeman, "Landscapes, Indians, and Photography in the Age of Scientific Exploration," in *The Big Empty*, 62. Hegeman reads as symptomatic the preference in William Henry Jackson's landscape photography for vast spaces over detailed treatment of living natives: "The visible sign of the Indians' habitation and transformation of the landscape is to be portrayed as minor compared to the grand expanse of (empty) scenery itself, and what little there is 'ancient,' a relic of a receding presence" (57).

21. Anders Stephanson, *Manifest Destiny: American Expansionism and the Empire of Right* (New York: Hill and Wang, 1995), 23. Stephanson notes the sway of such criteria in the work of the legal thinker Emerich de Vattel, who proposed that the capacity to productively use land was tantamount to the right to eliminate those supposedly lacking the strength and initiative to subdue it. Greeley rather bluntly articulates this structure of belief: "God has given this earth to those who will subdue and cultivate it, and it is vain to struggle against His righteous decree." As for those who would impede that progress: "These people must die out—there is no help for them" (see Greeley, *Overland Journey*, 152).

22. As Cronon, "Telling Tales," 51, points out, this convention persisted in spite of the fact that significant populations of Native Americans were settled and primarily agricultural. Nonetheless, "the visual models for creating equally striking images of women weeding corn or digging ground nuts or cleaning intestines were not nearly so readily available."

23. See Amy Dru Stanley, *From Bondage to Contract* (Cambridge: Cambridge University Press, 1998). The question of the economic unproductivity of the southern slave economy has been widely treated. For a range of angles on this question, see, among others, the 1905 analysis by Ulrich B. Phillips, "The Economic Cost of Slaveholding in the Cotton Belt," in *Slavery and the Southern Economy*, ed. Harold D. Woodman (New York: Harcourt, Brace and World, 1966), 35–44, which blends essentialist notions about the unfitness of slaves for disciplined labor with economic analysis of the damning tendencies of slave production toward overcapitalization and labor force inelasticity. On the unproductivity of the South in comparison with the North, consider Hinton Rowan Helper, *The Impending Crisis of the South: How to Meet It* (New York: Burdick Brothers, 1857); for a comparison of the readiness for industrialization on the southern versus the western economic frontier, see Douglas F. Dowd, "A Comparative Analysis of Economic Development in the American West and South," *Journal of Economic History* 16 (December 1956); the latter are excerpted in Woodman, *Slavery and the Southern Economy*, 200–205 and 243–54, respectively.

24. Of course, as Stanley indicates, this principle stopped short of extending contract protection to the bodies of women, in keeping with the tradition of the marriage contract

and patriarchal usufruct with regard to the various activities of the household (see *From Bondage to Contract,* esp. chaps. 4 and 5*)*. Walter Benn Michaels, *The Gold Standard and the Logic of Naturalism: American Literature at the Turn of the Century* (Berkeley: University of California Press, 1987), 113–36, argues critically that contract's assurance of free disposition over the body as property nevertheless assumes as constant the property-character of the body—what changes is only the right of jurisdiction over it. At the time, Karl Marx rather sarcastically asserted the apparently inevitable condition of servitude in either system—whether bondage or contract—in a footnote paraphrasing Carlyle on the American Civil War: "the Peter of the north wants to break the head of the Paul of the south with all his might, because the Peter of the north hires his labor by the day, and the Paul of the south his by the life. . . . The sum of all is—slavery!" (Karl Marx, *Capital: A Critique of Political Economy,* vol. 1, trans. Samuel Moore and Edward Aveling [Chicago: Kerr, 1908], 281).

25. Quoted in Stanley, *From Bondage to Contract,* 79.

26. Helen E. Brown, *John Freeman and his Family* (1864; repr., New York: AMS Press, 1980), 31.

27. Ibid., 10–11.

28. Ibid., 18.

29. Prince's exploits and the response they generate recur throughout Brown's text. Instances of his dangerous laziness appear ibid., 39–40, 42, 65, and 71.

30. Ibid., 70.

31. Clinton Bowen Fisk, *Plain Counsels for Freedmen* (1866?; repr., New York: AMS Press, 1980), 45, helpfully explains this higher motivation in terms more transparent than those of *John Freeman:* "When you were a slave, it may have been your habit to do just as little as you could to avoid the lash. But now that you are free, you should be actuated by a more noble principle than fear."

32. Ibid., 17, italics in original.

33. Ibid., 23, helpful italics in original.

34. Ibid., 33.

35. *Sloth and Thrift; or, the Causes and Correctives of Social Inequality* (Philadelphia: American Sunday-School Union, 1847). A similar tactic is employed much earlier by the anonymous author of *The Instructive History of Industry and Sloth* (Philadelphia: John Adams, 1806), a children's book in which the narrator contrasts the two modes by visiting, alternately, the homes of industry ("Here peace and plenty, order and regularity, seemed to reign throughout") and sloth ("what contention and strife, what poverty and shame, what misery and destruction") (see 6, 20).

36. *Sloth and Thrift,* 18–19.

37. Ibid., 39, 43, italics in original.

38. Ibid., 144–45.

39. Fisk, *Plain Counsels,* 62–63. The description borrows heavily from "American Farm Houses," *Plow* (April 1852): 120–22, which contrasts the "tumbledown mansion" of "Farmer Slack" with the more upright domain of "Farmer Snug."

40. Ibid., 63.

41. In Fisk's *Plain Counsels*, 41, one explanation of this seductiveness is, in fact, made explicit: "I know that it is quite natural that you should associate work with slavery and freedom with idleness."

42. Epigraph: William Cullen Bryant, "The Prairies," in *Poems* (New York: D. Appleton, 1855), 150.

43. On the "subversive" effect of Irving's "mock-heroic" or otherwise satirical tone, see William Bedford Clark, "How the West Won: Irving's Comic Inversion of the Westering Myth in *A Tour on the Prairies*," *American Literature* 50, no. 3 (November 1978): 346; and Peter Antelyes, *Tales of Adventurous Enterprise: Washington Irving and the Poetics of Western Expansion* (New York: Columbia University Press, 1990).

44. Such was the verdict of an anonymous critic in *Western Monthly Magazine* 3 (June 1835): 329–37, quoted in *Critical Essays on Washington Irving* (Boston: G. K. Hall, 1990), 106. Moreover, Irving's headlong plunge into western adventure reanimates a well-established conception of the American land as a theater for European exertion. Before the American Revolution, the British had long regarded the New World as the sphere in which their own endemic national lassitude would be redeemed by masculine adventure and religious righteousness, buoyed by America's abundant natural and human resources. See Shannon Miller's treatment of this in her *Invested with Meaning: The Raleigh Circle in the New World* (Philadelphia: University of Pennsylvania Press, 1998), 28: "A national concern about England's idleness, promoted by England's belated role in New World exploration, develops simultaneously in tracts that describe and encourage New World activity," in an effort to redeem what was in the sixteenth century regarded domestically as England's perceived national idleness—"no New World involvement, no religious conversions, no sexual reproduction."

45. Bryce Traister, "The Wandering Bachelor: Irving, Masculinity, and Authorship," *American Literature* 74, no. 1 (March 2002): 112, 124. As Kristie Hamilton argues in *America's Sketchbook: The Cultural Life of a Nineteenth-Century Literary Genre* (Athens: Ohio University Press, 1998), Irving's contribution to the increased moral value of bourgeois leisure can hardly be separated from his popularization of amateur literary expression in the form of the sketch: "The aspiration to leisure that was a mark of the middle class thus inscribed in the genre, as Irving executed it . . . pleasure was itself constructed as moral" (42). See 35–46 for further expansion on the stakes of this formal innovation.

46. Traister, "The Wandering Bachelor," 128.

47. For Traister's take on the bachelor-author's investment in romantic plots, see "The Wandering Bachelor," 129.

48. See, on Irving's representational strategy, Robert Thacker, "The Plains Landscape and Descriptive Technique," *Great Plains Quarterly* 2, no. 3 (Summer 1982): 151. On Irving's deployment of prairie sublimity, see also Kris Lackey, "Eighteenth-Century Aesthetic Theory and the Nineteenth-Century Traveler in Trans-Allegheny America: F. Trollope, Dickens, Irving, and Parkman," *American Studies* 32, no. 1 (Spring 1991), esp. 42–44.

49. Though Daniel F. Littlefield Jr., "Washington Irving and the American Indian," *American Indian Quarterly* 5, no. 2 (May 1979): 136, credits Irving with an "intelligent, enlightened attitude toward the Indians," Irving's depiction of the natives he encountered tends to romanticize and mythologize certain traits he found noble while subjecting other aspects to the comic treatment that typifies the rest of the text. He expressed, in a letter to S. G. Drake, dated 10 October 1837, the hope that his descriptions would serve as part of "a complete depository of facts concerning these singular and heroic races that are gradually disappearing from the face of the earth" (quoted in Williams, *Life*, 354).

50. Irving, *Tour*, 167.

51. Ibid., 172.

52. Ibid.

53. Ibid., 180.

54. Ibid., 180–81.

55. The "Bee Hunt" chapter was also excerpted in the *New-York Mirror*, 4 April 1835.

56. "How doth the little busy bee / Improve each shining hour, / And gather honey all the day / From every opening flower! . . . In works of labour or of skill / I would be busy too; / For Satan finds some mischief still / For idle hands to do" (Isaac Watts, "Against Idleness and Mischief," *A Catechism for Children* [Windham, Ct.: Byrne, 1795]).

57. Consider the character of Benjamin Boden in Cooper's *Oak Openings*, (1848; repr., New York: R. F. Fenno, 1900), 9–10, for example, who "by the *voyageurs*, and other French of that region . . . was almost universally styled *le Bourdon*, or the 'Drone'; not, however, from his idleness or inactivity, but from the circumstance that he was notorious for laying his hands on the products of labor that proceeded from others." The bee in Bryant is "a more adventurous colonist than man." See "The Prairie," 147. Irving's fascination with this man-as-bee motif resonates with John Hall's *Letters from the West; Containing Sketches of Scenery, Manners, and Customs; and Anecdotes Connected with the First Settlements of the Western Sections of the United States* (London: Henry Colburn, 1828), 8: "Our curiosity is excited to know what powerful attraction has drawn these multitudes from their native plains, and why, like bees, they swarm as it were to the same bough."

58. Irving, *Tour*, 61–62.

59. This lost fragment was brought to light in Richard D. Rust, "Irving Rediscovers the Frontier," in *Washington Irving: The Critical Reaction*, ed. James W. Tuttleton (New York: AMS Press, 1993), 158.

60. Irving, *Tour*, 62, emphasis added.

61. Ibid., 65.

62. Ibid., 66. Irving's exploration of the man-bee indeterminacy reaches this climax: "The poor proprietors of the ruin . . . seemed to have no heart to do anything. . . . [They] crawled backwards and forwards, in vacant desolation, as I have seen a poor fellow, with his hands in his breeches pocket, whistling vacantly and despondingly about the ruins of his house that had been burnt " (67).

63. Antelyes, *Tales of Adventurous Enterprise*, 127.

64. Ibid. Attending to the way that Irving's comic tone addresses this matter throughout is the observation that in Irving's portrayal, "the blood lust of the troop, once aroused, endangers even the innocuous and inedible prairie-dog" (see Clark, "How the West Won," 340).

65. Edward Gibbon Wakefield, *England and America: A Comparison of the Social and Political State of Both Nations*, vol. 2 (London: Richard Bentley, 1833), 191–92. Wakefield's argument is addressed in Marx, *Capital*, 1: 845.

66. The reputation of New England industrialists for discouraging western migration in order to preserve the stability of their workforce is discussed in Smith, *Virgin Land*, 204. It should also be noted, however, that the hegemonic desire to keep women *out* of the workforce (for moral reasons, as well as to avoid the downward pressure they exerted on wages) resulted in their being *encouraged* to move west—where they might find husbands to provide for their needs (see Alice Kessler-Harris, *Out to Work: A History of Wage-Earning Women in the United States* [Oxford: Oxford University Press, 1982], 98).

67. Smith, *Virgin Land*, 201–10, provides an account of the myriad and contradictory political deployments of the "safety valve" theory, tracing its emergence to Massachusetts Bay in the mid-seventeenth century. Ray Allen Billington, *The American Frontier Thesis: Attack and Defense* (Washington, D.C.: American Historical Association, 1971), 21, offers a helpful account of Turner's adoption of the idea, and especially of the efforts of twentieth-century historians that have disproved its demographic and economic presuppositions. Nevertheless, he avers that the theory of the "psychosociological" impact of the frontier— its ability to conjure visions of flight, despite the demographic improbability of actual escape—is sustainable.

68. Consider John Bellers's early use of a natural motif that would have stung Washington Irving, in "Proposals for Employing the Poor in a College of Industry" (1714): "The Poor without employment are like rough diamonds; their worth is unknown. . . . The best horses, whilst wild at grass, are but useless and chargeable; and the same are mankind, until they are regularly and usefully employed" (quoted in Sir Frederic Morton Eden, *The State of the Poor: A History of the Labouring Classes in England, with Parochial Reports*, ed. A.G.L. Rogers [London: Routledge, 1928], 47).

69. In the course of this transition, "value existing as money-wealth is enabled, on one side, to buy the objective conditions of labor; on the other side, to exchange money for the living labor of the workers who have been set free" (Marx, *Grundrisse*, trans. Martin Nicolaus [New York: Penguin, 1973], 507).

70. Eden, *State of the Poor*, 5, 7.

71. Ibid., 5.

72. Marx, *Capital*, 843.

73. Greeley, *Overland Journey*, 157.

74. Martineau, quoted in James E. Davis, *Frontier America 1800–1840: A Comparative Demographic Analysis of the Frontier Process* (Glendale, Calif.: Arthur H. Clark, 1977), 136.

75. Thoreau, "Walking," 668.

76. Michael Walzer, *Exodus and Revolution* (New York: Basic Books, 1985), 17, points out the different possibilities of the two models: "Exodus is a model for messianic and millenarian thought, and it is also a standing alternative to it—a secular and historical account of 'redemption,' an account that does not require the miraculous transformation of the material world but sets God's people marching through the world toward a better place within it." An interesting side note to this discussion of the discourse of exodus is provided by the envisioning, by millennial Protestantism, of posthistorical Utopia as an "extended Sabbath" spatially located in the New World (see Stephanson, *Manifest Destiny*, 9).

77. Walzer, *Exodus and Revolution*, 17.

78. Ibid., 17.

79. Ibid., 126.

80. As Walzer notes, "there is no ultimate struggle, but a long series of decisions, backslidings, and reforms. The apocalyptic war between 'the Lord's people' and 'their enemies' can't readily be located within the Exodus" (56).

81. Turner, *Frontier in American History*, 206. Billington, *American Frontier Thesis*, 28, subsequently stresses the "adaptation" of preexisting organs of government, in contrast to the untenable assertion (often ascribed to Turner) that such institutions were created out of a vacuum. According to him, Turner "insisted only that American democracy derived from the democracy imported from Europe, and that the deviation was sufficiently great to constitute a new species."

82. See Paolo Virno, "Virtuosity and Revolution: The Political Theory of Exodus," in *Radical Thought in Italy*, trans. Ed Emory, ed. Michael Hardt and Virno (Minneapolis: University of Minnesota Press, 1996), 199. There he proposes the nondialectical strategy of "exodus" from the contemporary subsumption of all activity by capital, arguing that "nothing is less passive than flight."

83. Quoted in Marx, *Capital*, 771. See also Wakefield, *England and America*, 1: 314–31, on "Some Social Peculiarities of the Americans," specifically the relationship between dispersion, crudeness, and civilization. Wakefield attributes discovery of the relationship between these terms to Adam Smith.

84. Jackson, *Crabgrass Frontier: The Suburbanization of the United States* (New York and Oxford: Oxford University Press, 1985), 75, notes Thomas Jefferson's role in the 1787 establishment of the Northwest Ordinance, an act which rationalized the Appalachian outback. That precedent would achieve its ultimate realization in the Homestead Act of 1862, which succeeded in quartering each square mile into sections bordered by straight lines.

85. Charles Dickens, *Works of Charles Dickens*, vol. 4, *Great Expectations, Pictures from Italy, and American Notes* (New York: G. W. Carleton, 1883), 691.

86. One such case was Francis Baily, whose *Journal of a Tour in Unsettled Parts of North America in 1796 and 1797* (London, 1856) took early umbrage: "I think that oftentimes it is a sacrifice of beauty to prejudice, particularly when they persevere in making all their streets cross each other at right angles, without any regard to the situation of the ground, or the face of the surrounding country" (quoted in John W. Reps, *Town Planning in Frontier America* [Princeton: Princeton University Press, 1969], 429).

87. Jackson, *Crabgrass Frontier*, 54–72.

88. Ibid., 76.

89. Ibid., 80.

90. Ibid., 85.

91. Ibid., 83.

92. Lewis Mumford, *The City in History: Its Origins, Its Transformations, and Its Prospects* (New York: Harcourt Brace Jovanovich, 1961), 486.

93. It is safe to say that Willis is among the century's most influential and ardent advocates of idleness. On some of the paradoxes of his position, see Sandra Tomc's excellent essay "An Idle Industry: Nathaniel Parker Willis and the Workings of Literary Leisure," *American Quarterly* 49, no. 4 (December 1997), as well as my own "Money, Mobility, and the Idle Speculation of Nathaniel Parker Willis," *ATQ*, n.s., 22, no. 4 (December 2008).

94. James Grant Wilson reports that Idlewild's fitting moniker stemmed from a conversation between Willis and the previous owner of the then undeveloped property. The seller, uncertain about the motivations of the plot's new "poet-owner," is reported to have said to him, "What on earth can you do with it? It's only an idle wild" (see *Bryant, and His Friends: Some Reminiscences of the Knickerbocker Writers* [New York: Fords, Howard, and Hulbert, 1886], 314). Willis himself provides an account of Idlewild's development in *Outdoors at Idlewild; or, the Shaping of a Home on the Banks of the Hudson* (New York: Charles Scribner, 1860).

95. T. Addison Richards, "Idlewild: The Home of N.P. Willis," *Harper's New Monthly Magazine*, January 1858, 154, 156.

96. Nathaniel Parker Willis, *Health Trip to the Tropics* (New York: Charles Scribner, 1853), 210. His *Rural Letters and Other Records of Thought at Leisure* (1849) and *The Convalescent* (1859) offer extended meditations on these themes.

97. Wilson, *Bryant, and His Friends*, 326.

98. Nathaniel Parker Willis, *Rural Letters and Other Records of Thought at Leisure* (New York: Baker and Scribner, 1849), 187.

99. Richards, "Idlewild," 156.

100. Jackson, *Crabgrass Frontier*, 135.

101. Mumford, *City in History*, 486, notes wryly that all this pretense to freedom has ultimately resulted in "a multitude of uniform, unidentifiable houses, lined up inflexibly, at uniform distances, on uniform roads, in a treeless communal waste . . . a low-grade uniform environment from which escape is impossible." Mumford quotes Francis Parkman, who makes the relationship between suburban and frontier pioneers explicit: "The sons of civilization, drawn by the fascinations of a fresher and bolder life, thronged to the western wilds in multitudes which blighted the charm that had lured them" (491).

102. "A Plea for Idleness," *Putnam's Monthly Magazine of American Literature, Science, and Art* 10, no. 57 (September 1857): 360.

103. Ibid., 361.

104. Ibid., 362, emphasis added.

105. A.K.H.B., "Concerning Hurry and Leisure," *Littell's Living Age* 66, no. 852 (September , 1860): 793. The piece was reprinted for American readers from *Fraser's Magazine*.

106. Such "intervals" also frequently provided an alibi for trifling literary works, which would be prefaced with a disclaimer stressing that the work had been "penned in the intervals of more robust literary labors," or something of that sort. Finally, recall Washington Irving's suggestive description of the frontier heartland (in his *Astoria*) as "a lawless interval between the abodes of civilized man" (quoted in Clark, "How the West Won," 346).

107. An American, "A Glance at the Streets of Paris during the Winter of 1849–50," *Southern Literary Messenger* 16, no. 5 (May 1850). The reflections of this "American" couldn't help but be catalyzed by Paris's reputation as the ultimate "promised land of the flaneur," as Walter Benjamin later put it in *The Arcades Project*, ed. Rolf Tiedemann, trans. Howard Eiland and Kevin McLaughlin (Cambridge and London: Harvard University Press, 1999), 417. On *flanerie* as a privileged practice of European leisure, see Baudelaire's *The Painter of Modern Life* (London: Phaidon, 1964); Benjamin, *Arcades Project*, 416–55; and "On Some Motifs in Baudelaire," trans. Harry Zohn, *Illuminations*, ed. Hannah Arendt (New York: Schocken Books, 1969), esp. 172–74; and, for a theoretical context, Susan Buck-Morss, *The Dialectics of Seeing: Walter Benjamin and the Arcades Project* (Cambridge and London: MIT Press, 1989).

108. An American, "A Glance at the Streets of Paris," 264.

109. Ibid., 264.

110. "Concerning Hurry and Leisure," 793.

111. Ibid., 795.

112. "A Plea for Idleness," 360.

113. A.K.H.B., "Concerning Hurry and Leisure," 796.

114. Ibid., 792.

115. Irving letter (18 December 1850), University of Virginia Special Collections, accession 6256–a.

116. Ibid.

117. Consider the argument of James Freeman Clarke, *Self-Culture: Physical, Intellectual, Moral, and Spiritual* (Boston: James R. Osgood, 1882), 351, that "work which is not finished is not work at all. The difference between active work and active idleness lies just at this point."

118. Irving, *Tour*, 35.

119. Ibid., 21.

120. Mark Twain, *Mark Twain's Letter to the California Pioneers* (1869; repr., Oakland: Dewitt and Snelling, 1911), 13.

121. Davis, *Frontier America*, 136.

122. The most stunning attempt to account for the infinity of activity beyond the scope of "productive" industry was undertaken in the English context by Henry Mayhew, *London Labor and the London Poor: A Cyclopaedia of the Condition and Earnings of Those That Will Work, Those That Cannot Work, and Those That Will Not Work (1851–1862)* (New York: A. M. Kelley, 1967). There he elaborates an apparently exhaustive inventory

of marginals, including ratcatchers, match girls, street-sellers of grease-removing composition, fly-papers, and beetle-wafers, and others. But Mayhew's considerable disdain for these marginals is mild compared to his treatment of the nomadic and transient, who make up, he claims, one of two "distinct and broadly marked races." The nomad "is distinguished from the civilized man by his repugnance to regular and continuous labor and by his want of providence in laying up a store for the future—by his inability to perceive consequences ever so slightly removed from immediate apprehension—by his passion for stupefying herbs and roots, and, when possible, for intoxicating fermented liquors . . . by his comparative insensibility to pain" (2). Of note here is the "insensibility to pain," which mobilizes a secondary definition of the word "indolence" not uncommon in English at the time. Mayhew goes on to malign the nomad for gaming, pleasurable dances, an absence of chastity and female honor, and an indifference to religion.

123. Francis Whiting Halsey, quoted in Davis, *Frontier America*, 154.

124. Cobbett concludes that "full pocket or empty pocket, these American labourers are always the *same men.* . . . This, too, arises from the free institutions of government. A man has a voice *because he is a man*, and not because he is the *possessor of money*. And, shall I *never* see our English labourers in this happy state?" (quoted in Allan Nevins, ed. *America Through British Eyes* [New York: Oxford University Press, 1948], 65–67).

125. Antonio Negri, *Insurgencies: Constituent Power and the Modern State*, trans. Maurizia Boscagli (Minneapolis: University of Minnesota Press, 1999), 143–44.

126. Ibid., 151.

127. Gilles Deleuze and Félix Guattari, *A Thousand Plateaus*, trans. Brian Massumi (Minneapolis and London: University of Minnesota Press, 1987), 481. In contrast to this distribution in "smooth" space, consider their explanation of striated spatial exploration: "In striated space, one closes off a surface and 'allocates' it according to determinate intervals, assigned breaks."

128. Negri, *Insurgencies*, 147.

129. Ibid. Davis, *Frontier America,* 142–43, demonstrates how the reputation of the pioneer as a "raucous hell-raiser" is in fact belied by the development of various organic means of horizontal governance charged not only with maintaining order, but also with preventing the disagreeable incursion of speculators, lawyers, and other agents of vertical power.

130. Turner, *Frontier in American History,* 258.

131. Ibid., 15, 212. Turner hails the concreteness of this immanent social constitution of governance with a juridical example: "crime was more an offense against the victim than a violation of the law of the land." For an additional discussion of the horizontal orientation of frontier power see Davis, *Frontier America*, 142.

132. Norton, quoted in Turner, *Frontier in American History,* 209.

133. A similar discomfort with the political productivity of the frontier is expressed by John Randoph: "We are the first people that ever acquired provinces . . . not for us to govern, but that they might govern us—that we might be ruled to our ruin by people bound to us by no common tie of interest or sentiment" (quoted in Russell Kirk, *Randolph of*

Roanoke: A Study in Conservative Thought [Chicago: University of Chicago Press, 1951], 145).

134. As Negri, *Insurgencies*, 159, notes, constituent power is reduced by representative democracy to a *model* for governance; it is no longer the *means* of governance. This reduction, by which "American democracy becomes republican democracy," is established by the *Federalist* numbers 9 and 10. Negri argues that the repudiation of the spatial organization of political power is established in the machinery of the Senate: "In the Senate the frontier of American freedom is definitely erased: with a sublime irony, it is the constitutional 'spatial' organ that defines this closure."

135. Gilles Deleuze and Claire Parnet, "On the Superiority of Anglo-American Literature," in *Dialogues*, trans. Hugh Tomlinson and Barbara Habberjam (New York: Columbia University Press, 1987), 40, suggest that the "rails, boundaries and surveys" are the tools of transcendent gods, the imposition from outside of order onto space calibrated to other regimes.

136. Ralph Waldo Emerson, "The Young American," in *Manifest Destiny*, ed. Norman A. Graebner (Indianapolis and New York: Bobbs-Merrill, 1968), 6.

137. Deleuze and Guattari, *A Thousand Plateaus*, 474, offer the concept of "translation" as a means of understanding the relationship between the smooth and the striated. Their opposition of these terms does not posit an initial identity between the two; rather, the smooth and striated designate a *process* of translation and not a fixed binary. "[S]mooth space is constantly being translated, transversed into a striated space; striated space is constantly being reversed, returned to a smooth space." Finally, "the two spaces in fact exist only in mixture."

138. John O'Sullivan, quoted in Stephanson, *Manifest Destiny*, 44. In the subsequent debate over whether to forego further annexation of Mexican territory, the persuasiveness of the natural boundary of the Rio Grande is supplemented, no less, by an explicit invocation of the essential idleness of the Mexican people—O'Sullivan's expansionist *Democratic Review* drew the line against pushing farther south, describing Mexicans as "too proverbially indolent to pursue industrial employments," and therefore unworthy of incorporation (see "Occupation of Mexico," *United States Magazine and Democratic Review* 21 [November 1847]: 202).

139. See Lewis C. Levin's address, reprinted in the appendix of the *Congressional Globe* (29th Cong., 1st sess., 1846): 96.

140. Charles F. Lummis, *A Tramp Across the Continent* (New York: Scribner's, 1892), 1, echoes the sentiments voiced in A.K.H.B.'s "Concerning Hurry and Leisure," 787: "A man flying through this peaceful valley in an express-train at the rate of fifty miles an hour, might just as reasonably fancy that to us, its inhabitants, the trees and hedges seem always dancing, rushing, and circling about, as they seem to him in looking from the window of the flying carriage, as imagine that, when he comes for a day or two's visit, he sees these landscapes as they are in themselves, and as they look to their ordinary inhabitants.... Trees, fields, sunsets, rivers, breezes, and the like, must all be enjoyed at leisure, if

enjoyed at all. There is not the slightest use in a man's paying a hurried visit to the country. He may as well go there blindfold, as go in a hurry. He will never see the country."

141. For Emerson, "The Young American," 6, it is the indifference of the railroad to the particularities of not only nature, but also of the nation's inhabitants, that burnishes the railroad's appeal: "Not only is the distance annihilated, but when, as now, the locomotive and the steamboat, like enormous shuttles, shoot every day across the thousand various threads of national descent and employment, and bind them fast in one web, an hourly assimilation goes forward, and there is no danger that local peculiarities and hostilities should be preserved."

142. Ibid., italics in original.

143. Deleuze and Guattari, *A Thousand Plateaus*, 490.

NOTES TO CHAPTER 4

1. Max Horkheimer and Theodor Adorno, *Dialectic of Enlightenment*, trans. John Cumming (New York: Continuum, 1972), 137.

2. Anson Rabinbach, *The Human Motor: Energy, Fatigue, and the Origins of Modernity* (Berkeley and Los Angeles: University of California Press, 1990), 19. This chapter will suggest the pertinence of Rabinbach's argument to the American context; though he does acknowledge the important contributions to this discourse by Americans such as Frederick Taylor and George Miller Beard, his work is chiefly concerned with the circulation of their ideas in Europe.

3. In addition to Rabinbach's germinal work, I have found particularly useful the frameworks provided by William Gleason's *The Leisure Ethic: Work and Play in American Literature, 1840–1940* (Stanford: Stanford University Press 1999); and Tom Lutz's *American Nervousness, 1903: An Anecdotal History* (Ithaca and London: Cornell University Press, 1991). I believe it impossible to conduct a proper study of the history of American idleness without in some ways echoing many of the choices made by these authors in identifying the key figures in this discourse: Gilman, James, Dreiser, etc. However, this chapter proposes to explore different texts than those made canonical in previous work, and to produce an alternative conceptual constellation, isolating and emphasizing the definition of unproductivity, the limits of the body, and especially the question of what James called "vital reserves." In short, despite the valuable contributions of these works, there yet remains work to be done on American unproductivity at the turn of the century.

4. The Charlotte Perkins Gilman quotes that appear in this chapter's section heads are drawn from her journals and notes, which are a rich source of insight into her thought. As is evident from the scraps collected in the folders entitled "Thoughts and Figgerings," Gilman was an enthusiastic keeper of detailed notes to herself, which often consisted of lists of works written or yet to write, along with ledgers of accounts receivable, grocery lists, and other quotidian documents. These notes suggest that her birthdays were a day of self-evaluation, often according to a calculus actuarially measuring the work she anticipated

being able yet to finish (Gilman Papers, mf-1, folder 16, Schlesinger Library on the History of Women in America, Harvard University).

5. The key James works to be discussed here are collected in *On Vital Reserves: "The Energies of Men" and "The Gospel of Relaxation"* (New York: Henry Holt, 1911). Hereafter the two James essays are cited parenthetically as EM and GR, respectively. Theodore Dreiser's *Sister Carrie*, 3rd Norton Critical Edition, ed. Donald Pizer (New York and London: Norton, 2006) is hereafter cited as *SC*.

6. For an interesting account of the germination of many of these ideas in James's own biography, as well as an account of his critique of prevailing theories of neurasthenia, see Lutz, *American Nervousness*, 66–74.

7. Lutz reads across James's oeuvre to provide a helpful summary of his complicated stance toward Rooseveltian imperialism in *American Nervousness*: "Despite the fact that James was a pacifist and an ardent and active-anti-imperialist, his final statement on these issues argued that a culture could simply not survive and progress without the martial spirit.... [He, however,] hoped to see the day that these energies would be turned to entirely peaceful ends" (94–95).

8. Frederick Jackson Turner, "Contributions of the West to American Democracy," in *The Frontier in American History* (New York: Henry Holt, 1985), 243, emphasis added.

9. Ibid. See also Turner, "Significance of the Frontier," 2.

10. For this quote, and more on the Turner-Loria connection, see Lee Benson, *Turner and Beard: American Historical Writing Reconsidered* (Glencoe, Ill.: Free Press, 1960), 27.

11. Ruskin, quoted in John F. Sears, *Sacred Places: American Tourist Attractions in the Nineteenth Century* (New York and Oxford: Oxford University Press, 1989), 141.

12. Ibid., 174.

13. Horace Greeley, *An Overland Journey from New York to San Francisco in the Summer of 1859*, ed. Charles T. Duncan (New York: Knopf, 1964), 97.

14. Quoted in Sears, *Sacred Places*, 128, emphasis added.

15. James Freeman Clarke, *Self-Culture: Physical, Intellectual, Moral, and Spiritual* (Boston: James R. Osgood, 1882), 395–96. This instrumentalization is economically more transparent in the parallel development by which forest reservations were set aside on public lands; the aim, as the 1897 Organic Act (alternately known as the Forest Management Act) promised, was that such land would act as a reserve of latent potential and would "furnish a continuous supply of timber for use . . . of the citizens of the U.S" (see William D. Rowley, "From Open Range to Closed Range on the Public Lands," in *Land in the American West*, ed. William G. Robbins and James C. Foster [Seattle: University of Washington Press, 2000], 100).

16. Ibid., 391.

17. Mary Roberts Rinehart, *Through Glacier Park: Seeing America First with Howard Eaton* (Boston and New York: Houghton Mifflin, 1916), 74–75. This mentality seems to have been demographically significant. J. Valerie Fifer, *American Progress: The Growth of the Transport, Tourist, and Information Industries in the Nineteenth-Century West* (Chester, Conn: Globe Pequot Press, 1988), 265, suggests that "the most common (and reasonable)

estimate is that as many as one-quarter of Southern California's and one-third of Colorado's total population originated as health-seekers in the late nineteenth century."

18. Rinehart, *Through Glacier Park*, 65–66.

19. Frank Norris, "The Frontier Gone at Last," in *Complete Works of Frank Norris: Blix, Moran of the Lady Letty, Essays on Authorship* (New York: P. F. Collier and Son, 1899), 285, 287.

20. Theodore Roosevelt, *The Strenuous Life* (New York: Century, 1904), 252, 6. On the relationship between economic "surplus" and discourses of "over-civilization," and its implications for the construction of an "imperial manhood," see chap. 6 of Lori Merish, *Sentimental Materialism: Gender, Commodity Culture, and Nineteenth-Century American Literature* (Durham and London: Duke University Press, 2000), esp. 283.

21. Quoted in Fifer, *American Progress*, 6.

22. *The American Alps*, Great Northern Railway promotional brochure, 1914, Great Northern Archives, 132.G.8.5 (B), Minnesota Historical Society, St. Paul.

23. Sears, *Sacred Places*, quoting Senator Conness, 130.

24. Sears, *Sacred Places*, 162. On the directly productive fruits of collusion between railroad companies, parks advocates, and advocates of tourism, see 130–31, 160–62, as well as Fifer, *American Progress*, passim.

25. Rinehart, *Through Glacier Park*, 6.

26. Martin Heidegger, "The Question Concerning Technology," in *Basic Writings*, ed. David Farrell Krell (San Francisco: HarperCollins, 1977), 322, emphasis added.

27. Marguerite S. Shaffer, "Seeing America First: The Search for Identity in the Tourist Landscape," in *Seeing and Being Seen: Tourism in the American West*, ed. David M. Wrobel and Patrick T. Long (Boulder: University Press of Kansas, 2001), 165. And, as Sears points out, guidebooks and parks literature of the time reveal the ordering, and especially *measurement*, of natural attractions to be a profound source of tourist appeal. Somewhat ironically, measurement, the reduction of an object to a system of common equivalences, here "is the means of validating an object's uniqueness" (*Sacred Places*, 137).

28. Rinehart, *Through Glacier Park*, 13, 80.

29. Norris, "The Frontier Gone at Last," 285. Darkly amusing in this connection is an anecdote, reported by Sears and others, in which the playacting became quite literal. A group of tourists, equipped for "pleasure camping" with wagons and carriages, a cook, and musical instruments, were a week into their 1877 junket when they were reached by word warning them of rebellious Nez Perce Indians nearby (who were themselves violently refusing to be reserved). Scared and depressed by the news, the campers entertained themselves by putting on a campfire western show, theatrically playing out roles as frontier outlaws and forgetting their cares. Their performance, however, was "suddenly overrun by the actual West," as the Indians, who were apparently watching this spectacle from the cover of the woods, emerged in the morning and took the party of tourists captive, killing one (see Sears, *Sacred Places*,180–81, for his account of this episode).

30. Theodor Adorno, "Valery Proust Museum," in *Prisms*, trans. Samuel Weber and Shierry Weber (Cambridge: MIT Press, 1981), 175, emphasis added. For more on the museal

quality of the tourist encounter, see Simon Evans and Martin Spaul, "Straight Ways and Loss: The Tourist Encounter with Woodlands and Forests," in *Visual Culture and Tourism*, ed. David Crouch and Nina Lübbren (Oxford and New York: Berg Press, 2003), 212.

31. *Vacations for All* (1920s?). Despite the claim in *Walking Tours: Glacier National Park* (1915) that "these tours are not confined to members of the male sex," one has cause to suspect that these expeditions hardly constituted vacations "for all," after all. Such is suggested by *With the Mountaineers in Glacier National Park* (1915) , where Lulie Nettleton offers not only "equipment hints for women walkers," but also a final call to domestic duty in her closing exhortation to "above all, leave the camp clean." All are located in the Great Northern Archives, 132.G.8.5(B), Minnesota Historical Society, St. Paul.

32. *Walking Tours: Glacier National Park*, 1915, Great Northern Archives, 132.G.8.5(B), Minnesota Historical Society, St. Paul.

33. Shari M. Huhndorf, *Going Native: Indians in the American Cultural Imagination* (Ithaca: Cornell University Press, 2001), 25.

34. Ibid., 33, 35. And this, at roughly the same moment that the geographical reserve of western space was quite literally integrated into the rational model of national industry by the General Allotment Act of 1887. Also known as the Dawes Act, it "mandated that reservation land be divided into individual parcels [. . . and attempted] to transform Natives from communal occupants of collective property into individual farmers (in other words, into western proprietors). Agents further reduced tribal landholdings by opening vast tracts of 'surplus' reservation land to white settlement" (see 60–61).

35. Referring to this "playground," Huhndorf quotes the description given by one commentator of this supposed "terra incognita." As she notes, "the Midway bore distinct similarities to the wild and barbaric land that Columbus had found, at least according to popular myth" (*Going Native*, 46). "If the White City signified the coherence and order ostensibly characterizing white civilization," Huhndorf argues, "the ethnological displays on the Midway evoked pure chaos and savagery" (42).

36. Moreover, as Huhndorf concludes, the allegorical dimensions of the 1893 fair had recursive ramifications capable of implicitly policing emergent social cleavages as well. Not only did the fair directly provide "white, middle-class viewers with a comforting vision of stability, control and order in the face of racial, ethnic, and class-based challenges," but this comfort also enabled a symbolic neutralization of other unproductive bogeys, including those responsible for strikes and other intense forms of labor conflict, in broader discourses through which working-class agitators were "frequently dubbed 'Indians' or 'savages'" (ibid., 50).

37. Leigh Ann Litwiller Berte, "Geography by Destination: Rail Travel, Regional Fiction, and the Cultural Production of Geographical Essentialism," in *American Literary Geographies: Spatial Practice and Cultural Production, 1500–1900*, ed. Martin Brückner and Hsuan L. Jsu (Newark: University of Delaware Press, 2007), 180–81.

38. See Huhndorf's discussion of transformations in the ideological stakes of "going native" in her work of that same title. In some respects, this development culminates a century-long reworking of the European tradition that viewed wilderness as merely an

"antithetical" space, as is described in Robert E. Abrams, *Landscape and Ideology in American Renaissance Literature: Topographies of Skepticism* (Cambridge: Cambridge University Press, 2004), 7. The romantic revision of this idea produced by midcentury the nascent possibility of "an alternative, less escapist aesthetic whose liberating power lies immediately *within* rather than *beyond* culture and history" (7, 9).

39. *Great Northern Recreational Map of Glacier National Park*, flyer, n.d., Great Northern Archives, 132.G.8.5(B), Minnesota Historical Society, St. Paul. This representation of the Indians thereby finds a compromise between the twin prospects of extermination and sheer museality raised by an Edward S. Curtis article in *Scribner's*: "It is true that advancement demands the extermination of these wild, care-free picturesque Indians, and in the language of our President, we cannot keep them on their lands for bric-a-brac" (quoted in Mary Lawlor, *Recalling the Wild: Naturalism and the Closing of the American West* [New Brunswick, N.J., and London: Rutgers University Press, 2000], 41).

40. *Hotels and Tours*, flyer, 1913(?), Great Northern Archives, 132.G.8.5(B), Minnesota Historical Society, St. Paul. The triumph of ease and regularity at Yellowstone is also telling: while in 1872 that park was several days' journey from the nearest railroad station, by April 1902 the Northern Pacific reached directly to the park. Sears argues with incisive snark that "Old Faithful became Yellowstone's principal symbol because only it behaved to suit the tourist's schedule" (see Sears, *Sacred Places*, 173).

41. Quoted in Fifer, *American Progress*, 308.

42. Ibid., 5.

43. Alice Kessler-Harris, *Out to Work: A History of Wage-Earning Women in the United States* (Oxford: Oxford University Press, 1982), is a particularly useful chronicle of changes in women's participation in the labor force during the nineteenth century. On the specific demographic changes under way leading up to and at century's end—by which time America had 5 million working women (though they remained largely confined to certain "acceptable" sectors of the economy)—see especially her chapter 2. It is also necessary to keep in mind the variability of women's experience in the work force, depending on social class, geography, and economic sector. These developments were unevenly distributed and historically discontinuous in ways that make perilous most attempts to generalize, including this one.

44. See Gillian Hewittson, *Feminist Economics: Interrogating the Masculinity of Rational Economic Man* (Cheltenham, U.K., and Northampton, Mass.: Edward Elgar, 1999), 47–53; 130–38, for a discussion of how postwar economists, in particular those of the neoclassical "Chicago school," have problematically attempted to address the exclusion of women's work, often with the consequence of naturalizing women's activity anew.

45. Karl Marx, *Economic and Political Manuscripts of 1844* (Moscow: Progress, 1977), 113.

46. Ibid., 94.

47. Christine Delphy, *Close to Home: A Materialist Analysis of Women's Oppression*, ed. and trans. Diana Leonard (Amherst: University of Massachusetts, 1984), 64.

48. See Gayle Rubin's classic essay "The Traffic in Women: Notes on the Political Economy of Sex," in *Toward an Anthropology of Women*, ed. Rayna Reiter (New York: Monthly Review Press, 1975), for a thoroughgoing account of this persistent dynamic.

49. Mary Ann Dimand, "The Economics of Charlotte Perkins Gilman," in *Women of Value: Feminist Essays on the History of Women in Economics*, ed. Mary Ann Dimand, Robert W. Dimand, and Evelyn L. Forget (Aldershot U.K., and Brookfield, Vt.: Edward Elgar, 1995), 130.

50. Ibid., 125.

51. Though Gilman does here devote some pages to the question of the gendering of productive activity, her argument aims less at analyzing "women's" work, she insists, than at defining *human* work (see Charlotte Perkins Gilman, *Human Work* [Lanham, Md.: AltaMira Press, 2005], 214 and passim). *Human Work* is hereafter cited parenthetically as *HW*.

52. Rabinbach, *The Human Motor*, 46–47. For another semantic distinction on this point, see also Gilles Deleuze and Félix Guattari, *A Thousand Plateaus* (Minneapolis: University of Minnesota Press, 1987), 397: "The two ideal models of the motor are those of work and *free action*. Work is a motor cause that meets resistances, operates upon the exterior, is consumed and spent in its effect, and must be renewed from one moment to the next." And yet in Gilman's model there seems to be no such *exterior*, and hence work for her is more compatible with Deleuze and Guattari's idea of free action, "also a motor cause, but one that has no resistance to overcome, operates only upon the mobile body itself, is not consumed in its effect, and continues from one moment to the next."

53. Gilman's letters and their advocacy of *Human Work* are quoted in a series of articles commemorating her death, in the *Amerikanische Turnzeitung*, no. 45–46 (10 November 1935):13.

54. Emphasis added. Gilman Papers, mf-1, folder 16, Schlesinger Library.

55. Gilman describes in her diaries for January 1903 how McClure, Phillips and Co., in receipt of four chapters of *Human Work* and one provisional chapter of *The Home*, initially expressed interest only in the latter volume (see Gilman Papers, mf-1, volume 46, Schlesinger Library). The letter (17 January 1903) expressing the publisher's ambivalence is housed in folder 130.

56. *The Home* paid royalties in the amount of 10 percent on its first five thousand copies. This information, among other documents pertaining to the publication history of *Human Work*, including the royalty receipt for sales in the first half of 1906 (indicating five copies sold between January and June!), may be found in the Gilman Papers, mf-1, folder 130, Schlesinger Library. Reviews of the work were mixed, ranging from the cagily and vaguely positive to the mean-spirited, as in the *Chicago Post*'s bluntly derisive description of the book as "crude, shallow, [and] fallacious."

57. As the subsequent discussion will suggest, her analysis appears to anticipate, in descriptive fashion at least, the neoclassical account of the body as a range of "diverse and separable behaviors and functions . . . revealed in their interactions with external objects," as described by Jack Amariglio and David F. Ruccio, "From Unity to Dispersion: The Body in Modern Economic Discourse," in *Postmodernism, Economics and Knowledge*, ed. Stephen Cullenberg, Amariglio, and Ruccio (London and New York: Routledge, 2001), 152–53. Rejecting in this way so many of the humanisms that have long defined the economic

body, the radical socialism of *Human Work* paradoxically resists its own title, advancing a surprisingly anti-*human*ist argument.

58. A persuasive account on this point is supplied by Amariglio and Ruccio, "From Unity to Dispersion," 166.

59. The "romantic" novel, as Norris terms it, busies itself with "prying, peeping, peering into the closets of the bedroom, into the nursery, into the sitting-room; yes, and into that little iron box screwed to the lower shelf of the closet in the library.... [It would] pick here a little and there a little, making up a bag of hopes and fears and a package of joys and sorrows—great ones, mind you." ("A Plea for Romantic Fiction," in Norris, *Complete Works*, 343). He closes this screed with a challenge to those readers content with mere bourgeois realism: "You, the indolent, must not always be amused" (344).

60. Philip Fisher, *Hard Facts: Setting and Form in the American Novel* (New York and Oxford: Oxford University Press, 1987), 172.

61. Fisher, *Hard Facts*, 174. In other contexts, however, Fisher is commendably alert to manifestations of "collective identity" in Dreiser (see 143–45).

62. Ellen Moers, "The Finesse of Dreiser," in *Critical Essays on Theodore Dreiser*, ed. Donald Pizer (Boston: G. K. Hall, 1981), 206, notes the local use of the figure in this scene, but neglects to trace its applications elsewhere in the novel. Her citation of an original paragraph excised by Dreiser also allows us to glimpse another application of hands as a signifier for intersubjective interests: "We are inclined sometimes to wring our hands much more profusely over the situation of another than the mental attitude of that other, towards his own condition, would seem to warrant" (207).

63. Dreiser revisits these "helping" hands in another significant scene from the Hurstwood–Carrie courtship, when the inexperienced Carrie is taught to play euchre, and again Hurstwood's magic touch augments her capacity for affection. Upon taking a trick, Carrie "laughed gleefully as she saw the hand coming her way. It was as if she were invincible when Hurstwood helped her" (*SC* 70).

64. A similar connection is made by Engels in *Anti-Duhring*, where, as Rabinbach summarizes it, "Energy is the universal equivalent of the natural world, as money is the universal equivalent of the world of exchange" (see *The Human Motor*, 82).

65. George Simmel, *The Philosophy of Money*, trans. Tom Bottomore and David Frisby (London and Boston: Routledge and Kegan Paul, 1978), 510–11.

66. Ibid., 303–4.

67. For a radical account of how the universal differentiality of all values, linguistic, economic, or otherwise, defines the ontological fabric of secular modernity, see Kiarina Kordela, $surplus: Spinoza, Lacan$ (Albany: State University of New York Press, 2008).

68. Simmel, *Philosophy of Money*, 304.

NOTES TO CHAPTER 5

1. Ross Posnock, "The Politics of Nonidentity: A Genealogy," in *National Identities and Post-Americanist Narratives*, ed. Donald E. Pease (Durham and London: Duke University Press, 1994), 36.

2. Ibid., 60.

3. See, on the call for a restoration of "span"—that is, a liberal comparativity—to Americanist criticism, Wai-Chee Dimock, "Planet and America, Set and Subset," in *Shades of the Planet: American Literature as World Literature*, ed. Dimock and Lawrence Buell (Princeton and Oxford: Princeton University Press, 2007), 5–6.

4. It must be noted not only that Adorno's critique is deeply informed by the cultural experience of his exile amid the coalescing structures of American mass culture, but also that his observations continue a dignified tradition of subtle critiques of American life from an outsider's perspective. An unprejudiced rereading of Adorno in this light yields considerable evidence of his often surprising sensitivity to the tensions between democratic ideals and capitalist cultural practices, and of his value for the analysis of "American" themes. This argument is well made in David Jenemann, *Adorno in America* (Minneapolis: University of Minnesota Press, 2007), esp. the coda, "Theodor Adorno, American," 179–91. One suspects that as the radical dislocations of the mode of production in the second half of the twentieth century are increasingly brought under analytical consideration, Adorno will read more and more like a nineteenth-century thinker (but that is a thesis for another time).

5. Adorno is not unique in finding in the shadow a rich figure for activity conducted at its limit. In addition to the manifestations toward which I have gestured in the preceding chapters, the trope functions widely in critical analyses not only of productivity but also of the unformed outside of thought. Hence, we might note its importance from the outset of Branka Arsić's *Passive Constitutions* (Stanford: Stanford University Press, 2007)—see chapters "0" and "7 ½" especially—as well as Laura Rigal's deployment of the figure in her *American Manufactory: Art, Labor, and the World of Things in the Early Republic* (Princeton: Princeton University Press, 1998), 141, which in one illuminating paragraph describes the American "lounger" as not only "a shadowy figure of Napoleonic federalism," but also "a shadow in the increasingly hard-working world of American productivity."

6. Theodor W. Adorno, *Minima Moralia*, trans. E. F. N. Jephcott (London and New York: Verso, 1974), 175. In light of these compulsions, the greater threat to humanity is not its potential "lapse into luxurious indolence," but rather "the savage spread of the social under the mask of universal nature, the collective as a blind fury of activity" (see Adorno, *Minima Moralia*, 156).

7. Ibid., 164.

8. On the bi-phasic approach, see Theodor W. Adorno, "The Stars Down to Earth," in *Stars Down to Earth and Other Essays on the Irrational in Culture*, ed. Stephen Crook (London and New York: Routledge, 1994), esp. 56–77. The essay explores, among other issues, the relationship of work to pleasure in the idealized life world constructed by the

astrology column of the *Los Angeles Times*. Perhaps the most frugal summary of this problematic is Adorno's observation that "the complete severance of work and play as an attitudinal pattern of the total personality may justly be called a process of disintegration strangely concomitant with the integration of utilitarian operations for the sake of which this dichotomy has been introduced." He laconically adds that "the column does not bother about such problems" (72).

9. Theodor W. Adorno, "Free Time," trans. Gordon Finlayson and Nicholas Walker, in *The Culture Industry: Selected Essays on Mass Culture*, ed. J. M. Bernstein (London: Routledge, 1991), 168.

10. Ibid., 162, emphasis added.

11. Adorno, *Minima Moralia*, 157.

12. Ibid., 138, emphasis added.

13. Theodor W. Adorno, *Negative Dialectics*, trans. E. B. Ashton (New York: Continuum, 1973), 4, 6.

14. Henry David Thoreau, "Walking," in *The Selected Works of Thoreau* (Boston: Houghton Mifflin, 1975), 683–84.

15. Ibid., 684.

16. Thoreau, "Life Without Principle," in *The Writings of Henry David Thoreau*, vol. 4, *Cape Cod and Miscellanies* (New York: AMS Press, 1968), 456.

17. Ibid., 457.

18. Ibid., 463.

19. Ibid., 458–59.

20. Ibid., 463.

21. Ibid., 475.

22. See Thoreau, "Walking," 665; and Robert E. Abrams, *Landscape and Ideology in American Renaissance Literature: Topographies of Skepticism* (Cambridge: Cambridge University Press, 2004), 43. For an extended discussion of Thoreau's radical conception of space, see Abrams's chapter 2.

23. Abrams, *Landscape and Ideology*, 11.

24. Thoreau, "Walking," 660.

25. Vincent J. Bertolini, "Fireside Chastity: The Erotics of Sentimental Bachelorhood in the 1850s," in *Sentimental Men: Masculinity and the Politics of Affect in American Culture*, ed. Mary Chapman and Glenn Hendler (Berkeley and London: University of California Press, 1999), argues that "the bachelor's fireside revery" tends to be represented as "a moment of discursive pressure, intrasubjective conflict, and emergent identity," in which the thinker thinks normative thoughts of "what it would be like *not* to be a bachelor"—it is depicted as housing, that is, a longing for convention and domesticity (see 19–20).

26. Thoreau, "Walking," 660; see also 685: "we are growing rusty and antique in our employments and habits of thought." Branka Arsić discovers in Melville quite a similar argument, that "to the extent that our thinking is 'familiar,' it is also always partial" (see Arsić, *Passive Constitutions or 7 ½ Times Bartleby* [Stanford: Stanford University Press, 2009], 5).

27. Abrams, *Landscape and Ideology*, 48–49.

28. Wai-Chee Dimock, *Through Other Continents: American Literature across Deep Time* (Princeton and Oxford: Princeton University Press, 2006), 9. There is much to say about Dimock's readings across "deep time," and I will return to the premise in the section devoted to Hawthorne below. In relation to Thoreau, however, the intertextual relays that she exposes between *Walden* and the *Bhagavad Gita* are particularly interesting for pivoting precisely on the question of the value of activity. Thoreau's reading of the *Bhagavad Gita*, Dimock argues, enables him to think an indeterminate practice at the limits between action and inaction—an "improper action" that violates the integrity of the antithesis and renders its terms "vexed partners, with a space intervening in between. There is such a thing as inaction in action, and action in inaction, Krishna [via Thoreau] now says" (see 17–18). My sympathy with such a reading should, at this point, pretty much go without saying. But it is additionally important to note that her example reveals how it is precisely when Thoreau is at his most radical in unraveling spatial and temporal categories that he must simultaneously conduct an unraveling of the fraught value of activity as well. Which is another way of saying that the limits of productive space and time and the limits of productivity are often coexistent and codependent.

29. "We have heard of a Society for the Diffusion of Useful Knowledge. It is said that knowledge is power, and the like. Methinks there is equal need of a Society for the Diffusion of Useful Ignorance. What we will call Beautiful Knowledge, a knowledge useful in a higher sense: for what is most of our boasted so-called Knowledge but a conceit that we know something, which robs us of the advantage of our actual ignorance. What we call knowledge is often our positive ignorance; ignorance our negative knowledge" (Thoreau, "Walking," 681).

30. Ibid., 667.

31. Freud's classic description of the "work" of condensation and displacement is outlined in the magisterial sixth chapter of *The Interpretation of Dreams*, ed. and trans. James Strachey (New York: Avon, 1965), esp. 312–44; consider as well his insistence upon the unapproachable negative kernel of any knowledge resulting from interpreting such a work: "There is often a passage in even the most thoroughly interpreted dream which has to be left obscure . . . at that point there is a tangle of dream-thoughts which cannot be unraveled and which moreover adds nothing to our knowledge of the content of the dream. This is the dream's navel, the spot where it reaches down into the unknown" (564).

32. Thoreau, "Life Without Principle," 482.

33. Michael T. Gilmore, *Surface and Depth: The Quest for Legibility in American Culture* (Oxford: Oxford University Press, 2003), 89: "*Moby-Dick*, as a compendium of America, inventories the culture's favorite ways of knowing." On the location of Ishmael between empiricism and romanticism, see Michael Rogin, *Subversive Genealogy: The Politics and Art of Herman Melville* [New York: Knopf, 1983], 109).

34. Herman Melville, *Moby-Dick, or, The Whale* (Indianapolis and New York: Bobbs-Merrill, 1964), 253. Hereafter cited parenthetically as *MD*.

35. The chapter thus reproduces the recurring pattern identified by Gilmore, *Surface and Depth*, 89, in which "Ishmael undertakes a thorough investigation of some part of the whale's

anatomy or behavior only to reach the conclusion that reliable knowledge is impossible." A chorus of critical concurrence rightly aligns this idea with Melville's critique of Enlightenment rationality, as in Tony Tanner, *The American Mystery: American Literature from Emerson to DeLillo* (Cambridge: Cambridge University Press, 2000), 68, who explores how the "Cetology" chapter is doomed to failure in trying to "systematize" the whale; or the argument of John Bryant, *Melville and Repose: The Rhetoric of Humor in the American Renaissance* (New York and Oxford: Oxford University Press, 1993), 186, that Ishmael must discover that "knowing . . . is forever contingent, hence marginal and picturesque." Resonating with the thrust of my earlier observations about the "Bartleby Industry," Tanner goes on to link Ishmael's obsessive classifications with the nineteenth century's penchant for "ambitious, comprehensive, exhaustive, philosophical and taxonomic 'systems,. . . .[T]he categorizations proliferate impossibly, perhaps even parodically, as if to show the hopeless arbitrariness of all our categorisings, the hopelessness of our categorizing ambition. Ishmael leaves his 'system' deliberately and wisely 'unfinished'" (68). See also John Seelye, *Melville: The Ironic Diagram* (Evanston: Northwestern University Press, 1970).

36. Rogin, *Subversive Genealogy*, 117. Gilmore, *Surface and Depth*, 88, stresses the violent will fueling Ahab's uses of knowledge: "Ishmael wants to understand; Ahab wants to exterminate that which eludes his understanding."

37. Bainard Cowan, *Exiled Waters: Moby-Dick and the Crisis of Allegory* (Baton Rouge and London: Louisiana State University Press, 1982), 94.

38. Ibid. For a memorable discussion that uses the play of light to depict this brand of dialectics—and does so in a vein sympathetic to Adorno's own stance on the productivities of thought—see Fredric Jameson, *Marxism and Form: Twentieth-Century Dialectical Theories of Literature* (Princeton: Princeton University Press, 1971), 307: "It is, of course, thought to the second power: an intensification of the normal thought processes such that a renewal of light washes over the object of their exasperation. . . . Faced with the operative procedures of the nonreflective thinking mind . . . dialectical thought tries not so much to complete and perfect the application of such procedures as to widen its own attention to include them in its awareness as well."

39. Rogin, *Subversive Genealogy*, 110.

40. As Charles Feidelson Jr.'s editorial note explains on *MD* 207.

41. John Bryant, *Melville and Repose*, 187, highly attuned to repose's ambivalences, notes its "precariousness" in this scene, in which "self-awareness vies with transcendence."

42. Bryant, *Melville and Repose*, 196, concludes that this sacrifice, producing nothing, is a total loss: "There is no artful transformation of experience here [as in *White-Jacket*]; thus philosophy without art, like idea without action, is useless."

43. Arsić, *Passive Constitutions*, 87, emphasis added.

44. See Arsić's discussion of Jonathan Edwards's attempt—complicated by "Bartleby"—to produce a total system in which every identity, along with its "thoughts, desires, and volitions [might be] accountable" (ibid., 23).

45. Herman Melville, *Redburn: His First Voyage* (New York: Holt, Rinehart and Winston, 1971), 198.

46. Arsić, *Passive Constitutions*, 140.

47. Nathaniel Hawthorne, *The Scarlet Letter* (New York: Modern Library, 1926), 7, 22, 19, 24, 14, 23, 15, 13. Hereafter cited parenthetically as *SL*.

48. These materials were placed in the corner of a drawer, it should be noted, by a former Surveyor, Jonathan Pue, who was apparently "little molested . . . with business pertaining to his office," and thus was able to devote himself to historical researches. "These supplied material for petty activity to a mind that would otherwise have been eaten up with rust" (*SL* 34).

49. Dimock, *Through Other Continents*, 4, 86 (the latter page critiquing Bakhtin's theory of epic's relationship to novel). Dimock's theoretical exploration of "deep time" makes a profound contribution to the important work of demystifying the central categories of literary study. This trajectory, arguably initiated by the shift "from work to text" and by the declaration of the "death of the author," is reenergized here, though there is a danger that the radical intertextuality of Dimock's practice of "deep time" might tend to unwork the limits of the text at the same time that it inadvertently reinforces the category of the author. She is therefore laudably careful to insist that the textual reference points in her retemporalization of literary history are always to some extent collective; reading acts are instantiations of a global civil society (8). Yet the very availability of salient texts culled from the deep recesses of history nevertheless indicates the success of the author-function defining them as readable. This aside is simply an observation, and in no way a claim that the present work has succeeded in skirting this risk.

50. Gilles Deleuze and Félix Guattari, *What Is Philosophy?*, trans. Hugh Tomlinson and Graham Burchell (New York: Columbia University Press, 1994), 59.

51. Ibid., 40.

52. Ibid., 41.

53. Adorno, *Negative Dialectics*, 8. Translation slightly modified. The word "individuality" in this passage demands further comment, given that the individuality of production is a central myth that this study is dedicated to questioning (see, in particular, chapters 1 and 4). Adorno notes, in *Minima Moralia*, Hegel's "serene indifference" to the "liquidation of the particular," but furthermore contests Hegel's unreflective and "naïve" hypostatization of the individual "as an irreducible datum," impervious to further reflection as a category that must itself be mediated with reference to the capitalist social order upon which it depends. See Adorno, *Minima Moralia*, 17, for this moment in which "the Master has now been rather magisterially treated as a moment in the preface of the son. Exit Daddy, Teddie arrives"—as Tom Pepper memorably put it his *Singularities: Extremes of Theory in the Twentieth Century* (Cambridge: Cambridge University Press, 1997), 29, a work that is itself uncompromising in its attention to and exemplification of the restless possibilities of thought.

54. Adorno, *Negative Dialectics*, 12.

55. Ibid., 14. The citation in the original German is Theodor W. Adorno, *Negative Dialektik* (Frankfurt: Suhrkamp, 1966), 26.

56. Ibid., 31.

57. Ibid., 27, emphasis added. Consider also the reminder offered in Theodor W. Adorno, *Hegel: Three Studies*, trans. Shierry Weber Nicholsen (Cambridge and London: MIT Press, 1993), 21: "the strains and toils of the concept are not metaphorical."

58. Adorno, *Negative Dialectics*, 21, emphasis added.

Index

Abrams, Robert E., 160, 161
acedia, 15, 42, 184nn33–34
Adorno, Theodor W.: *Aesthetic Theory*, 54, 84–85, 198n11; critical theory, 152–57, 226n4–6; on dissolution of work/play binary, 124, 170, 226–27n8; "Free Time," 152; *Minima Moralia*, 154, 155, 156, 230n53; on the "museal," 134; *Negative Dialectics*, 157, 177–78, 230n53
affect, 9–10, 11, 21–22, 65–71, 82, 186n45
Agamben, Giorgio, 183n22
agency, 21, 32, 77, 92, 106, 119, 153, 186n45
A.K.H.B., "Concerning Hurry and Leisure," 111–13
Allston, Washington, 57–65, 205n91; *Elijah in the Desert*, 57–59, *58*, 64–65, 199–200n25; "The Hypochondriac," 57, 60–61, 62, 66, 200n28; *Lectures on Art*, 52, 53, 61–65, 200n36, 200–201n40; *Moonlit Landscape*, 59, 73; paintings, 77; on procrastination, 200n27
Althusser, Louis, 48
Antelyes, Peter, 102
Aquinas, Thomas, 15, 17, 184n33
arbitrariness, 6, 7, 126, 182n13
architecture, 3, 38–41, 108–11, 197n4
Arsić, Branka, 168, 188n1, 189n3, 190n12, 227n26, 229n44
asceticism, 16–17
assemblage(s): in "Bartleby, the Scrivener," 44; city as, 150–51; of concepts, 174–75;

social body as, 143–44, 146–51; theory, 9–10, 182n17
Astor, John Jacob, 189n6
Atlantic, 158
Augst, Thomas, 26, 189n5

bachelordom, 20–22, 98–99, 161, 227n25
Baily, Francis, 214n86
Bartleby Industry, 25–26, 229n35
"Bartleby, the Scrivener" (Melville), 3, 22, 25–50, 162; B.'s alleged previous employment, 27; B.'s effect on coworkers, 28–29, 31–33, 34, 41, 45–46, 49; B.'s enigma, 26; B.'s imprisonment, 31, 40–41, 42, 49; B.'s initial productivity, 33–34, 45; B.'s passivity, 28, 29, 31–33, 168; B.'s perpetual presence, 13, 33–34, 44–45, 169; consumption in, 45; individualism in, 27–29, 32, 34, 35, 48–49; method *vs.* prudence in, 26–27, 28–29; narrator's character, 26–28, 29, 49; narrator's offer to B., 49–50; office's "natural arrangement," 43–45; the "residual" in, 33–37; source text, 26, 29–33, 191n19; spatial unworking, 37–41; temporal unworking, 42–50; Wall Street setting, 38–40
Baur, John, 72, 203n72
Baxter, Richard, 16, 17
Becker, Gary, 35
Beecher, Catharine, 139
Bellers, John, 213n68

233

About the Author

Andrew Lyndon Knighton is Associate Professor of English at California State University, Los Angeles.

Lightning Source UK Ltd.
Milton Keynes UK
UKHW010040110221
378607UK00007B/395